Role Portrayal
and Stereotyping
on Television

Recent Titles in
Bibliographies and Indexes in Sociology

Cubans in the United States: A Bibliography for Research in the Social
and Behavioral Sciences, 1960-1983
Compiled by Lyn MacCorkle

Demography of Racial and Ethnic Minorities in the United States: An
Annotated Bibliography with a Review Essay
By Jamshid A. Momeni

Sociology of Poverty in the United States: An Annotated Bibliography
Compiled by H. Paul Chalfant

Biological, Psychological, and Environmental Factors in Delinquency and Mental
Disorder: An Interdisciplinary Bibliography
Compiled by Deborah W. Denno and Ruth M. Schwartz

Role Portrayal and Stereotyping on Television

An Annotated Bibliography of Studies Relating to Women, Minorities, Aging, Sexual Behavior, Health, and Handicaps

Compiled and edited by NANCY SIGNORIELLI

With the assistance of ELIZABETH MILKE *and* CAROL KATZMAN

Research sponsored by The Corporation for Public Broadcasting

Bibliographies and Indexes in Sociology, Number 5

Greenwood Press
Westport, Connecticut • London, England

Ref.
Z 7711
S 53
1985

Library of Congress Cataloging in Publication Data

Signorielli, Nancy.
  Role portrayal and stereotyping on television.

  (Bibliographies and indexes in sociology, ISSN 0742-6895; no. 5)
  Includes indexes.
  1. Television broadcasting—Social aspects—United
States—Bibliography. I. Milke, Elizabeth.
II. Katzman, Carol. III. Corporation for Public
Broadcasting. IV. Title. V. Series.
Z5784.M9S53   1985   [PN1992.6]   016.3022'345   85-9823
ISBN 0-313-24855-9 (lib. bdg. : alk. paper)

Library of Congress Catalog Card Number: 85-9823
ISBN: 0-313-24855-9
ISSN: 0742-6895

First published in 1985

Greenwood Press
A division of Congressional Information Service, Inc.
88 Post Road West
Westport, Connecticut 06881

Printed in the United States of America

The paper used in this book complies with the
Permanent Paper Standard issued by the National
Information Standards Organization (Z39.48-1984).

10   9   8   7   6   5   4   3   2   1

To Robert, David and Laura

Contents

Preface

   This annotated bibliography of television portrayals
began as a project of the Office of Human Resources
Development at the Corporation for Public Broadcasting.
The work examines five specific areas: women and
sex-roles, racial and ethnic minorities, age-roles, sexual
behavior and orientations, and health and handicaps.
Consisting primarily of articles published in scholarly
journals and books, this bibliography also includes
articles from popular journals and reports published by the
U.S. government, but not conference papers and
dissertations due to the general inaccessibility of this
material.

   Each annotation consists of a bibliographic citation,
a description of the sample used in the research (if
described and/or appropriate), and an abstract of the
results.

   Several important sources of information were tapped
to compile this book. A number of authors examined and
wrote a large amount of the material in this bibliography.
The most prolific authors include George Gerbner, Larry
Gross, Michael Morgan, and Nancy Signorielli of the
Cultural Indicators Project at The Annenberg School of
Communications at the University of Pennsylvania and
Bradley S. Greenberg and his associates and students at
Michigan State University. Bardley Greenberg's collection
of studies, Life on Television: Content Analyses of
U.S. TV Drama (Ablex, 1980), is an especially good overview
of portrayals on prime-time and weekend-daytime dramatic
programming on network television.

   Portrayals on children's weekend-daytime and late
afternoon programming have been neatly gathered by F. Earle
Barcus in Images of Life on Children's Television (Praeger,
1983). Role portrayals on public television have been
explored by Isber and Cantor and by Signorielli and
Gerbner.

Preface

    The world of daytime serial dramas has been studied extensively by a number of different authors. A good review of soap operas may be found in Cassata and Skill's <u>Life on Daytime Television</u>: <u>Tuning-In American Serial Drama</u> (Ablex, 1983). For portrayals in television commercials, readers should refer to research conducted by Courtney and Whipple and by Dominick and Raugh among others.

    This bibliography includes most, if not all, relevant articles published through 1984. For future reference, readers should refer to the following scholarly journals for studies relating to television portrayals and effects: <u>Journal of Communication</u>, <u>Journal of Broadcasting and Electronic Media</u> (formerly the <u>Journal of Broadcasting</u>), <u>Journalism Quarterly</u>, and <u>Public Opinion Quarterly</u>.

Acknowledgments

I am especially grateful to Mildred R. Morse and
Thomas W. Fuller of the Office of Human Resources
Development at The Corporation for Public Broadcasting for
their continued interest and support of this project.
Elizabeth Milke and Carol Katzman were invaluable in the
preparation of the first draft of this bibliography.
Special thanks go to Rachel Simon for her help in preparing
the final draft for publication and Hillary Gunther for her
help in preparing the camera-ready copy. Finally the
continued support and encouragement of my husband, Robert
Penneys, has been instrumental in bringing this project,
and many others, to fruition.

Introduction

Television is the mainstream of our popular culture
and the primary leisure time activity and entertainment of
most Americans. It is also our most common and vivid
learning environment. In most homes, the television set is
on about six hours each day; the average person watches
more than three hours each day, most of which during the
evening.

The world of television, however, is one created
primarily to attract viewers for commercials. In this
synthetic environment, every character, prop, theme,
locale, action, and story is manufactured to allure the
largest audience at the least possible cost. Television is
ruled by the principle of cost per thousand or how much it
costs to attract a thousand viewers.

Television, especially in dramatic programming,
presents a translucent and compelling world of times,
places, social types, strivings, powers, and fate. Here
people do not live or die but are created or destroyed to
tell a story. The message of all television stories
emerges from aggregate patterns of casting,
characterization, and fate. Although programs are
structured to make the casting of its characters appear
natural, casting conveys a message of its own.

Roles are created in direct relation to their
usefulness on television. The most numerous, and hence
most useful roles involve jobs, adventure, sex, power, and
other opportunites and chances in life. Like most
resources, these values are distributed according to status
and power. Dominant social groups tend to be
overrepresented and overendowed, not only absolutely but
even in relation to their actual percentage in the real
population. Minorities are defined by having less than
their proportionate share of values and resources, meaning
less usefulness, less opportunities, and fewer but more
stereotyped roles. Underrepresentation signifies

restricted scope of action, stereotyped roles, diminished life chances, and under-evaluation ranging from relative neglect to symbolic annihilation.

This does not imply that faithful proportional representation of reality is necessarily fair or just. Artistic and dramatic functions require selection, amplification, and invention, all of which may deviate from what the census reports or independent experiences reflect. Reality provides a standard by which the nature and extent of deviations can be measured. The important question is not so much whether deviations exist, but rather what tendencies occur and with what consequences for thinking, action, and policy.

OVERVIEW OF THE RESEARCH FINDINGS

Women and Sex-Roles

The most striking revelation of this bibliography is the overall similarity and stability of the research findings. In regard to women, study after study reveals that men outnumber women by two or three to one; in addition, women are generally younger than the men and are cast in very traditional and stereotypical roles. Women are less aggressive than men, take more orders than men, and are generally limited in their employment possibilities. Television does not recognize that women can successfully mix marriage, homemaking, and raising children with careers. Programs in which married women work outside the home focus on their home-related roles. Nor does television adequately acknowledge the importance of homemaking and raising children: a woman who stays home has less status than one who has a career.

Women in the daytime serials generally have parity with the men and are sometimes presented as equal. But the overall impression, however, is that the traditional woman has life just a little easier; she often triumphs while the liberated or modern woman is punished or has a harder time.

Women are especially short-changed and under-represented on children's programs broadcast during weekend-daytime and prime-time hours. In cartoons, studies consistently reveal that men outnumber women by four or five to one. Moreover, women are likely to be cast in very stereotypical roles. Nor do men fare well in this genre; they are more likely to rely on aggression and to receive disapproval.

Like children's programs, commercials are sex-typed
and stereotoyped. Women's voices are rarely used as the
voice-over. Men remain authoritative, even for products
used primarily by women: women are the consumers. While
women and men are more equally represented in prime-time
commercials than programming, women are underrepresented in
commercials aired during children's programs. Even
children's programs on public television do not provide a
good image of women.

The few studies of television news that have focused
on sex-role portrayals have found that women are
underrepresented and appear mainly in stories that deal
with women's issues.

Some of these studies reveal a degree of improvement
over the past decade. There are also some very positive
aspects of the stereotyped portrayal of women. Women
generally exhibit prosocial and affectionate behaviors;
are in nurturant roles, and are able both to request and
receive support. Nevertheless, women usually talk about
feminine matters (even to men), interact mostly with men,
and often spend their time trying to attract men. Thus,
the overall picture of women on television is very
restricted.

Racial and Ethnic Minorities

Studies on the portrayal of minorities (especially
blacks) show a similar stability. Many of these studies
have found that the exposure blacks receive reflects their
proportion in the U.S. population. Blacks are often found
in situation comedies and in programs with predominantly
black casts. Like women, blacks are generally portrayed as
less powerful and less important in stereotyped roles. The
work of Gerbner and his colleagues focuses on the portrayal
of black men and that of white men. They found that white
men are older, powerful, and in roles of dramatic
authority; they are the least likely group to be
victimized, and those who are victimized are quite likely
to commit violence and to come out the victor. Black men,
on the other hand, are younger and less powerful; they are
more likely to be the victims of violence than the
victimizers.

Blacks exhibit about the same number and type of
antisocial acts as whites and show similar patterns of
giving and receiving orders. While blacks are less
aggressive than whites, non-black minorities are more
aggressive than whites. An important race-sex interaction

found that black males are less aggressive than white males, but black females are more aggressive than white females. Other studies discovered that blacks are more dominant in situation comedies, and whites in crime dramas.

Black families are especially stereotyped in that they are less likely to be portrayed in a nuclear family constellation than white families. Black families are often single parent families. Black women, however, are more likely to be married than white women.

The use of black English on television has also been examined. Studies found that black characters are likely to use black English, though usually in a form that is not too black. Finally, black characters are somewhat more likely to be overweight than white characters.

Similar patterns are found for minorities in commercials. Over the years blacks have increasingly appeared in commercials. Minority children appear more frequently than minority adults.

Members of other minority groups are also underrepresented. While Asians are underrepresented to a lesser degree than other racial minorities, their appearances are due to one or two programs. Hispanics have been especially underrepresented; they have not benefited from token appearances.

Age-Roles

In addition to blacks, Hispanics, and women, both the very young and the very old are also stereotyped and underrepresented on television. Research reveals that the elderly have a very negative image in programs and commercials. The age-sex interaction is also important. Old women are more likely to fail than succeed in achieving their goals. They are only killed and are never the killers. Old women are often presented as eccentric and foolish. Though still underrepresented, old men are portrayed in a more flattering light than old women. Many elderly men are active in their careers and might even be romantically involved. Older characters are the only group whose body-images are closest to reality; characters with weight problems are almost all middle-aged or old. Beck neatly sums up the differences beween old men and old women on television: Older men's handsome and weathered faces reveal that they have lived, loved, suffered, and learned; older women, on the other hand, have to hide their age lines, dye their hair, and stay trim lest the world discover that they, too, have lived, loved, suffered, and learned.

Sexual Behaviors and Orientations

The existing work reveals that sex has become an important part of many television programs (especially the serial dramas) and commercials. It is, however, usually presented as an innuendo or in a passing comic reference. As Roberts indicates, sex on television is important: Characterizations provide insight into what it means to be a man or woman in our society and how to express intimacy and affection. Sex as it is currently presented, however, does little to enhance our sexual identities. Women have a negative sexual image; they are often portrayed as decorations or sex objects in commercials, particularly for men's products.

Homosexuality rarely appears on television. When homosexuality does occur it is usually treated in a comic or negative way or as a discouraged sexual practice.

Health and Handicaps

Like homosexuals, handicapped persons are rarely presented. When they do appear they are almost never found among background characters but are usually the focus of attention. Mental illness, however, does occur rather frequently, often in the context of violence and with negative connotations. Physical illnesses and other related medical problems also appear somewhat frequently, especially in the daytime serials.

Doctors and nurses are among the most frequently appearing professionals, though their images are divergent. Doctors are usually presented as demigods--the heroes who can do no wrong--and are always cast in roles that put them in full control. On the other hand, nurses are often seen as handmaidens to doctors and are usually in the position of following, rather than giving orders. Moreover, in recent years, nurses have often been presented as sex-objects.

Drinking, especially social drinking, occurs very frequently on television and is often used to indicate sophistication, facilitate social interactions, or provide an escape from reality. Drinking also often accompanies crises. The negative consequences of drinking or any

expression of disapproval toward drinking and drunkeness
rarely occur.

Smoking and drug abuse rarely appear and when they do
appear, they are generally presented with negative
connotations. In the past few years, however, marihuana
has been presented as a relatively harmless substance
offering escape from care and boredom.

Can television change? Can the wrongs be rectified?
These important questions are not easy to answer. Although
the industry claims to be concerned and has made some
changes, evidence indicates that a great deal still needs
to be done.

Negative images abound. Findings from studies
conducted in the early days of television (especially in
regard to the portrayal of women) are remarkably similar to
findings from studies conducted in the past few years.

Television is a business. Programs exist to make
money by attracting the viewers who will eventually buy the
products advertised. Producers want to spend the least
amount of money that they possibly can. They also want to
be able to quickly bail out if they find they have produced
a bomb. A program must be an immediate hit, an overnight
sensation that everyone talks about, in order to survive.

Television both mirrors and leads society. What we
see on television reflects our own life experiences.
Writers take daily happenings and turn them into stories.
Television is also a teacher. Research (controlled for
demographic characteristics) has consistently revealed that
those who watch more television tend to view many aspects
of the the world as they are reflected on television.
Therefore it is extremely important that television
programs eliminate stereotyping and underrepresentation.

A few simple changes could be made to improve
programming. First, and most important, women and
minorities must become actively involved in the television
industry. They must be hired as writers and producers and
move into positions of power to make changes. Second,
writers and producers should make sure that more women and
minorities are written into television scripts, not just as
incidental or minor characters, but ones with power and
authority, which is used in constructive ways. Scripts
should be monitored for stereotypical characterizations and
storylines. Writers should not rely on formulas, quotas,
or procedures that try to pinpoint the demographic mix to

attract the largest audience. Finally, new and different programs should be given a chance to catch, they should be promoted, not cancelled, because their debut drew a small audience. Viewers must be educated as to what is good programming, then given enough time to select these programs.

Though numerous programs have come and gone over the past twenty years, the negative images of being a woman, old, or member of a minority have essentially remained the same. Nor are men immune from negative portrayals; The presentation of macho heroes is just as problematic and does not make men aware of alternative modes of behavior. This is not to say that there have not been any changes or any good programs. Good programs do exist, but they are few and far between and very often have to fight to survive. We must also realize that just because there are a few good shows on television the problem has not disappeared. We cannot lose sight of the overall picture and the overwhelming number of stereotypical images on television. Only when we can turn on the television set and not be faced with negative images and stereotypes will we truly know that progress has been made.

Role Portrayal
and Stereotyping
on Television

1.
Women and Sex-Roles

1. Abelman, Robert and Kimberly Neuendorf. "Religion in Broadcasting: Demographics." Cleveland, Ohio: Cleveland State University, 1983.

> sample: three episodes of each of the "top 27" religious programs in the U.S.; 81 episodes, 514 characters.

> Males were 67 percent and females 33 percent of all speaking roles; one percent of the characters could not be classified by gender. Females were the majority among adolescents (56 percent) and most underrepresented among mature adults (22 percent). Most of those shown working for the church were men (93 percent). Blue collar workers were mostly men (93 percent); students were equally divided between males and females. Two-thirds of those who could be identified as married were men while those who were single or widowed were equally divided among men and women. Women were also found in lower socio-economic status roles than men: the lower class was 58 percent women and 42 percent men; the middle class was 35 percent women and 65 percent men; and the upper class was 16 percent women and 84 percent men.

2. Adams, William and Suzanne Albin. "Public Information on Social Change: TV Coverage of Women in the Workforce." The Policy Studies Journal, 1980, 8(5), pp. 717-734.

> sample: every story about women in the work force and sex discrimination in employment on evening network news from 1968 to 1978 compiled from Vanderbilt University's TV News Index and Archives; 74 stories.

> Stories about women in the work force and sex discrimination in employment appeared once every five months on the early evening network news. The average length of the story was one and a half

3

minutes and the story generally was aired halfway
through the broadcast. Out of a total of over
120,000 newstories broadcast by the three networks
during this time, only 74 such stories appeared.
Two-thirds focused upon litigation regarding
discrimination in employment (pregnancy, etc.);   12
percent focused upon status and role of women in
workforce, 7 percent on congressional debate, and 9
percent were "first woman" stories. Most stories
appeared between 1970 and 1972.

3. Arliss, Laurie, Mary Cassata, and Thomas Skill.
"Dyadic Interaction on the Daytime Serials: How Men and
Women Vie for Power." In Mary Cassata and Thomas Skill
(eds.), Life on Daytime Television: Tuning-In American
Serial Drama. Norwood, New Jersey: Ablex Publishing, 1983,
pp. 147-156.

sample: 316 dyadic transactions from two months'
episodes of daytime serial drama (One Life to Live,
Another World, and Guiding Light) broadcast in
1981-1982.

Transactions involved 97 characters (50 females and
47 males). The majority of the dyads (197 or 62
percent) were composed of a male and a female, with
equal percentages (19 percent) of male-male and
female-female dyads. Men were most likely to be part
of business-related dyads while women were most often
found in social-related dyads. Topics discussed in
male-female dyads were family (31 percent), social
(26 percent), business (22 percent), and romance (21
percent). In these dyads, men were not always
depicted as controlling the women; but women were
seldom seen dominating the men.

4. Baker, Robert K. and Sandra J. Ball. "The Television
World of Violence." In Violence and The Media.
Washington, D.C.: GPO, 1969, Vol. IX., pp. 313-340.

sample: week-long samples of prime-time and
weekend-daytime network dramatic programs broadcast
in the fall of 1967 and 1968; 455 major characters.

Male characters dominated the world of television
drama by a four-to-one ratio, and committed six times
more violence than females. Males killed eight times
more frequently than females, and were killed seven
times as often. Violent deaths were suffered by six
percent of all males and three percent of all

females. Middle-aged characters were the most likely
to commit violence.

5. Barabatsis, Gretchen S., Martin R. Wong, and Gregory
M. Herek. "Struggle for Dominance: Relational
Communication Patterns in TV Drama." Communication
Quarterly, 1983, 31(2), pp. 148-155.

sample: 3 randomly selected episodes from each of the
top ten prime-time serial dramas (30 programs, 1,878
20-second messages), plus 8 daytime serials (434
20-second messages) and 11 cartoons (612 20-second
messages).

The predominant form of interaction was the dyad,
accounting for 96 percent of the messages in
prime-time drama, 99 percent of the messages in
daytime serials, and 74 percent of the messages in
cartoons. One-quarter of the messages in cartoons
were directed toward the viewers. Males sent and
received the majority of messages in all three
samples (63 percent in prime-time drama, 61 percent
in daytime serials, and 81 percent in cartoons).
There were no significant differences by sex between
the frequency of messages sent and received. The
most pervasive message was an assertion of dominance
(54 percent of messages in prime-time drama, 44
percent in daytime serials, and 49 percent in
cartoons). The most frequently occurring message was
male dominance (33 percent of dyadic messages in
prime-time drama, 26 percent in daytime serials, and
41 percent in cartoons). While there was no
significant difference in the control direction of
messages sent or received by men or women, in
prime-time drama women sent significantly more
noncomplete messages and received significantly more
messages in the form of answers than did males.
Males received significantly more messages in the
form of initiation/termination and nonsupport than
did females. Nevertheless, females were spoken to
similarly by both males and females, and males were
spoken to similarly by both males and females.
Overall, the predominant model of interpersonal
interaction for both male and female characters was a
dominant masculine style of interaction resulting in
the portrayal of a struggle for dominance.

6.   Barcus, F. Earle.   "Commercial Children's Television on
Weekends and Weekday Afternoons: A Content Analysis of
Children's Programming and Advertising Broadcasting in
October 1977." Newtonville, Mass.: Action for Children's
Television, 1978.

> sample: network and independent weekend morning
> programming and independent weekday afternoon
> programming broadcast in 1977; 228 program segments,
> 899 characters, and 1,022 commercial announcements.

> The weekday afternoon sample was 26 percent female
> and the weekend sample was 23 percent female. The
> male-female distribution was somewhat more equitable
> among teenagers but greatly distorted among adults.
> In both the weekend and weekday samples of
> commercials, less than one in five spokespersons were
> women. Cereal commercials used only male
> spokespersons while toy commercials, because of those
> for dolls, were somewhat less dominated by male
> spokespersons. Females made up 40 percent of the
> characters in commercials and they were usually found
> in commercials for personal care products. Children,
> both boys and girls, were a prominent age group in
> the commercials.

7.   Barcus, F. Earle.   Images of Life on Children's
Television. New York: Praeger Publishers, 1983.

> sample: one weekend and several weekday afternoons of
> network and independent children's programming
> broadcast in 1981; 235 program segments, 1,145
> characters.

> Male dominance was prevalent in children's
> television. Slightly more than three-quarters of the
> characters were male, about one-fifth were female,
> and the remainder could not be classified. Although
> 56 percent of the segments were sexually integrated,
> with males and females appearing together, 35 percent
> contained only male characters, and two percent
> contained only female characters. Relative to males,
> females were portrayed as younger, more likely to be
> married or widowed, and more likely to be found in
> family roles (primarily as wives, mothers, and
> grandmothers). Women were less likely to be
> employed; when they were, their opportunities were
> limited and they were assigned less prestigious
> occupations. Males were important figures in
> children's TV, and often joined together in
> single-sex groups to have fun, fight, or solve

problems. This pattern of single-sex companionship was denied females, who seldom appeared without the company of men.

8. Barcus, F. Earle. "Saturday Children's Television; a Report on Television Programming and Advertising on Boston Commercial Television." Newtonville, Ma.: Action for Children's Television, 1971.

> sample: one Saturday morning (7 a.m. to 1:45 p.m.) of network and independent programming and commercials broadcast in 1971; 132 different commercials.

> About half of these commercials featured characters of only one sex. Of these 13 had female children and two had female adults; 12 had male children, 19 had male adults, and eight had at least one male adult and child. Girls were associated mostly with dolls and boys were associated mostly with toy vehicles.

9. Barcus, F. Earle. "Television in the After-School Hours: A Study of Programming and Advertising for Children on Independent Stations Across the United States." Newtonville, Ma.: Action for Children's Television, 1975.

> sample: three hours of afternoon programming for each of ten independent stations (located in different cities) broadcast in 1975; 92 program segments, 405 major characters, and 487 commercials.

> Females made up 26 percent of the 390 characters who could be sex-typed. The casts of cartoons and action-adventure programs had about ten percent more males than comedy and variety programs; females were one-fifth of the characters in the former and one-third of the characters in the latter. Minority males outnumbered minority females by two to one.

> In the commercials, voice-overs were 90 percent male; women were more likely to be used for the voice-over in commercials for personal care products, household products, cereals, and restaurants. Girls were more likely than boys to do voice-overs for cereal, while boys were more likely than girls to do voice-overs for candy. Thirty-six percent of the sex-typed characters in commercials were females and 64 percent were males. Boys formed the largest group of characters followed by men, girls, and women.

10. Barcus, F. Earle. "Weekend Commercial Children's
Television -- 1975." Newtonville, Ma.: Action for
Children's Television, 1975.

> sample: one weekend of network and independent
> children's programs and commercials broadcast in
> 1975; 97 program segments with 389 sex-typed major
> characters, 403 commercials with 1,182 sex-typed
> characters.
>
> Females made up 22 percent of the 389 sex-typed
> characters in this sample. Informational programs
> had a greater proportion of females (36 percent)
> while cartoons had a somewhat smaller proportion of
> females (19 percent). Minority males outnumbered
> minority females by five to one. The sample of
> commercials was 31 percent female and 69 percent
> male, with an emphasis upon male children. The
> sample was 39 percent boys, 21 percent men, 22
> percent girls, and 7 percent women. Voice-overs were
> 90 percent male.

11. Bardwick, Judith M. and Suzanne I. Schumann.
"Portrait of American Men and Women in TV Commercials."
Psychology, 1967, 4(4), pp. 18-23.

> Authors describe, with a qualitative analysis, the
> people who inhabit "Commercial Land." The woman
> abhors dirt and bad odors, seldom works outside the
> home, is diet-conscious but provides appetizing meals
> for her family, is health-custodian for the family,
> and is concerned about her appearance. The man is
> knowledgeable, dominating, sexy, and athletic only
> outside of the home; in the home, "his judgment and
> authority are limited to his ability to recognize
> good coffee." The themes of commercials were
> seduction, wealth and status, and acceptance.
> Commercials with men also had themes of power and
> violence and the nurturant female.

12. Baxter, Leslie A. and Stuart J. Kaplan. "Context
Factors in the Analysis of Prosocial and Antisocial
Behavior on Prime Time Television." Journal of
Broadcasting, 1983, 27(1), pp. 25-36.

> sample: 2 episodes of each of the top 15 dramatic
> programs (based on Nielson ratings) broadcast during
> two months in 1981.

Analysis of characters' prosocial acts (to help,
cooperate, or support) and antisocial acts (to harm
or cause physical/mental discomfort) in the context
of overall behavior. Of all acts by males, 19
percent were antisocial; of all acts by females, 12
percent were antisocial. About a third of
high-importance acts for both males and females were
antisocial. Proportionately fewer low-importance
acts were antisocial: among males 14 percent were
antisocial and among females, 8 percent were
antisocial. Antisocial behaviors by females were
significantly more likely to be internally motivated
(optional, deep-seated) than those by males. In both
antisocial and prosocial behaviors, males were more
likely to respond to situational (essential,
immediate) pressure. The authors found that
television allowed females to be praised only if
their behavior was compatible with sex-role
stereotypes.

13. Beck, Kay. "Television and the Older Woman."
Television Quarterly, 1978, 15(2), pp. 47-49.

sample: no information given.

Content analysis revealed that the older woman had no
clearly defined role on television and was generally
underrepresented. She made up less than 5 percent of
all female characters. Most women in TV drama were
between 25 and 29 while most men fell into the 35-45
age group. Men were seen in terms of power, women in
terms of sexual attractiveness. Men were always
older and wiser than women. The average woman was
about ten years younger than her male partner. As
she aged she became decreasingly important to the
plot. The aging male, on the other hand, took on
added importance. While men became problem solvers,
women became nags or adoring attendants. The older
man's handsome and weathered face revealed that he
had lived, loved, suffered, and learned. The older
woman had to hide her age lines, dye her hair, and
stay trim lest the world discover that she too had
lived, loved, suffered, and learned.

14. Bond, Jean Carey. "The Media Image of Black Women."
Freedomways, 1975, 15, pp. 34-37.

*** see racial-ethnic groups ***

15. Busby, Linda J. "Defining the Sex-role Standard in
Network Children's Programs." Journalism Quarterly, 1974,
51(4), pp. 690-6.

>   sample: 20 network cartoon episodes (up to 30 minutes
>   in length) broadcast in the 1972-1973 season; 48
>   major and minor characters.

>   There were more than two male major characters for
>   each female major character. For minor characters,
>   the ratio was four to one. Network cartoons
>   reflected a traditional sex-role orientation.
>   One-fifth of the women (none married) worked out of
>   the home. Women were in traditional or low-level
>   jobs, and performed routine, home-related chores.
>   Men's jobs ranged from professional to blue collar
>   worker. Of 40 personality traits coded, 24 showed
>   significant male-female differences. Men were
>   independent and brave; women were dependent, weak,
>   affectionate, and sensitive.

16. Busby, Linda J. "Sex-role Research on the Mass
Media." Journal of Communication, 1975, 25(4),
pp. 107-131.

>   Author summarizes research on sex-role portrayals in
>   television and print, covering advertising and
>   programming for adults and children. An extensive
>   bibliography is included.

17. Butler, Matilda and William Paisley. Women and the
Mass Media: Sourcebook for Research and Action. New
York: Human Sciences Press, 1980, pp. 69-92.

>   Summary and description of content studies about the
>   portrayal of women in television programs and
>   commercials. Studies overwhelmingly revealed the
>   underrepresentation of women and the restricted roles
>   they portrayed.

18. Butsch, Richard and Lynda M. Glennon. "Social
Class: Frequency Trends in Domestic Situation Comedy,
1946-1978." Journal of Broadcasting, 1983, 27(1),
pp. 77-81.

>   sample: prime-time network family situation comedy
>   series from 1946-1978 as described in TV Guide and
>   similar sources; 189 series.

The working wife, an important source of income for
many families, appeared in only 13 of the 189 series.
The portrayal was almost exclusively a middle class
wife in pursuit of a professional career.

19. Cantor, Muriel G. "Children's Television: Sex-Role
Portrayals and Employment Discrimination." In Keith
W. Mielke, Rolland C. Johnson, and Barry G. Cole. The
Federal Role in Funding Children's Television Programming,
Vol. II. Bloomington, In: Indiana University, Institute for
Communication Research, 1975.

> sample: one week of children's programming broadcast
> by PBS in 1975; 15 episodes from a total of six
> series.

> Cites the greater visibility of males in these
> programs (66 percent) and as the voice-over (75
> percent) in programs where a voice-over is an
> essential part of the format (Sesame Street, Electric
> Company, and Villa Alegre). Describes the narrow,
> traditional portrayal of sex roles on several of
> these public television programs and concludes that
> public television shares the same limited vision of
> sex-role portrayals as commercial television.

20. Cantor, Muriel G. "Where are the Women in Public
Broadcasting?" In Gaye Tuchman, Arlene K. Daniels, and
James Benet (eds.), Hearth and Home: Images of Women in the
Mass Media. New York: Oxford University Press, 1978,
pp. 78-89.

> sample: one week of programming (37.5 hours)
> distributed by PBS in 1974-1975.

> Recapitulates the findings of Isber and Cantor (99)
> for the Task Force on Women in Public Broadcasting
> but goes further in comparing the public broadcasting
> data with several studies on commercial programming.
> Concludes that "women are not represented as integral
> to American life" in either place and discusses the
> general philosophy toward women and "women's issues"
> within the public television industry which generates
> this neglect.

21. Cantor, Muriel G. "Women and Public Broadcasting."
Journal of Communication, 1977, 27(1), pp. 14-19.

>   Summarizes Isber and Cantor's (99) work and includes
>   consideration of the report's impact on employment
>   and programming.

22. Cantor, Muriel G. and Suzanne Pingree. The Soap
Opera. Beverly Hills, Ca.: Sage Publications, 1983,
especially pp. 69-96.

>   Sketches predominant trends in soap opera content
>   (locale, sex, moral standards, interpersonal
>   relations, social issues and health) using a number
>   of studies (including Cassata, Skill and Boadu
>   (25); Downing (41); Greenberg et al. (87); Katzman
>   (108); Turow (172)).

23. Cassata, Mary. "The More Things Change, The More They
Are The Same: An Analysis of Soap Operas from Radio to
Television." In Mary Cassata and Thomas Skill (eds.), Life
on Daytime Television: Tuning-In American Serial Drama.
Norwood, New Jersey: Ablex Publishing, 1983, pp. 85-100.

>   sample: informal survey of radio and television soap
>   operas.

>   Looks at the difference between radio and television
>   soap operas, including some of the transitions made
>   by the soaps from radio to television. A number of
>   radio serials aired between 1932 and 1939 had women's
>   names in their titles. Although television soap
>   operas were not titled for women (or men), women
>   continued to be the strong and central characters.
>   Women were half the population of daytime serials but
>   only one-quarter of the population of prime-time
>   dramatic programs.

24. Cassata, Mary B., Patricia A. Anderson, and Thomas
D. Skill. "The Older Adult in Daytime Serial Drama."
Journal of Communication, 1980, 30(1), pp. 48-49. See
also, "Images of Old Age on Daytime." In Mary Cassata and
Thomas Skill (eds.), Life on Daytime Television: Tuning-In
American Serial Drama. Norwood, New Jersey: Ablex
Publishing, 1983, pp. 37-44.

*** see age roles ***

sample: ten consecutive episodes of each of thirteen
daytime network serial dramas broadcast in 1978; 365
characters, 58 aged 55 or older.

Women comprised 50 percent of the overall daytime
serial drama population and 48 percent of the
characters in these programs who were 55 or older.
In general, older characters had important roles and
older women had more significant roles than older
men. The image of older men and women was generally
positive. More older males (63 percent) than older
females (40 percent) were categorized as upper-middle
class or wealthy, while more women (61 percent) than
men (34 percent) were middle or lower-middle class.

25. Cassata, Mary B., Thomas D. Skill, and Samuel
D. Boadu. "In Sickness and in Health." Journal of
Communication, 1979, 29(4), pp. 73-80.

sample: summaries (from Soap Opera Digest) of
thirteen daytime serial dramas broadcast in 1977; 341
characters.

Women made up 50 percent of this sample. Slightly
more than half (53 percent) of the 144 characters
involved in health-related occurrences were women.
Psychiatric disorders were more common than
cardiovascular disease (the most common serious
ailment). Of the 25 characters with psychiatric
disorders, 18 were women between the ages of 22 and
45.

26. Ceulemans, Mieke and Guido Fauconnier. Mass
Media: The Image, Role, and Social Conditions of Women -- A
Collection and Analysis of Research Materials. Paris,
France: UNESCO, 1979, pp. 7-10; 17-24.

Concise and comprehensive summary of research
(international and U.S.) of various media.
Discusses portrayal of women in advertising and
programming and documents several areas of sex
distinction. Women were portrayed as housewives or
sex objects in commercials. In dramatic programs
they appeared less frequently and were cast in less
central roles, marriage and parenthood were more
important in their characterizations, there were
traditional divisions of work in the home, women in
the labor force generally were in more subordinate
and less important positions, they were more passive
and generally more interested in relationships than

13

in professions. Women were underrepresented in news broadcasts as reporters and newsmakers; women's issues were rarely covered.

27. Comstock, George, Steven Chaffee, Natan Katzman, Maxwell McCombs, and Donald Roberts. Television and Human Behavior. New York: Columbia University Press, 1978, pp. 33-45.

Concise presentation of the theoretical framework of media image research and summaries of widely-cited analyses of ethnic and sex-role portrayals up to the U.S. Commission on Civil Rights Report (Window Dressing on the Set) of 1977 (174).

28. Courtney, Alice E. and Thomas W. Whipple. Sex Stereotyping In Advertising. Lexington, Ma.: Lexington Books, 1983.

Review of ten years of content studies focusing upon the image of men, women, and children in television commercials confirmed that sex stereotyping (both adults and children) still existed and that little progress and improvement had been made. The typical woman was usually found in the home and her labor force role was underrepresented. She was shown as housewife and mother, dependent upon men for her decisions. Women, overall, had two roles: (1) attracting and attaining a man and (2) serving him in the role of housewife and mother. The image of both men and women in television commercials reflected the status quo of a time gone by.

29. Courtney, Alice E. and Thomas W. Whipple. "Women in TV Commercials." Journal of Communication, 1974, 24(2), pp. 110-118.

sample: three days of afternoon and evening commercials broadcast on Canadian television; 434 commercials, 151 using a product representative.

Authors summarize and compare methods and results of their research to three other studies of women in American television commercials: Dominick and Rauch (37), a New York chapter of NOW, and the National Capital area chapter of NOW. The four studies were comparable: women were presented stereotypically and in traditional roles; females were young housewives who performed domestic chores, while the males were older, told her what to do, and why.

The Canadian study found that women appeared in 58 percent of daytime and 35 percent of prime-time commercials. Voice-overs usually were male (85 percent) both during day and prime-time hours. Females were significantly more likely than males to appear in commercials for female cosmetics and household products while males were more likely to be featured in commercials for drugs and medicines. More than half of the women were concerned with home and family, while only 12 percent of the men were similarly involved. Males appeared considerably more often in business/sales/management positions (19 percent) than females (two percent). More than four-fifths of the women and two-thirds of the men were categorized as young.

30. Culley, James D. and Rex Bennett. "Selling Women, Selling Blacks." Journal of Communication, 1976, 26(4), pp. 160-174.

sample: one week of prime-time commercials broadcast on one network affiliate in 1974; 359 commercials, 395 adult characters in non-background roles.

Authors replicated and updated Dominick and Rauch (37). Women were 42 percent and men were 58 percent of the sample. Women were overrepresented in commercials for female cosmetics and household products and underrepresented in advertisements for cars and car-related items, pet foods, home appliances, and banking and insurance. As in other studies, voice-overs were predominantly male (84 percent). Earlier differences in the percentage of men and women in business and outdoor settings disappeared. Males were somewhat less likely to be found in business/outdoor settings and somewhat more likely to be found in the home. Women continued to be portrayed essentially as housewives/mothers with a drop from 56 precent to 45 percent; men portrayed as fathers remained stable at 15 percent. There was a slight increase in the number of women in the white collar occupational category. No women were portrayed as lawyers, doctors, scientists, engineers, or judges. Overall, commercials revealed stereotyped areas of decision-making: women made decisions about the home and personal appearances, while men made decisions about major purchases and business matters.

15

31. Davis, Richard H. <u>Television</u> and <u>the</u> <u>Aging</u> <u>Audience</u>.
Los Angeles, Ca.: The Ethel Percy Andrus Gerontology
Center, 1980.

*** see age roles ***

> Summarizes research that revealed, contrary to
> U.S. Census figures, older men outnumbered older
> women in television commercials. Men were permitted
> to look older so long as the image of virility and
> sexual appeal was maintained. Older women were
> seldom seen in commercials; when they appeared they
> often played less than attractive characters. In
> dramatic programs, older men were more likely to be
> presented as bad or evil; they often were victims
> and suffered fatal punishment. Women over the age of
> 30 were less likely to be seen on screen and were
> rarely presented as romantic partners. Older women
> in leading roles were shown in mid-life. The older
> male was more interesting; he gained in power and
> experience.

32. DeFleur, Melvin. "Occupational Roles as Portrayed on
Television." <u>Public</u> <u>Opinion</u> <u>Quarterly</u>, 1964, 28,
pp. 57-74.

> sample: 250 randomly-selected half-hour periods of
> network programming, excluding cartoons and
> westerns; 436 occupational portrayals.

> Of the 436 occupational portrayals, 84 percent were
> males and 16 percent were females. This is an
> underrepresentation of women compared to their
> proportion in the television population and a
> significant underrepresentation compared to real life
> (1960 Indiana Census reported a state labor force
> that was 31 percent female). Women were
> overrepresented in the professional/technical field,
> as craftsmen/foremen, and as domestics. They were
> underrepresented as sales workers, operatives and
> service workers. Men were overrepresented in the
> professional/technical field (to about the same
> degree as women), as managers and proprietors, and as
> domestics and other service workers. They were
> underrepresented as clerical and sales workers, and
> as craftsmen/foremen, operatives and laborers. The
> overall pattern of difference from real-world
> statistics is similar for men and women -- there is
> an overrepresentation of upper-middle class
> occupations and an underrepresentation of some middle
> and lower class occupations. Significant sex-related

16

differences appeared in specific types of jobs within
these broad occupational categories.

33. DeGooyer, J. and F. Borah. "What's Wrong with This
Picture?: A Look at Working Women on Television."
Washington, D.C.: National Commission on Working Women,
1982.

> sample: 25 top rated programs broadcast from 1972 to
> 1981.
>
> While some change in the portrayal of women was found
> between 1976 and 1978, the overall image of women
> changed very little between 1972 and 1981. Women on
> television were younger than women in real life and
> women over 60 were almost totally absent. There was
> also an underrepresentation of black women; black
> women have appeared in only eight of the top 25
> shows. Moreover, in 1977 and 1978 there were no
> black women. Working women were more likely to be
> professionals on television than in real life. Women
> were also young and single with an overabundance of
> wealthy and upper-middle class women. Women were
> also more likely to be found in situation comedies
> than other types of programs.

34. Dohrmann, Rita. "A Gender Profile of Children's
Educational TV." Journal of Communication, 1975, 25(4),
pp. 56-65.

> sample: two episodes each of Sesame Street, The
> Electric Company, Mister Roger's Neighborhood, and
> Captain Kangaroo, broadcast in 1974; 345 human
> characters (about half from Sesame Street).
>
> Females made up 21 percent of major characters and 25
> percent of minor characters; their proportion
> increased among ethnic characters. Voice-overs
> (N=54) were 74 percent male and 26 percent female.
> Occupational portrayals (N=144) were dominated by
> males: 15 percent of these portrayals were females.
> Characters' behavior (N=613 acts) was coded as
> "active mastery" (aggression, leadership, task
> completion and intelligence) or "passive dependent"
> (routine service, incompetence, praise and altruism).
> Twice as many acts were "active mastery" as "passive
> dependent." Eighteen percent of "active mastery"
> acts were performed by women and 82 percent were
> performed by men. Females performed 32 percent of
> the "passive dependent" acts. Women were likely to

17

perform more passive than active acts; girls,
however, were more active than passive.

35. Dominick, Joseph R. "Crime and Law Enforcement on
Prime-Time Television." Public Opinion Quarterly, 1973,
37(2), pp. 241-50.

sample: one week of prime-time network drama,
including comedy and excluding feature films,
broadcast in 1972; 51 programs, 269 speaking
characters, 119 crimes.

Comparison of sex distribution of criminals and
murder victims on television to FBI Uniform Crime
Reports for the same period. Women made up 16
percent of the 96 TV criminals in the sample and 20
percent of the 26 murder victims (approximate parity
with FBI data). Women comprised 17 percent of the 90
overall victims of crime on television and 5 percent
of the 83 law enforcers.

36. Dominick, Joseph R. "The Portrayal of Women in Prime
Time, 1953-1977." Sex Roles, 1979, 5(4), pp. 405-11.

sample: annual week-long samples of prime-time
network drama and comedy drama (excluding movies)
from 1953 to 1977, based on TV Guide
descriptions; 1,314 programs, 2,444 characters in
regular starring roles.

Women played about 30 percent of all starring roles.
They continued to be more highly concentrated than
men in situation comedies, although the percentage of
women in this genre dropped from 80 percent in the
1950s to 60 percent in the 1970s. The percentage of
men in situation comedies also dropped -- from 44
percent to 34 percent. The percentage of women
portrayed as housewives dropped from 53 percent in
the 1950s to 36 percent in the 1960s, and remained
fairly stable (39 percent) in the 1970s. The
analysis of characters in identifiable occupations
for two time periods (1956-1965 and 1966-1975)
indicated that the job distribution on television for
both men and women differed significantly from the
census figures. Women and men in professional and
managerial occupations were considerably
overrepresented while those in other occupations
(clerical, sales, operatives) were significantly
underrepresented. In the second time period, the
distribution of occupations for women was more

similar to the distribution for men, indicating less
stereotyping.

37. Dominick, Joseph R. and Gail E. Rauch. "The Image of
Women in Network TV Commercials." Journal of Broadcasting,
1972, 16(3), pp. 259-265.

NAS.

    sample: one composite week of evening network
    commercials broadcast in 1971; 986 commercials,
    including 381 featuring 462 females. Plus an
    additional sample of commercials featuring 235 males.

    In the first sample of 986 commercials, 87 percent of
    voice-overs were male. Women were more likely to be
    associated with kitchen/bathroom products and less
    likely to be associated with heavy machinery and
    related products. When females in these commercials
    were compared to males from the second sample, 71
    percent of the women were in the 20-35 age group
    compared to 43 percent of the men. Of those females
    with identifiable occupations, 56 percent were
    housewives/mothers. Only 14 percent of the males
    were portrayed as husbands/fathers. Women were more
    likely to be pictured in the home (38 percent) than
    males (14 percent). Females were more likely to be
    portrayed as decorations/sex objects in ads for
    products directed to males (54 percent of females in
    these ads) than in ads for products directed to women
    or to both sexes (25 percent of the females in these
    ads).

38. Dominick, Joseph R., Shanna Richman, and Alan Wurtzel.
"Problem-Solving in TV Shows Popular with Children:
Assertion vs. Aggression." Journalism Quarterly, 1979,
56(3), pp. 455-463.

    sample: 623 problem-solving attempts from three
    episodes of each of the top 15 prime-time programs
    broadcast during the 1976-1977 season and 800
    problem-solving attempts from three episodes of each
    of the top eight Saturday morning programs for
    children.

    The authors examined the range of behavior used by
    characters in dealing with some imbalance or conflict
    and contrasted the use of aggression with the use of
    assertion (direct but non-injurious actions to uphold
    rights, defend values, or secure personal goals,
    including initiative, self-confidence,
    outspokenness, etc.) and helping.

In prime time, approximately 15 percent of the
problem-solving attempts were aggressive. This
behavior was significantly more common in Saturday
morning programs, where 46 percent of the problems
were solved by aggression. Males were more likely
than females to use aggression in both prime-time and
Saturday morning programs. Males displayed more
positive behavior overall than aggression in prime
time; this was not the case on Saturday morning
programs. The difference between males and females
in the use of aggression on Saturday morning programs
was offset by a greater display of helping behavior
by females. Most aggressive characters also
exhibited non-aggressive problem-solving behaviors.

39. Donagher, Patricia C., Rita Wicks Poulos, Robert
M. Liebert, and Emily S. Davidson. "Race, Sex, and Social
Example: An Analysis of Character Portrayals on
Inter-Racial Television Entertainment." Psychological
Reports, 1975, 37, pp. 1023-1034.

sample: one episode of each of nine prime-time
network series (drama and comedy) broadcast in 1974
that featured one regularly appearing black and males
and females of both races; 60 major characters.

One-third of the major characters were female and
two-thirds were male. No significant differences
were found between the races and sexes in terms of
amount of time on screen. Women were generally in
traditional roles, but white women had more
non-traditional options than black women. (This
represented progress for white females from earlier
portrayals.) Men were more aggressive than women and
there was a significant sex-race interaction (black
women were more aggressive than white women). Men
were significantly more persistant at tasks than
women. Women were more likely than men to share
feelings; again, there was a significant sex-race
interaction (e.g., black women were most likely to
engage in this behavior). While the frequencies of
portrayals increased and occupational categories
expanded, characterizations based on sex and race
continued to be stereotypical.

40. Doolittle, John and Robert Pepper. "Children's TV Ad
Content: 1974." Journal of Broadcasting, 1975, 19(2),
pp. 131-142, esp. pp. 137-9.

sample: 49 Saturday morning commercials broadcast in 1974.

Examines several forms of dominance in commercials. Male voices were used in 91 percent of commercials using announcers. Half of the ads portrayed an authority figure -- males exercised the authority in 85 percent of these. In those commercials displaying dominance in the way in which products were presented or used, the vast majority were dominated by males. Females were most dominant/least subordinate in toy commercials.

41. Downing, Mildred H. "Heroine of the Daytime Serial." Journal of Communication, 1974, 24(2), pp. 130-137.

sample: 20 episodes of each of 15 serial dramas broadcast in 1973; 300 episodes, 256 characters.

This sample contained approximately as many men (127) as women (129). Women were younger than men; for every age group past youth (20 to 24), men outnumbered women. Two-thirds of all the characters were or had been married; two-thirds of those who had never been married were women. Marital status was more salient for women -- it was clearly identifiable for 85 percent of the women and 73 percent of the men. Occupation, however, was more salient for males -- identifiable for 89 percent of the males and 80 percent of the females. The occupational distribution was different for men and women: 58 percent of the men were professionals (greatly exaggerated compared with census figures), ten percent were proprietors or managers, and ten percent were law enforcers. The distribution was somewhat more realistic for women: 30 percent were housewives, 19 percent were professionals, and nine percent were clerical workers. Professional women were portrayed sympathetically; housewives were intelligent, self-reliant, articulate, and devoted to the family. Overall, the daytime serial heroine aged gracefully and remained effective and needed.

42. Downs, A. Chris. "Sex-Role Stereotyping on Prime-Time Television." Journal of Genetic Psychology, 1981, 138, pp. 253-258.

sample: four episodes of each of 14 popular evening comedy and action-drama network series (e.g., Lou Grant, Alice, Bionic Woman) broadcast in 1977; 56 episodes, 8 male leads and 6 female leads.

The men were usually in action-drama programs while the women were in comedies. The level of sex-role stereotypes and problem-solving behavior was assessed using a list of behaviors including "home/family" vs. "employment" orientation, sociability, verbal aggression, confidence, and empathy. Portrayals were generally non-stereotyped but with some exceptions. Of 11 stereotypes, there were significant sex-related differences for employment orientation and emotional expression. Women were less likely to be shown in employment-related duties and more likely to be shown at home while men were more stereotyped in being generally restricted to employment settings. Women were more likely to be emotionally expressive. They were less likely to solve their own problems (13 percent of the women compared to 42 percent of the men); but women and men were equally likely to help someone with a problem.

43. Downs, A. Chris and Darryl C. Gowan. "Sex Differences in Reinforcement and Punishment on Prime-Time Television." Sex Roles, 1980, 6(5), pp. 683-94.

sample: one week of network prime-time programming (excluding movies and specials) broadcast in 1976; 41 programs.

Authors analyzed positive and negative behaviors of adult characters, expressed as mean frequencies and proportions per program. Smiling and verbal interference were the two most frequent categories of behavior. Overall, males were equally likely to reinforce and to punish; females were more likely to reinforce than punish (male rates were higher, especially for punishing). There were sex-related differences in rates of specific behaviors: males were more likely to praise, agree, interfere verbally, and hit, while females were more likely than males to give affection, smile, and ridicule. As targets of behavior, females were more likely than males to receive reinforcement; males were more likely than females to be punished.

44.   Estep, Rhoda and Patrick T. Macdonald.   "How Prime
Time Crime Evolved on TV, 1976-1981." Journalism
Quarterly, 1983, 60, (2), pp. 293-300.

sample: 50 crime programs broadcast in 1976-77, 49
crime programs broadcast in 1978-79, and 30 in
1980-81.

Televised crime continued to overrepresent violent
crime (murder, robbery, assault) compared to property
crime. The analysis focused upon suspects
(characters depicted as responsible for committing a
crime) and victims (characters receiving the direct
impact of a crime). There was a persistent trend in
overrepresenting middle class, middle-aged whites in
suspect and victim roles. In the later sample, more
women than men were depicted as murder victims,
further increasing inaccuracy. The most recent
sample also depicted robbery suspects as lower or
working class rather than middle class. There had
also been a gradual shift in placing more blacks and
young characters in suspect and victim roles. The
motivation for violent crime on TV remained
psychological. Finally television police were
totally adequate in dealing with the problem of
crime: almost 9 out of 10 television crimes were
solved.

45.   Fine, Marlene G.   "Soap Opera Conversations: The Talk
That Binds." Journal of Communication, 1981, 31(3),
97-107.

sample: random samples of five episodes of each of
four soap operas broadcast in 1977; 20 episodes, 232
dyadic conversations.

Conversations were predominently male-female (N=151),
followed by female-female (N=49), and male-male
(N=32). Dyads were also classified by
relationship; the most frequently occurring primary
relationships were personal friends, blood relatives,
spouses and co-workers. Women most often related to
each other as family members; men related to each
other as professionals. Men and women related to
each other as spouses and/or romantic partners.
While these male-female relationships provided the
most frequent channel for intimacy (self-definition
and disclosure, affection, and conflict),
female-female dyads were more often intimate (47
percent) than male-male dyads (34 percent).

23

46. Fine, Marlene G. and Carolyn Anderson. "Dialectical Features of Black Characters in Situation Comedies on Television." Phylon, 1980, 41(4), pp. 396-409.

*** see racial-ethnic groups ***

   sample: three episodes of each of three situation comedies with primarily black casts (Good Times, The Jeffersons, and What's Happening).

   Generally, female black characters used Black English Vernacular (BEV) less than black males, with some black females displaying occasional high usage rates. The rate of usage also varied with the program and was most noticeable in The Jeffersons.

47. Foster, June E. "Father Images: Television and Ideal." Journal of Marriage and the Family, 1964, pp. 353-355.

   sample: five episodes of four selected TV series featuring a mother and father with children under 18 (Lassie, Danny Thomas, Dennis the Menace, Father of the Bride).

   Fathers in these series were rated on a personality scale by 28 middle/upper-middle class real-life fathers. Their images were then compared to an "ideal" image formulated by the real-life fathers. Only the father in Lassie approached the ideal (moral, rational, calm, sociable, competent, decisive, independent); nevertheless, he varied considerably from the "ideal" image. The other three fathers were significantly less adequate, wise, decisive, predictable, and were, in fact, very similar to each other. TV father images were generally very stereotyped.

48. Fox, Harold W. and Stanley R. Renas. "Stereotypes of Women in the Media and their Impact on Women's Careers." Human Resource Management, Spring 1977, pp. 28-31.

   sample: no information given.

   The monitored television commercials revealed 110 off-camera and 62 on-camera announcers. Men were a near monopoly of off-camera speakers and outnumbered women 2.5 to 1 as on-camera speakers. Vocational castings revealed similar patterns: one-half of the men compared to one-fifth of the women were shown in

work situations. Commercials exaggerated the actual
difference in the U.S. labor force (three-fourths of
the men and almost one-half of the women among adults
over 16). In commercials men outnumbered women 5 to
1 in semi-professional, sales, or middle-level
business roles. Moreover, all 37 blue collar workers
were men (in reality, one-sixth of U.S. blue collar
workers are women). Overall, females appeared in
fewer occupational categories than males.
Commercials with women in vocational settings cast
them primarily as white collar nonprofessionals.
Women also played decorative roles much more
frequently than men: feminine attractiveness was
featured three times as often as masculine. In many
ads men made financial decisions or played ball with
their sons; women changed diapers. Traditional
roles dominated the portrayal of the sexes.

49. Franzwa, Helen. "The Image of Women in Television: An
Annotated Bibliography." In Gaye Tuchman, Arlene Kaplan
Daniels and James Benet (eds.), Hearth and Home: Images of
Women in the Mass Media. New York: Oxford University
Press, 1978, pp. 273-299.

    Annotated bibliography compiled in 1975. Articles
    suggested that the portrayal of women on television
    changed very little over the past twenty years. Men
    generally outnumbered women by three to one, even
    though women were over 50 percent of the
    U.S. population. Women on television were usually
    young and were portrayed primarily as housewives; if
    presented in paid employment, they were restricted to
    traditional careers such as nurse and secretary.
    Women were portrayed stereotypically as weak,
    vulnerable, submissive, dependent, and often as sex
    objects.

50. Friedman, Leslie J. Sex Role Stereotyping in the Mass
Media: An Annotated Bibliography. New York: Garland
Publishing, Inc., 1977.

    Annotated bibliography on sex role
    stereotyping; includes television, advertising,
    films, print media, popular culture (comic strips,
    science fiction, music, pornography) and children's
    media.

51. Gade, Eldon M. "Representation of the World of Work in Daytime Television Serials." Journal of Employment Counseling, 1971, 8(1), pp. 37-42.

> sample: one month of nine daytime serials broadcast in 1970; 90 leading characters in occupations (20 females) and 35 housewives.

> In these serials, 62 percent of the women and 89 percent of the men were in the professional, technical, or managerial fields. By comparison only 19 percent of women in the U.S. labor force were similarly employed. On television, 24 percent of the women and three percent of the men were employed in sales or as clerical workers and 14 percent of the women and seven percent of the men were employed as sevice workers. Actual labor statistics showed that 42 percent of employed women were clerical workers or in sales, and 20 percent were service workers.

52. Gallagher, Margaret. Unequal Opportunities: The Case of Women and the Media. Paris, France: UNESCO Press, 1981.

> Review of studies dealing with different aspects of the relationship between women and the media, including the portrayal of women on North American television. These studies revealed that women were underrepresented and occupied less central roles than men. Marriage and parenthood were considered more important to women than to men and the traditional division of labor was shown as typical in marriage. Women were more passive than men. Employed women were shown in traditionally female occupations, as subordinate to men, with little status or power. Television ignored or distorted the women's movement. Author discusses similar research in other countries.

53. Gerbner, George. "Communication and Social Environment." Scientific American, September, 1972, pp. 5-12. Reprinted in Communication: A Scientific American Book. San Francisco, Ca.: W.H. Freeman and Co., 1972.

> sample: annual week-long samples of prime-time and weekend-daytime network dramatic programming broadcast between 1967 and 1971.

> Analysis revealed a "pecking order" in which white males were the least likely to be victimized while

26

women and minorities were the most likely to be
victimized.

54. Gerbner, George. "Cultural Indicators: The Case of
Violence in Televison Drama". The Annals of the American
Academy of Political and Social Science, 1970, 388,
pp. 69-81.

*** see racial-ethnic groups ***

55. Gerbner, George. "Death in Prime Time: Notes on the
Symbolic Functions of Dying in the Mass Media." The Annals
of the American Academy of Political and Social Science,
1980, 447, pp. 64-70.

> sample: annual week-long samples of prime-time and
> weekend-daytime network dramatic programming
> broadcast between 1969 and 1978; 3,949 major
> characters.

> Overall, 63 percent of all characters were involved
> in violence: for every 10 violents there were 12
> victims but for every 10 killed there were 19
> killers. If and when involved in violence, women and
> minorities, and especially young and old women, were
> the most vulnerable. The pecking order of both
> mayhem and killing was dominated by men -- American,
> white, middle class, and in the prime of life. At
> the top of the general order of "victimizers" were
> "bad" women, old men and "bad" men, in that order.
> Heading the rankings of killers over killed were
> "good" and other majority-type males. Lowest on the
> power scale were women, lower class, and old people.
> Of the 20 most victimized groups (both total violence
> and killing), all but three were women. Old women
> were at the bottom of the heap of both the battered
> and the killed. "Good" women were among the
> characters most likely to be both general and fatal
> victims of violence rather than the perpetrators.
> "Good" men had power, indicated by their heading the
> killer-killed list; "good" women, on the other hand,
> were near the bottom of the power hierarchy.

56. Gerbner, George. "Interpreting the TV World." Irish
Broadcasting Review, Spring 1980, pp. 7-11.

> sample: annual week-long samples of prime-time and
> weekend daytime network dramatic programming
> broadcast between 1967 and 1979.

Annual monitoring of network television drama showed
a remarkably consistent pattern despite changes in
program titles, formats and styles. The lion's share
of representation went to the types that dominated
the social order. Less fully represented were those
lower in the domestic and global power hierarchy and
characters involved in familiar social context, human
dependencies, and other situations that impose the
real-life burdens of human relationships and
obligations upon freewheeling activity. Men
outnumbered women by four to one. Violence was the
key to power; it was committed by 46 percent and
suffered by 55 percent of all major characters.
Violence as a demonstration of power, examined in
terms of differential risks of social groups in the
population, revealed that in comparison to the
majority types, women, nonwhites, and the elderly,
when involved in violence, were more likely to be
hurt than to hurt others.

57. Gerbner, George. "Television: The American
Schoolchild's National Curriculum Day In and Day Out." PTA
Today, April 1981, pp. 3-5.

sample: annual week-long samples of prime-time and
weekend-daytime network dramatic programming
broadcast between 1967 and 1979; over 1,600 programs,
5,000 major and 14,000 minor characters.

Analysis revealed stable patterns that changed little
from year to year despite shifts in program format
and genre. Men outnumbered women by at least three
to one. Most women did not work outside the home and
were younger than the men with whom they dealt.
Young people comprised one-third and older persons
one-fifth of their true proportion in the
U.S. population. Nonwhites, especially Hispanics,
were underrepresented. White male Americans and all
characters in the "prime of life" numbered more than
their true share of the population. An average of
five acts of violence an hour in prime-time and 18
acts an hour in weekend-daytime programs victimized
half of the prime-time characters and two-thirds of
those on children's programs. Pain, suffering, or
medical help rarely followed this mayhem. Symbolic
violence demonstrated power: who could get away with
what against whom. Adult white males were most
likely to get involved in violence and, along with
older males, the most likely to get away with it.
Old, young adult and minority group women, as well as
young boys, were the most likely to be victims rather

28

than victimizers in violent conflict. Children's
programming increased these unfavorable ratios of
risk, especially among young women.

58. Gerbner, George. "Violence in Television
Drama: Trends and Symbolic Functions." In George
A. Comstock and Eli A. Rubinstein (eds.), Television and
Social Behavior, Vol. I, Media Content and Control.
Washington, D.C.: GPO, 1972, pp. 28-187.

> sample: annual week-long samples of prime-time and
> weekend-daytime network dramatic programming
> broadcast in 1967, 1968, and 1969; 762 major
> characters.

> More than three-quarters of the characters were male,
> American, middle and upper class, unmarried, and in
> the prime of life. While only one in three male
> leads was shown as intending to or ever having been
> married, two of every three female leads were married
> or expected to marry in the story. Violence was part
> of the role of most males but part of only about half
> of all female roles. Females' chances of being a
> victim of violence were greater than their chances of
> committing violence.

59. Gerbner, George (ed). "Women: Nine Reports on Role,
Image, and Message." Journal of Communication, 1974,
24(2), pp. 103-155.

> Collection of articles concerning women's
> participation and portrayal in media and the arts.
> Also included are articles dealing with children's
> vocational choices vis-a-vis their sex and concerted
> efforts to change media image and increase female
> representation in the television industry.

60. Gerbner, George and Larry Gross. "Living with
Television: The Violence Profile." Journal of
Communication, 1976, 26(2), pp. 173-199.

> sample: annual week-long samples of prime-time and
> weekend-daytime network dramatic programming
> broadcast between 1967 and 1975.

> Casting the symbolic world of television has a
> meaning all its own: the lion's share of
> representation goes to the types that dominate the
> social order. About three-quarters of all leading

29

characters were male, American, middle and upper
class, and in the prime of life. Less fully
represented were those lower in the domestic and
global power hierarchy. While only one in three male
major characters was shown as married (or intending
to marry), two of every three females were married.
Women were also disproportionately represented among
the very young and old. Children, adolescents, and
old people together accounted for less than 15
percent of the total fictional population.
Approximately five in ten characters were identified
as gainfully employed; three were proprietors,
managers, and professionals, the fourth from the
ranks of labor, and the fifth a law enforcer. Old
men, married men, lower class, foreign, and nonwhite
males were more likely to get killed than to inflict
lethal injury. Among females, both young and old,
unmarried, lower class, foreign and nonwhite women
were especially likely to be victimized. Old, poor
and black women were shown only as killed and never
as killers. "Good" women, unlike "good" men, had no
lethal power, but "bad" women were even more lethal
than "bad" men.

61. Gerbner, George and Larry Gross. "The Scary World of
TV's Heavy Viewer." Psychology Today, April, 1976,
pp. 41-45.

    sample: annual week-long samples of prime-time and
    weekend-daytime network dramatic programming
    broadcast between 1969 and 1975.

    About three-fourths of all leading characters on
    prime-time network television were male, mostly
    single, middle and upper class white Americans in
    their 20s and 30s. Most of the women represented
    family or romantic interests. While only one out of
    three male leads intended to or had ever been
    married, two out of every three females leads were
    either married, expected to marry, or were involved
    in some romantic relationship. Except in comic
    roles, one rarely saw a leading man burdened by
    real-life constraints, such as family, that inhibited
    freewheeling activity.

62. Gerbner, George and Larry Gross. "Violence Trends in
Television." The Journal of the Producers Guild of
America, 1975, pp. 9-12.

sample: annual week-long samples of prime-time and
weekend-daytime network dramatic programming
broadcast between 1967 and 1973.

Although women were less likely to get involved in
violence than men, for five of the seven years
studied they were more likely to be victimized and
always more likely to be killed. Although more than
eight out of ten young men and nearly six out of ten
young women were involved in some violence, young
adult women were more likely to be victimized than
young adult men. Single women were the most likely
of all groups to be killed; they had five killed for
every two killers. The odds were reversed for both
married women and all males. In the world of
television drama, men lost and women gained power in
marriage, narrowing but not closing the gap of sex
role inequality. Most likely to get involved in
violence were lower class, foreign and nonwhite men,
in that order. Old men had the most favorable, and
male children the most unfavorable, odds of general
male victimization. Women were the most
victimization prone, especially lower class,
nonwhite, and old women.

63. Gerbner, George and Larry Gross. "The Violent Face of
Television and Its Lessons." In Edward L. Palmer and Aimee
Dorr (eds.), Children and the Faces of
Television: Teaching, Violence, and Selling. New
York: Academic Press, 1980, pp. 149-162.

sample: annual week-long samples of prime-time and
weekend-daytime network dramatic programming
broadcast between 1969 and 1978.

Summarizes findings from Cultural Indicators annual
message system analyses. In one week the typical
prime-time viewer will encounter about 300 dramatic
characters playing speaking roles (217 males, 80
females and 3 of no clear gender). The racial
composition of the television world was 262 whites,
35 members of other races, and 3 whose race could not
be determined. Children who watch weekend-daytime
programs met an additional 137 dramatic characters.
Overall, the world of television was three-fourths
American, three-fourths between the ages of 30 and 60
(compared to one-third of the real population), and
three-fourths male. Approximately five in ten
characters could be identified as gainfully
employed; of these, three were proprietors, managers

31

and professionals, one came from the ranks of labor, and the fifth enforced the law or preserved the peace. Violence was committed by 46 percent and suffered by 55 percent of the major characters and it served as a scenario of power: women, especially old and minority women, were more likely to be victimized than to commit violence. These findings have been remarkably consistent despite changes in program titles, formats, and styles. Research also examined relationships between television images and people's conceptions of social reality.

64. Gerbner, George, Larry Gross, Stewart Hoover, Michael Morgan, Nancy Signorielli, Harry E. Cotugno, and Robert Wuthnow. "Religion on Television and in the Lives of Viewers." Report prepared for the Ad Hoc Committee on Religious Television Research, National Council of the Churches of Christ, New York, New York, 1984.

sample: one week of local and syndicated religious television programs broadcast in 1982; 101 programs and 752 characters.

The demographic distribution of characters in this sample of local and syndicated religious programming revealed patterns remarkably similar to those found on dramatic programs: women made up 34 percent, the elderly 3 percent, and blacks 10 percent of the characters. Four out of ten children and adolescents, almost half of the young adults and more than half of the elderly characters were women. There were also fewer women among the black characters: 27 percent of the blacks as compared to 34 percent of the whites were women. Only 8 percent of the women as compared to 11 percent of the men were black. Women were somewhat less likely to appear on local programs (one-quarter of the characters in local programs as compared to one-third of the characters in syndicated programs were women), and blacks were somewhat more likely to appear on local programs than syndicated programs (14 percent of the characters on local programs as compared to 10 percent of those on syndicated programs).

65. Gerbner, George, Larry Gross, Marilyn Jackson-Beeck, Suzanne Jeffries-Fox, and Nancy Signorielli. "Cultural Indicators: Violence Profile No. 9." _Journal of Communication_, 1978, 28(3), pp. 176-207.

sample: annual week-long samples of prime-time and weekend-daytime network dramatic programming broadcast between 1967 and 1977; 3,651 major characters.

Men outnumbered women by three to one in these annual samples of network dramatic programming. More than six out of ten major characters were involved in some type of violence: nearly seven out of ten men as compared to less than five out of ten women. The characters most involved in violence were men classified as "bad," foreign, or lower class, and women categorized as "bad," lower class, or unmarried. The least involved were old and married characters of both sexes. The order of victimizers were "bad" women, old men, and "bad" men; the most likely to be victimized, in order, were women, lower class people, and old people. Of the 20 most victimized groups (both for total mayhem and killing), all but three were women. While "good" men had power as indicated by their heading up the killer-killed list, "good" women were near the bottom of the power hierarchy. Research also examined relationships between television images and people's conceptions of social reality.

66. Gerbner, George, Larry Gross, Michael Morgan and Nancy Signorielli. "Aging with Television Commercials: Images on Television Commercials and Dramatic Programming, 1977-1979." Annenberg School of Communications, University of Pennsylvania, 1981.

sample: commercials in three annual samples of prime-time and weekend-daytime network dramatic programs broadcast in 1977, 1978, and 1979 plus commercials from the evening network news broadcast during the same week as the 1979 dramatic sample; 1,949 prime-time, 510 weekend-daytime, and 97 news commercials.

The world of television commercials, like the world of dramatic programming, was a very stable world with little change between 1977 and 1979. Women appeared frequently in the commercials broadcast during prime-time programs and the news, but rather infrequently in the commercials during children's programs; women appeared in about 70 percent of the former, but in less than 20 percent of the latter. Most of the commercials had announcers (75 percent of prime-time commercials, 87 percent of news commercials, and 82 percent of children's commercials) but women were rarely presented in this role: over seven out of ten commercials had male announcers and only one in twenty had a female announcer. When female announcers were found, they were more likely than male announcers to be both seen and heard. While the proportion of women was about equal to the proportion of men in prime-time and evening news commercials (44 percent women vs. 54 percent men), women were outnumbered by three to one in weekend-daytime commercials. Women of all ages, but especially young women, were in commercials relating to hygiene and beauty aids; men were in car commercials.

67. Gerbner, George, Larry Gross, Michael Morgan, and Nancy Signorielli. "Charting the Mainstream: Television's Contributions to Political Orientations." Journal of Communication, 1982, 32(2), pp. 100-127.

sample: annual week-long samples of prime-time network dramatic programming broadcast between 1969 and 1981; over 1,600 programs and 14,000 characters.

Men outnumbered women by three to one; most women attended to men or home and were younger (but aged faster) than the men they met. Young people (under 18) comprised one-third and older people (over 65) one-fifth of their true proportion in the population. Blacks represented three-fourths and Hispanics one-third of their share of the U.S. population; a disproportionate number of minorities were minor rather than major characters. Asians were overrepresented in these samples, mostly as minor characters. Nearly seven out of ten characters were middle class, and most of them were professionals and managers. Blue collar and service work occupied 67 percent of all Americans, but only ten percent of television characters. Each week the typical prime-time viewer saw 30 police officers, 7 lawyers, and three judges, but only one engineer or scientist and very few blue collar workers. There was considerable violence in this world, but pain, suffering, and medical help rarely followed the mayhem. Symbolic violence demonstrates power: it shows who can get away with what against whom. White males were the most likely victimizers while old, young and minority women, and young boys were the most likely to be the victimized. Findings of the message system analyses were related to viewer conceptions of social reality.

68. Gerbner, George, Larry Gross, Michael Morgan, and
Nancy Signorielli. "The 'Mainstreaming' of
America: Violence Profile No. 11." Journal of
Communication, 1980, 30(3), pp. 10-29.

> sample: annual week-long samples of prime-time and
> weekend-daytime network dramatic programming
> broadcast between 1967 and 1979.
>
> An examination of some conceptual and behavioral
> correlates of growing up and living with a television
> world in which men outnumbered women three to one,
> young people comprised one-third and old people
> one-fifth of their real numbers, professionals and
> law enforcers dominated the occupations, and an
> average of five acts of violence per prime-time hour
> (and four times that number per weekend-daytime hour)
> involved more than half of all leading characters.
> About two-thirds of the males and nearly half of the
> females were involved in violence. When involved,
> female characters were more likely than male
> characters to be the victims rather than the
> perpetrators of violence. Only one group of male
> characters -- young boys -- were among the ten groups
> who were most likely to be victimized. Women cast in
> minority roles (old women, upper class women,
> nonwhite women, young women and lower class women)
> were especially likely to suffer rather than to
> inflict violence. Only two groups of characters --
> old men and "bad" women -- were more likely to hurt
> others than be hurt themselves. Research also
> examined relationships between television images and
> people's conceptions of social reality.

69. Gerbner, George, Larry Gross, Michael Morgan, and
Nancy Signorielli. "Media and the Family: Images and
Impact." Paper for the National Research Forum on Family
Issues, White House Conference on Families, April, 1980.

> sample: annual week-long samples of prime-time and
> weekend-daytime network dramatic programming
> broadcast between 1969 and 1978.
>
> Examination of image of the family in several media,
> including television. Authors' research reveals that
> the world of prime-time and weekend-daytime dramatic
> programming was predominantly male: year in and year
> out there were approximately three males for every
> female. Home, family, marriage were the domain of

35

the female: more women than men were portrayed as
married, as having children, as being involved
romantically, and as interested in family-related
issues. Women were not presented as able to mix
successfully homemaking activities with job success;
males were both married and employed and seemed to
succeed in both. One negative aspect of male
portrayals was that married men were portrayed as
less important and powerful than their unmarried
counterparts.

70. Gerbner, George, Larry Gross, Michael Morgan, and
Nancy Signorielli. "Scientists on the TV Screen."
Society, May/June, 1981, pp. 41-44.

sample: annual week-long samples of prime-time and
weekend-daytime network dramatic programming
broadcast between 1969 and 1979; 1,833 prime-time
and 1,144 weekend-daytime characters.

Although science was a frequent theme of television
drama, the scientist was a relatively rare and
specialized dramatic character. The typical
prime-time viewer encountered science and technology
every night but a scientist only once a week, and a
scientist playing a major role once every two weeks.
Scientists comprised less than one percent of
prime-time working characters, less than half of the
corresponding percentage in the U.S. labor force.
Women scientists as dramatic characters were
overrepresented compared to their tiny actual
percentage in the country and to the small proportion
of working women in the world of prime-time drama.
By comparison, television doctors and other health
professionals numbered over seven times their real
percentage of the population.

71. Gerbner, George, Larry Gross, and Nancy Signorielli.
"The Role of Television Entertainment in Public Education
About Science." Annenberg School of Communications,
University of Pennsylvania, 1985.

*** see health ***

sample: annual week-long samples of prime-time
network dramatic programming broadcast between 1973
and 1983.

The television world was dominated by men in the
prime of life. Men were also more likely than women

to be portrayed as having an occupation. Men were
usually cast in traditionally male occupations and
women in traditionally female occupations. More than
90 percent of the television doctors were men and
more than 90 percent of the television nurses were
women. One-quarter of the scientists, however, were
women. The woman scientist on TV was overrepresented
compared to her tiny actual percentage in the
U.S. labor force.

72. Gerbner, George, Larry Gross, Nancy Signorielli, and
Michael Morgan. "Aging with Television: Images on
Television Drama and Conceptions of Social Reality."
Journal of Communication, 1980, 30(1), pp.37-47.

*** see age-roles ***

sample: annual week-long samples of prime-time and
weekend-daytime network dramatic programming
broadcast between 1969 and 1978; 1,365 programs,
3,700 major and 13,000 minor characters.

In prime time, women younger than 30 outnumbered
young males; but their numbers decreased as they got
older and their usefulness in the television world
decreased. The greatest percentage of women was in
the 25 to 34 age group and the largest percentage of
men was the 35 to 44 age group. In weekend-daytime
programs, the youthfulness of female characters was
accentuated -- the largest group of females were
those under 21. Moreover, females outnumbered males
in this group. Most males were in the 35-45 age
group.

73. Gerbner, George, Larry Gross, Nancy Signorielli, and
Michael Morgan. "Television Violence, Victimization, and
Power." American Behavioral Scientist, 1980, 23(5),
pp. 705-716.

sample: annual week-long samples of prime-time and
weekend-daytime network dramatic programming
broadcast between 1967 and 1979.

Overall, the world of television was three-quarters
American, three-quarters between the ages of 30 and
60 (compared to one-third of the U.S. population),
and three-quarters male. The age curve of the TV
world population was more like the curve of consumer
spending than like the real world: children and the
elderly were relatively neglected, old people

37

virtually invisible. The portrayal of these and
other minorities, as well as of women, are sensitive
barometers of the dramatic equities of life.
Two-thirds of all characters in prime-time and 80
percent of all characters in weekend-daytime programs
were involved in violence. Men were more likely to
be involved than women, and adults were more involved
than children, although about half of all women and
children still were involved. Television violence
serves primarily to support the established order and
its patterns show the power of dominant types to come
out on top. White males were the most likely
victimizers while old, young, and minority women and
young boys were the most likley to be victimized.
Research also examined the relationships between
television images and people's conceptions of social
reality.

74. Gerbner, George, Larry Gross, Nancy Signorielli,
Michael Morgan, and Marilyn Jackson-Beeck. "The
Demonstration of Power: Violence Profile No. 10." Journal
of Communication, 1979, 29(3), pp. 177-196.

sample: annual week-long samples of prime-time and
weekend-daytime network dramatic programming
broadcast between 1967 and 1978.

Males outnumbered females by three to one in these
samples of dramatic programming. The portrayal of
violence on television drama demonstrated a pattern
of unequal relative risks among characters of
different age, sex, and social groups: women of all
ages, but especially young adult and elderly women,
as well as young boys, nonwhites, foreigners, and
both members of the lower and upper (but not middle)
classes were more likely to be victimized than to
commit violence. In 1978, the relative risks of
female victimization further increased. In 1977
there were 1.05 male and 1.13 female victims for
every male or female violent. In 1978, the male
ratio of risk rose to 1.21 but the female ratio rose
to 2.14. Female victimization increased the most for
weekend children's programming, rising from 1.09 in
1977 to 2.80 in 1978. Research also examined
relationships between TV images and people's
conceptions of social reality.

75. Gerbner, George and Nancy Signorielli. "Women and
Minorities in Television Drama, 1969-1978." University of
Pennsylvania, Annenberg School of Communications, 1979.

38

sample: ten annual week-long samples of prime-time
and weekend-daytime network dramatic programming
broadcast between 1969 and 1978; 1,365 programs,
3,719 major characters, and 17,000 speaking
characters.

Presents comparative data for major and minor
characters in prime-time and weekend-daytime network
dramatic programs with U.S. Census figures. Females
were 27 percent of all characters on prime-time and
18 percent of characters on weekend-daytime programs.
Major characters were 29 percent female on prime-time
and 15 percent female on weekend-daytime programs.
Female representation in major roles increased to 37
percent in the 1978 sample. Women were concentrated
in comic, family centered, or romantic roles, which
limited their portrayal as serious, powerful
individuals.

76. Gerbner, George and Nancy Signorielli. "The World
According to Television." American Demographics, October,
1982, pp. 15-17.

sample: annual week-long samples of prime-time
network dramatic programming broadcast between 1969
and 1981.

Men outnumbered women by about three to one. They
make up 49 percent of the U.S. population but 73
percent of the prime-time population, while women, a
majority of the U.S. population, were only 27 percent
of the prime-time world. This finding fluctuated
very little from year to year. Women were most
underrepresented in action-adventure programs and
somewhat better represented in situation comedies
(but even in these programs were outnumbered by two
to one). In children's programming, women were
almost always outnumbered by four or more to one.
Information about marital status was not supplied for
about a third of the males compared to only 12
percent of the females. Women were attractive and
nurturing, often portrayed in the context of home and
family, and involved in romantic relationships.
Women who were employed (and they were usually not
married on television despite the fact that the
majority of married women in the U.S. also work
outside the home) were often cast in traditionally
female occupations -- nurses, secretaries,
waitresses. Men, on the other hand, were portrayed
as powerful and potent, and proportionally fewer were

married. More men were employed, and they usually
worked in traditionally masculine and prestigious
occupations such as medicine and law. Dominant white
males in the prime of life were relatively safe in
these programs and were more likely to be the
victimizers than the victims in violent encounters.
Conversely, old, young, and minority women and young
boys were relatively more likely to be the victims
rather than the perpetrators of violence. Television
told viewers more about police work, and the jobs of
selected professionals and celebrities, than about
all other working people combined.

77. Glennon, Linda and Richard Butsch. "Families on
TV: Looking for the Working Class." _Televisions_, 1980,
7(2/3), pp. 10-12.

sample: impressions of themes and portrayals of more
than 500 episodes of approximately 30 series
broadcast between 1947 and 1977.

Of more than 200 families in family series broadcast
in this period, only 11 were working class (about
five percent). By comparison, 160 families (80
percent) were categorized as middle class. In 40
percent of these, professionals were cast as heads of
households and portrayed as successful. The most
consistent characterization of working class was the
"husband/father as bumbling fool with little dignity,
often lovable but obviously unintelligent" ...
"often cast opposite a more sensible wife." On the
whole, these series had a very paternalistic attitude
toward the working class male. By comparison in many
middle class portrayals the wife was presented as the
"buffoon" with a sensible, more serious husband.

78. Glennon, Lynda M. and Richard Butsch. "The Family as
Portrayed on Television 1946-1978." In David Pearl,
Lorraine Bouthilet, and Joyce Lazar (eds.), _Television and
Behavior: Ten Years of Scientific Progress and Implications
for the Eighties_. Washington, D.C.: GPO, 1982,
pp. 264-271.

sample: descriptions of 218 prime-time network family
series broadcast between 1946 and 1978 from published
summaries and direct observation. Series usually
were situation comedies; about ten percent were
dramas.

Most of television's history has been typified by the
contrast between working class and middle class
families. From 1949 to 1966 the working class man
was usually presented as a "buffoon" accompanied by a
sensible, competent wife while the reverse was
typical of the middle class family. In the 1970s,
the dominant theme was the debunking of upper-middle
class professionals; and there was an increase in the
number of working class series. By the end of the
1970s, middle class mothers and fathers were both
portrayed as superparents; the inadequate working
class father was superceded by a theme of
upwardly-mobile children.

79. Greenberg, Bradley S. Life on Television: Content
Analyses of U.S. TV Drama. Norwood, New Jersey: Ablex
Publishing, 1980.

> An anthology of studies concerning the appearance and
> treatment of females, racial and ethnic minorities,
> the elderly, and sexual behavior. Listed under
> respective authors and titles.

80. Greenberg, Bradley S. "Television and Role
Socialization: An Overview." In David Pearl, Lorraine
Bouthilet, and Joyce Lazar (eds.), Television and
Behavior: Ten Years of Scientific Progress and Implications
for the Eighties. Washington, D.C.: GPO, 1982,
pp. 179-190.

> Concise summary of research conducted during the
> 1970s, including that of the author and his
> colleagues, focusing upon family, sex, race,
> occupation, and age-roles. Notes that although
> stereotyping is characteristic of both male and
> female portrayals, it is accentuated for females by
> their more limited appearance in the medium.
> Includes an extensive bibliography.

81. Greenberg, Bradley S. "Three Seasons of Television
Characters: A Demographic Analysis." Journal of
Broadcasting, 1980, 24(1), pp. 49-60.

> sample: characters in three composite weeks of
> network fictional series broadcast during prime time
> and Saturday morning in 1975 (N=1,212), 1976
> (N=1,120), and 1977 (N=1,217).

Each year males outnumbered females by three to one.
Women were younger than the males -- more than four
out of ten females were between 20 and 34. Females
were less likely to be lawbreakers (except for the
1976 season) and they were excluded from the middle
range job categories. A larger proportion of women
appeared in situation comedies and family dramas and
a smaller proportion appeared in the Saturday morning
cartoons.

82. Greenberg, Bradley S. and Charles K. Atkin. "The
Portrayal of Driving on Television, 1975-1980." Journal of
Communication, 1983, 33(2), pp. 44-55.

*** see health ***

sample: one week of prime-time commercial programs
broadcast in the fall of 1975, 1976, 1977, and 1979;
223 programs, 174.5 hours.

The analysis isolated 784 driving scenes that were 5
seconds or longer in duration. (3.5 scenes per
program and 4.5 scenes per program hour.) There were
a total of 869 drivers: 87 percent were males, 93
percent were white, and 72 percent were in their
twenties or thirties. The 479 passengers had similar
demographic patterns.

83. Greenberg, Bradley S., Nancy Buerkel-Rothfuss,
Kimberly A. Neuendorf, and Charles K. Atkin. "Three
Seasons of Television Family Role Interactions." In
Bradley S. Greenberg, Life on Television: Content Analyses
of U.S. TV Drama. Norwood, New Jersey: Ablex Publishing,
1980, pp. 161-172.

sample: 35 prime-time and Saturday morning family
dramatic series for each of three composite weeks
broadcast in 1975, 1976, and 1977; 115 programs,
approximately 50 families.

Male and female characters were equally as likely to
initiate and receive family role behaviors with other
family members, including offering information
(one-third of the interactions) and, less frequently,
seeking information, directing, and giving support.
Parents were more likely to interact with children of
the same sex.

84. Greenberg, Bradley S., Nadyne Edison, Felipe Korzenny,
Carlos Fernandez-Collado, and Charles K. Atkin.
"Antisocial and Prosocial Behaviors on Television." In
Bradley S. Greenberg, Life on Television: Content Analyses
of U.S. TV Drama. Norwood, New Jersey: Ablex Publishing,
1980, pp. 99-128.

     sample: characters in three composite weeks of
     network fictional series broadcast during prime time
     and Saturday morning in 1975 (N=1,212), 1976
     (N=1,120), and 1977 (N=1,217); approximately 2,500
     prosocial and antisocial acts per sample year.

     Verbal aggression was the most common antisocial
     behavior, followed by physical aggression. Altruism
     was the most common prosocial behavior. Male
     characters displayed more than twice as many acts of
     physical aggression as female characters. There was
     little difference between the sexes in the rates of
     verbal aggression and deceit, although male rates
     were consistently higher than female rates. Male and
     female characters had comparable rates for altruism.
     Affection was more likely to be given and received by
     females (over twice the rate of male characters).
     Female characters were also more likely to consider
     others' feelings and were somewhat more likely to
     explain their own feelings.

85. Greenberg, Bradley S., David Graef, Carlos
Fernandez-Colluado, Felipe Korzenny, and Charles K. Atkin.
"Sexual Intimacy on Commercial Television During Prime
Time." In Bradley S. Greenberg, Life on
Television: Content Analyses of U.S. TV Drama. Norwood,
N.J.: Ablex Publishing, 1980, pp. 129-136.

     sample: two weeks of prime-time network series aired
     in 1977 and 1978.

     There were 156 "agents" of intimate sexual references
     (e.g., characters who made references to intercourse,
     prostitution) and 146 "targets" of these references.
     Females, 30 percent of the characters in these
     samples, made up 58 percent of the "agents" and 50
     percent of the "targets" of these references.

86. Greenberg, Bradley S. and Carrie Heeter. "Television
and Social Stereotypes." In Joyce Sprafkin, Carolyn Swift,
and Robert Hess (eds.), Rx Television: Enhancing the
Preventive Impact of Television. New York: The Haworth
Press, 1983, pp. 37-52.

Summary and review of ongoing research on the
portrayal of sex-roles on television. The sexes have
been consistently portrayed in a stereotyped way.
Women have been proportionally underrepresented but
both men and women have been presented with a narrow
range of attributes. Women were younger, were more
likely than men to be clearly identified as married
or single, had fewer different types of jobs and
fewer high status jobs than men. Overall men were
more rational, more powerful, more stable, and more
tolerant while women were more concerned with family,
romance, and social relationships.

87. Greenberg, Bradley S., Kimberly A. Neuendorf, Nancy
Buerkel-Rothfuss, and Laura Henderson. "The Soaps: What's
On and Who Cares?" Journal of Broadcasting, 1982, 26(2),
pp. 519-536.

sample: three episodes per week of each of 13
afternoon serial dramas for a two week period in
1977; 308 speaking characters.

Authors outline demographics of soap opera
characters, comparing them to earlier data provided
by Gade (51), to 1975 U.S. Census figures and to the
prime-time population of characters described in
authors' own research (see, for example, Greenberg,
(81)). Of 308 speaking characters in this sample,
about half were female. Of 152 females, 31 percent
had identifiable employment; for males the figure was
81 percent. Professionals appeared at a rate that
was three times that of census reports. Males
generally were doctors, lawyers, and executives.
Females generally were nurses, secretaries, and
doctors. About an equal percentage of male and
female characters had children (50 to 55 percent).

88. Greenberg, Bradley S., Marcia Richards, and Laura
Henderson. "Trends in Sex-role Portrayals on Television."
In Bradley S. Greenberg, Life on Television: Content
Analyses of U.S. TV Drama. Norwood, New Jersey: Ablex
Publishing, 1980, pp. 65-87.

sample: characters in three composite weeks of
network fictional series broadcast during prime time
and Saturday morning in 1975 (N=1,212), 1976
(N=1,120), and 1977 (N=1,217).

Replicated and expanded Henderson et al. (96). Men
gave more orders on the average than did women in
each of the three seasons. Women received orders
equivalently from men and women, while men received
orders primarily from other men. In situation
comedies there was no significant difference between
the sexes in the rates of order-giving,
order-receiving, or order-following. In
crime/adventure shows, on the other hand, men
dominated in each sample week. Saturday morning
programs followed this pattern of male dominance.
Women were more likely than men to request support;
emotional support was particularly salient in female
portrayals. Moreover, men were significantly more
likely not to ask for support in situations in which
they would be expected to make such requests.

89. Greenberg, Bradley S., Katrina W. Simmons, Linda
Hogan, and Charles K. Atkin. "The Demography of Fictional
TV Characters." In Bradley S. Greenberg, Life on
Television: Content Analyses of U.S. Television Drama.
Norwood, New Jersey: Ablex Publishing, 1980, pp. 35-46.

sample: characters in three composite weeks of
network fictional series broadcast during prime time
and Saturday morning in 1975 (N=1,212), 1976
(N=1,120), and 1977 (N=1,217).

The proportion of females ranged from 27 percent to
29 percent over the three yearly samples and was
roughly equal for whites and blacks. This
distribution was influenced by program type. Women
appeared more frequently than expected in family
drama (41 percent female) and situation comedies (37
percent female). Women were significantly
underrepresented in Saturday morning cartoons (19
percent female). Women were overrepresented in the
younger age groups: they were 79 percent of the
characters under 20 years of age and 43 percent of
the characters 20 to 34 years of age. Women were
underrepresented in the older age groups: they were
20 percent of the characters aged 35 to 49 and 15
percent of those between 50 and 64. One-third of the
characters over age 65 were women. The data
indicated that occupational portrayals were moving
toward greater diversity, with women comprising 30
percent of professionals, 15 percent of managers, and
19 percent of service workers.

90. Harris, Adella J. and Jonathan F. Feinberg.
"Television and Aging: Is What You See What You Get?" The
Gerontologist, 1977, 17(5), pp. 464-468.

*** see age roles ***

91. Harris, Mary B. and Sara D. Voorhees. "Sex-Role
Stereotypes and Televised Models of Emotion."
Psychological Reports, 1981, 48(3), pp. 826.

   sample: two weeks of day and evening network
   programming broadcast in 1977; 470 characters.

   Female characters, compared to males, were
   predominantly happy: 75 percent of the females
   compared to 57 percent of the males. Slightly more
   females (17 percent) than males (13 percent) were
   unhappy. Female characters were more emotional than
   male characters. No emotion was displayed by eight
   percent of the females and 30 percent of the males.
   Interests were stereotyped by sex: women were more
   likely to be involved with home, romance, and
   physical appearances while men were more involved
   with work, cars, and sports. Women were concentrated
   in the younger age groups while men were more likely
   than women to be in the 50-to-59 age group.

92. Harvey, Susan E., Joyce N. Sprafkin, and Eli
Rubinstein. "Prime-Time TV: A Profile of Aggressive and
Prosocial Behaviors." Journal of Broadcasting, 1979,
23(2), pp. 179-189.

   sample: one week of network prime-time programming
   broadcast in 1975-1976; 66 programs, 946 human
   characters.

   Women made up only 28 percent of the sample. Men
   were more aggressive than women; women were more
   involved in the expression of feelings.

93. Haskell, Deborah. "The Depiction of Women in Leading
Roles in Prime-Time Television." Journal of Broadcasting,
1979, 23(2), pp. 191-196.

   sample: five episodes of each of 13 series, broadcast
   in 1977, featuring women as central characters; 76
   regularly appearing characters, 40 females.

Although the number of regularly appearing female and male characters was equal, males outnumbered females by two to one among characters appearing on a one-time basis. Black women made up 15 percent of the female characters. Several single women held jobs and headed households. Women who were not portrayed as homemakers were generally in middle- to lower-level jobs rather than in the professions. Female characters generally discussed "feminine" matters such as personal relationships and romance, regardless of program theme.

94. Head, Sidney W. "Content Analysis of Television Drama Programs." Quarterly of Film, Radio, and Television, 1954, 9, pp. 175-194.

sample: four episodes of each of 64 network dramatic series broadcast in 1952; 209 programs, 1,023 major and 740 minor characters.

One-third of these characters were females. Three-quarters of the characters had identifiable occupations: 17 percent were police or private detectives, 17 percent were criminals, 11 percent were housewives, and 10 percent were professionals.

95. Henderson, Laura and Bradley S. Greenberg. "Sex-Typing of Common Behaviors on Television." In Bradley S. Greenberg, Life on Television: Content Analyses of U.S. TV Drama. Norwood, New Jersey: Ablex Publishing, 1980, pp. 89-95.

sample: common behaviors of a subsample of 1,679 characters from 115 prime-time network and 43 Saturday morning network programs broadcast in 1975-76 and 1976-77; 2,322 speaking characters.

The sample of speaking characters was 28 percent female and 72 percent male. A subsample of 1,679 characters (half males and half females) was selected to analyze sex-typing of common behaviors. Of the common behaviors coded, 46 percent were sex-typed. Behaviors performed in disproportionately large amounts by females included entertaining, preparing and serving food, housework. Female characters were significantly less likely than males to drive, participate in sports, use firearms, make business calls, smoke and drink. Data indicated more stereotyping of male behavior than female behavior.

96. Henderson, Laura, Bradley S. Greenberg, and Charles
K. Atkin. "Sex Differences in Giving Orders, Making Plans,
and Needing Support on Television." In Bradley
S. Greenberg, Life on Television: Content Analyses of
U.S. TV Drama. Norwood, New Jersey: Ablex Publishing,
1980, pp. 49-63.

     sample: one composite week of network fictional
     series broadcast in 1975; 79 programs, 1,212 speaking
     characters.

     The sample was 27 percent female and 73 percent male.
     Males generated 80 percent of the orders but gave no
     more orders to females than to males. Orders given
     by males were more likely to be followed. There was
     proportionately more order-giving and receiving by
     females in situation comedies; however, these were
     not necessarily followed. Physical support was more
     likely to be needed by males, while females were more
     likely to need emotional support. Females were also
     more likely to request (and receive) support.
     Eighty-two percent of the plans (for both men and
     women) were made by male characters.

97. Hiemstra, Roger, Maureen Goodman, Mary Ann Middlemiss,
Richard Vosco, and Nancy Ziegler. "How Older Persons are
Portrayed in Television Advertising: Implications for
Educators." Educational Gerontology, 1983, 9, pp. 111-122.

*** see age-roles ***

     sample: 136 commercials broadcast during the summer
     of 1981 on the three major networks.

     Older women were especially underrepresented in this
     sample of commercials. Less than one percent of the
     characters were women over the age of 59.

98. Hodges, Kay Kline, David A. Brandt, and Jeff Kline.
"Competence, Guilt, and Victimization: Sex Differences in
Attribution of Causality in Television Drama." Sex Roles,
1981, 7(5), pp. 537-46.

     sample: eight one-minute segments from two to four
     episodes of each of four programs broadcast in
     1976; 96 minute-long segments.

     Authors examined sex differences in coping skills by
     analyzing characters' perceptions of self as a causal
     element ("origin" statements, including decisions,

48

plans, accepting responsibility, etc.) as opposed to statements reflecting perception of external control ("pawn" statements). On the whole, female characters made somewhat fewer "origin" statements proportionately and more "pawn" statements than male characters, especially in violent programs. In family drama, however, female characters made proportionately more "origin" statements and male characters made more "pawn" statements.

99. Isber, Caroline and Muriel Cantor. Report of the Task Force on Women In Public Broadcasting. Washington, D.C.: Corporation for Public Broadcasting, 1975.

sample: one week of programming distributed nationally through the Public Broadcasting Service in 1974-75; 37 programs, children's included.

Women are not found in these programs to the degree one would realistically expect. While women were not stereotyped in the 28 adult information/news programs, they were excluded. Eleven of these programs had no female participants and discussions of politics and economics were dominated by males. Nine out of ten programs had only male announcers. Overall, 85 percent of the participants were male and 15 percent were female. Women were as likely as males to be in high-salaried positions and in occupations generally associated with males. Only one program addressed a "woman's" issue. The two adult dramas in the sample had greatly different sex distributions and the female characters in these programs had traditional roles and traits. In the segments of six children's series, females comprised 32 percent of 1,155 characters. Twenty-six percent of male characters, compared to 16 percent of female characters, were in occupational roles. While most of the females were in traditional "women's" jobs, 17 percent were in jobs usually associated with males.

100. Jeffries-Fox, Suzanne and Nancy Signorielli. "Television and Children's Conceptions of Occupations." In Herbert S. Dordick (ed.), Proceedings of the Sixth Annual Telecommunications Policy Research Conference. Lexington, Mass: Lexington Books, 1978, pp. 21-38.

sample: annual week-long samples of prime-time network dramatic progamming broadcast between 1969 and 1976.

Major characters on prime-time programs were
three-quarters male and one-quarter female. While
males dominated in the portrayal of six occupations
(doctors, psychiatrists, paramedics, judges, lawyers,
and police), the male-female distributions mirrored
the actual distribution of men and women in these
jobs in the U.S.

101. Kalisch, Beatrice J., Philip A. Kalisch, and Margaret
Scobey. "Reflections on a Television Image: The Nurses,
1962-1965." Nursing and Health Care, May 1981,
pp. 248-255.

*** see health ***

102. Kalisch Philip A. and Beatrice J. Kalisch. "Nurses
on Prime Time Television." American Journal of Nursing,
1982, 82, pp. 264-270.

*** see health ***

sample: 20 percent random sample of each of the 28
series with a regular nurse character broadcast
between 1950 and 1980.

Nurses generally received stereotyped treatment on
television. They usually were presented as hand
maidens to the medical profession; doctor-nurse
interactions usually showed the nurse taking orders.
Doctors, usually men, were portrayed with more
ambition, intelligence, risk-taking, rationality,
adeptness, aggression, self-confidence, and
sophistication. They also were more sincere,
altruistic, honest, and perceptive than nurses.
Nurses were presented as more obedient, and showed
more permissiveness, conformity, and flexibility than
doctors. Doctors and nurses, however, did not differ
in efficiency, organization, or discipline.

103. Kalisch, Philip A. and Beatrice J. Kalisch. "Sex
Role Stereotyping of Nurses and Physicians on Prime Time
Television: A Dichotomy of Occupational Portrayals." Sex
Roles, 1984, 10(7/8), pp. 533-553.

*** see health ***

sample: 20 percent sample of all series with nurses and physicians in major roles broadcast between 1950 and 1980; 28 series, 320 episodes, 240 nurses, 287 physicians.

These programs presented extreme levels of both sexual and occupational stereotyping. Television nurses were 99 percent female and television doctors were 95 percent male. The cluster of sex and occupational role characteristics, personality attributes, primary values, career orientations, professional competencies, and the tone of nurse-physician relationships produced an image of the female professional nurse as totally dependent on and subservient to male physicians. Television nurses were most likely to be white (95 percent), under 35 (44 percent), single (82 percent), childless (95 percent). There was no change in this image over 30 years. Exceptions were unfavorable; older nurses were less attractive, more sadistic, and reprimanding toward patients. There was only a small increase in the number of women physicians: none in the 1950s, 2 (8 percent) in the 1960s, and 13 (7 percent) in the 1970s.

104. Kalisch, Philip A., Beatrice J. Kalisch, and Jacqueline Clinton. "The World of Nursing on Prime Time Television, 1950-1980." Nursing Research, 1982, 31(6), pp. 358-363.

*** see health ***

105. Kalisch, Philip A., Beatrice J. Kalisch, and Margaret Scobey. Image of Nurses on Television. New York: Springer Publishing Co., 1983.

*** see health ***

sample: survey of all television shows that have ever featured nurses.

Study chronicled and analyzed the development of the image of nurses and nursing on television. The most common stereotype was the nurse as the all-around doctor's helper; the nurse who devoted her life to the service of a single physician. Another stereotype was the presentation of nursing as an outlet for maternal feelings. These stereotypes have persisted: what was televised in 1980 was similar to what was seen in 1950, including uniforms.

106. Kaniuga, Nancy, Thomas Scott, and Eldon Gade.
"Working Women Portrayed on Evening Television Programs."
Vocational Guidance Quarterly, 1974, 23(2), pp. 134-7.

    sample: 44 evening series (excluding movies)
broadcast during two months in 1972; 140 principal
adult characters.

    Females made up 31 percent and males 69 percent of
the sample. Thirty percent of the women were
full-time housewives; the 70 percent who were
employed were mostly single and young. Only 10
percent of the employed women were married (compared
to 60 percent in real life), and their home-related
role was emphasized. These employed women were most
often cast in traditional jobs (such as nurses or
secretaries) even in crime and action shows.

107. Kaplan, Stuart J. and Leslie A. Baxter. "Antisocial
and Prosocial Behavior on Prime-Time TV." Journalism
Quarterly, 1982, 59(3), pp. 478-482.

    sample: one episode of each of 17 of the top 18 most
popular prime-time dramatic programs broadcast from
April to July, 1980; 12 hours.

    The majority of behaviors appeared to be internally
motivated. Physical as opposed to symbolic acts
(insults) were significantly more likely to be
attributed to an external locus. In addition,
antisocial physical acts were significantly more
likely to be attributed externally than were
prosocial physical acts. Antisocial symbolic acts,
however, were significantly more likely to be
internally attributed than were symbolic acts. Sex
differences were consistent with conventional
societal norms. Two-thirds of all antisocial acts
were committed by men. An internal causal locus for
antisocial behavior was more likely to be found for
female than male characters. Thus, women who engaged
in antisocial behavior were more likely than men to
be presented as dispositionally antisocial or
aggressive, i.e., cast in a disapproving light.

108. Katzman, Natan. "Television Soap Operas: What's Been
Going on Anyway?" Public Opinion Quarterly, 1972, 36(2),
pp. 200-12.

sample: one episode per week of each of 14 soap operas broadcast for four weeks in 1970; 371 characters, 884 conversations.

Although there was about an equal number of males and females, there were more younger women and older men. None of the seven infants and children was female. Almost two-thirds of the women were employed in traditional occupations (housewife, secretary, nurse), while 60 percent of the men were professionals. Women were more likely to discuss personal relationships and domestic matters; men were more likely to discuss professional or business matters.

109. Kaufman, Lois. "Prime-Time Nutrition." Journal of Communication, 1980, 30(3), pp. 37-46.

*** see health ***

sample: first 30 minutes of the top ten regularly scheduled series, including commercials, broadcast in 1977; 20 programs, 108 commercials.

Of 509 characters, 50 were overweight and ten were obese. Men were somewhat more likely to be overweight or obese than women: 15 percent of the men compared to 8 percent of the women. The overweight women usually were obese, while men's weight problems were not so severe.

110. Lemon, Judith. "Dominant or Dominated? Women on Prime-Time Television." In Gaye Tuchman, Arlene Kaplan Daniels, and James Benet, (eds.), Hearth and Home: Images of Women in the Mass Media. New York: Oxford University Press, 1978, pp. 51-68.

sample: characters in occupational interactions in a sample of situation comedy and crime drama (stratified for significance of female role) broadcast in 1975; 274 males and 84 females.

When occupational status was relevant in male-female interactions, males were more dominant than women, generally as a result of their higher occupational status. High-status males were dominant in 45 percent of their total appearances and were dominated in 14 percent. High-status females, however, were dominant in 29 percent of their appearances and

dominated in 38 percent. This high-status male
dominance was greater in crime drama; situation
comedy generated more equal interactions. There was
little difference among low-status males and females
except that males were somewhat more dominated (49
percent of appearances) than females (dominated in 41
percent of appearances). High-status women were
generally absent from situation comedies. Although
race influenced dominance patterns for women, sex was
the more important variable. Black women were more
dominant in family situations than white women, but
white women were given more latitude in non-family
related appearances.

111. Lemon, Judith. "Women and Blacks on Prime-Time
Television." Journal of Communication, 1977, 27(4),
pp. 70-79.

sample: 165 male-female verbal and non-verbal
interactions systematically sampled from eight crime
dramas and twelve situation comedies (stratified for
significance of female roles) broadcast in prime time
in 1975.

An analysis of dominance/equality in male-female
verbal and nonverbal interactions. Program type had
a significant effect upon dominance/equality. Women
were less dominated by men in situation comedies (23
percent of interactions) than in crime dramas (47
percent of interactions). There were few
interactions in which females dominated males in
either type of program (13 percent in situation
comedies and six percent in crime dramas). The
family context in situation comedies provided a more
egalitarian structure for male-female interactions
(64 percent equal interactions compared to 47 percent
in crime dramas). Occupational status was not
relevant in a majority of interactions. When it was
relevant, however, it was a stronger determinant of
dominance than was sex. Sex was a somewhat stronger
determinant of dominance than was race, with
considerable interaction between these two variables.

112. Levinson, Richard M. "From Olive Oyl to Sweet Polly
Purebread: Sex-role Stereotypes and Televised Cartoons."
Journal of Popular Culture, 1975, 9(3), pp. 561-72.

sample: three consecutive episodes of selected
Saturday morning network and independent regular
cartoon series broadcast in 1973; 58 starring
characters, 644 human and 101 non-human characters.

Overall, female characters made up 25 percent of the
sample (23 percent of the children, 34 percent of the
teenagers, 19 percent of the adults, and 23 percent
of the elderly). The percentage of female characters
rose to 33 percent among major characters (usually
teenagers in mixed groups). Females made up 23
percent of the animals who could be identified by
sex. Male characters played a greater variety of
roles. Females were usually teenagers or
housewives; those in paid employment were in
traditionally stereotypical ones (secretary, teacher,
entertainer, witch). Married women were not employed
(contrary to real life), though married men were.
Female characters performed "socio-emotional"
functions (defined by their relationship to the
males); males were "instrumental" (performing tasks
of bravery and strength). Female characters had two
major functions: to be rescued by the hero or to
"catch" the right male character for herself. Female
characters were stereotyped in more extreme ways than
the males: they were either dumb, or very smart and
catty. There were, however, a few non-stereotyped
female characters. Male characters were more stable
and intelligent without caricatured weaknesses.
Robots and animals frequently exhibited stereotyped
sex-role behavior.

113. Lichter, Linda S. and S. Robert Lichter. "Criminals
and Law Enforcers in TV Entertainment." Prime Time Crime.
Washington, D.C.: The Media Institute, 1983.

sample: six weeks of prime-time programs broadcast in
1980-81 in which at least one crime was committed or
a law enforcer appeared; 263 programs, 250 criminals
committing 417 crimes.

The male-female distribution of criminals on
television was about the same as in real life --
regardless of the crime, nine out of ten criminals
were men. Males also made up 89 percent of
television law enforcers. "Crime on TV is more
dangerous, more violent, and more likely to be
directed against persons than is actual crime.
Latest FBI statistics indicate that the most common
offenses are rarely seen on TV while the most brutal

and injurious crimes appear far out of proportion to
their occurrence in everyday life."

114. Lichter, S. Robert and Linda Lichter.
"Italian-American Characters in Television Entertainment."
Prepared for The Commission for Social Justice, May 1982.

   sample: 263 episodes from a six week sample of the
   1980-81 television season that contained at least one
   Italian-American; 96 Italian-American characters.

   Most Italian-American characters were males; only one
   in six was a woman. Negative portrayals of
   Italian-Americans outnumbered positive portrayals by
   a margin of nearly two to one. Almost half of the
   Italian-American characters were shown in a negative
   light; only one in four was portrayed positively.

115. Liebert, Robert M., John M. Neale, and Emily
S. Davidson (eds.). The Early Window: Effects of
Television on Children and Youth. New York: Pergamon
Press, Inc., 1973, pp. 18-22.

   Brief summary of studies dealing with the portrayal
   of television characters (DeFleur (32); Gerbner
   (58); Head (94); Smythe (164)) in regard to sex-role
   and racial/ethnic stereotypes.

116. Liebmann-Smith, Joan and Sharon L. Rosen. "The
Presentation of Illness on Television." In Charles Winick
(ed.), Deviance and Mass Media. Beverly Hills, Ca.: Sage
Publications, 1978, pp. 79-93.

*** see health ***

   sample: 50 episodes of Marcus Welby, M.D. and a
   qualitative analysis of other medical programs.

   There was a slow trend in casting more women and
   racial minorities as both physicians and
   paraprofessionals in medical programs. In the past,
   women have usually portrayed patients or nurses and
   only 7 percent of the doctors. The sample of Marcus
   Welby, M.D. programs had twice as many male as female
   patients, 36 percent of the patients were children
   under 18, 2 percent were 60 or older, 94 percent were
   white, 6 percent were black or Chicano, 52 percent
   were upper-middle class, 40 percent were middle
   class, and 8 percent were lower class.

117. Long, Michele L. and Rita J. Simon. "The Roles and
Statuses of Women on Children's and Family TV Programs."
Journalism Quarterly, 1974, 51(1), pp. 107-110.

   sample: 34 female characters in regular roles from
   five episodes of each of 22 shows (directed in part
   or primarily to children) broadcast in 1972.

   This sample included 14 married women, 14 mothers,
   three widows, seven unmarried adults, eight
   teenagers, and two fantasy characters. Females were
   in leading roles in eight of 16 shows, usually on
   screen more than half the time (cartoons were
   excluded from this analysis). Twelve of the 14
   married women were deferential to their husbands;
   only two shared authority and responsibility equally.
   No married mothers worked outside the home (one
   worked as a writer at home but was not portrayed at
   this work), as compared to the real world where 38
   percent of married women work outside the home. Six
   of the 10 unmarried women held jobs. Even the two
   women in higher-level professional jobs appeared
   subservient and less rational than male characters.
   Thirty of the 34 female characters were tall, thin,
   attractive, and well dressed; they were generally
   concerned about their own appearance, that of other
   characters, or that of the home. This was an element
   of interaction with male characters and subject to
   male evaluation. Overall, female characters were
   portrayed as dependent, functioning essentially in a
   "socio-expressive" capacity in the family. Unmarried
   females were generally involved in attracting male
   characters.

118. Lopate, Carol. "Daytime Television: You'll Never
Want to Leave Home." Feminist Studies, 1976, 3(3/4),
pp.69-82.

   sample: a qualitative description of daytime
   serials, game shows, and their commercials.

   The game shows, daytime serials and their commercials
   played down the nonbenign aspect of the power men
   hold over women. The game show's M.C. gave gifts,
   but he did not lay down correct behavior or chastize
   for incorrect actions. Men in the daytime serials
   also had the capacity to assist, protect, and give,
   without retaining the power to dominate that most men
   potentially have over most women. Despite career
   differences, women and men in the daytime serials

probably were more equal than in any other form of
drama or in any area of real life.

119. McArthur, Leslie Zebrowitz and Susan V. Eisen.
"Television and Sex-Role Stereotyping." Journal of Applied
Social Psychology, 1976, 6(4), pp. 329-351.

sample: 22 Saturday morning network children's
programs (110 characters) and 161 commercials (315
central characters) broadcast in 1974.

Females made up 32 percent of the characters in these
programs. They generally were found in nurturant
roles (e.g., family, friend) and displayed concordant
behavior such as affiliation, compliance, politeness,
and nurturance. Males, on the other hand, were more
often in occupational or villain roles and displayed
more activity, autonomy, aggression, and
problem-solving. In commercials, females comprised
20 percent of the characters overall (but 28 percent
of the children). Thirty-two percent of females were
authorities compared to 55 percent of males. Females
were found more often than males in familial roles
(43 percent of females were pictured in the home
compared to 29 percent of males).

120. McArthur, Leslie Zebrowitz and Beth Gabrielle Resko.
"The Portrayal of Men and Women in American TV
Commercials." Journal of Social Psychology, 1975, 97(2),
pp. 209-220.

sample: 199 commercials broadcast during a day in
1971; 299 central characters.

Women made up 43 percent of the sample. Men were
more likely to be presented as authorities and women
as product users: 70 percent of the males compared
to 14 percent of the females were "authorities,"
while 86 percent of the women compared to 30 percent
of the men were product users. Males usually were
presented as authorities on products used by women
(care of the home or body, and food). Females were
also in roles that showed a relationship with others
(housewife, parent), while males were in independent
roles (worker, celebrity). Women were more likely to
be found in the home while men were found, most
frequently, in occupational settings. In regard to
rewards gained by using the product, women were more
likely to gain approval of family and/or the opposite
sex; males were likely to gain approval of friends
and/or make social or career advancements.

121. Mackey, W.D. and D.J. Hess. "Attention Structure and Stereotypy of Gender on Television: An Empirical Analysis." Genetic Psychology Monographs, 1982, 106(2), pp. 199-215.

sample: randomly selected 10-minute intervals of evening network programs broadcast over a three week period in 1979; 623 scenes and 8,529 behaviors.

Males outnumbered females in program scenes by two to one. Six percent of the scenes contained females only, 32 percent contained males only, and 62 percent had both males and females. Female dyads were usually in comedies and family dramas. Fewer than four percent of the female-female scenes involved task-oriented behaviors compared to 18 percent of the male-male scenes.

122. McNeil, Jean C. "Feminism, Femininity, and Television Series: A Content Analysis." Journal of Broadcasting, 1975, 19(3), pp. 259-271. See also "Imagery of Women in TV Drama: Some Procedural and Interpretative Issues," pp. 283-288 and "Whose Values?", pp. 295-296.

sample: 43 prime-time network dramatic series broadcast in 1973; 279 major and supporting characters.

Women made up 30 percent of the entire sample: 40 percent of the characters in situation comedies and 25 percent of the characters in non-comedy dramatic programs. Marital and family relationships were central to women's roles, and out-of-home employment was significantly underrepresented. Women in out-of-home occupations were in traditionally female or low-level jobs subordinate to men. Female characters were presented as more passive than male characters: only two percent of the women compared to 13 percent of the men solved problems by themselves (a finding influenced by program type and more relevant in serious drama). Moreover, almost half of the women, compared to a third of the men, depended upon other characters to solve their problems.

123. Manes, Audrey L. and Paula Melnyk. "Televised Models of Female Achievement." Journal of Applied Social Psychology, 1974, 4(4), pp. 365-374.

sample: 62 female characters from a two-month sample
and another 95 female and 149 male characters from a
six week sample of Canadian prime-time network drama,
excluding old movies.

Generally, women employed at all occupational levels
were single or unsuccessfully married; employed women
were ten times more likely than housewives to have
unsuccessful marriages. Women in lower-level
occupations were usually depicted as engaged to be
married. In the 6 week sample (comparing males and
females), married, employed females were three times
more likely to be unsuccessfully married than males.
Females successful in having both a career and
marriage were not deeply committed to their
profession or were financially independent. On the
whole, programs offered negative reinforcement for
female aspirations and achievements outside the home
and family.

124. Marecek, Jeanne, Jane Allyn Piliavin, Ellen
Fitzsimmons, Elizabeth C. Krogh, Elizabeth Leader, and
Bonnie Trudell. "Women as TV Experts: The Voice of
Authority?" Journal of Communication, 1978, 28(1),
pp. 159-168.

sample: randomly selected day and evening network
commercials, excluding PSAs, aired in 1972 (N=500),
1973 (N=231), and 1974 (N=437).

In the three yearly samples, only 7 percent of the
commercials had female voice-overs and 4 percent had
both male and female voice-overs. Fifty-three
percent of the commercials featured a female product
representative; these often were for products
traditionally associated with women (food, household,
and feminine care). The female expert usually
appeared in conjunction with a male voice-over, thus
diluting her authority. What little opportunity
women had to show expertise was largely restricted to
areas of homemaking and personal care.

125. Meehan, Diana M. Ladies of the Evening: Women
Characters of Prime-Time Television. Metuchen, N.J.: The
Scarecrow Press, 1983.

A qualitative examination of 30 years of television
series.

The portrayal of women on television series has not
been fair or positive. Ten basic types of female
characters are presented: Imp, Goodwife, Harpy,
Bitch, Victim, Decoy, Siren, Courtesan, Witch, and
Matriarch. The overall underrepresentation of women
was discussed. Moreover, series featuring women also
had men portraying prominent roles while many
male-centered series had no female characters.

126. Miles, Beth. Channeling Children: Sex Stereotyping
in Prime-Time TV. Princeton, N.J.: Women on Words and
Images, 1975.

sample: 3 episodes of each of the 16 top rated
programs broadcast between 7:30 p.m. and 9:30
p.m. during November 1973.

There was considerable underrepresentation of women
in all programs; men made up 61 percent of the major
characters. In action-adventure programs men
outnumbered women by six to one. Men worked in
diverse occupations, nearly twice the number held by
women. Three-quarters of the adult men in programs
about families contributed to family support; only
one-third of the women made financial contributions.
All adult characters exhibited more negative than
positive behaviors, but the behavior of women was
more negative than that of men. More men than women
displayed competent behaviors, while more women than
men displayed incompetent or bungling behaviors. On
commercials, women took care of their houses, their
families, their shopping, and their own appearance;
men worked and played harder and provided the voice
of authority for the purchasing decisions made by
women.

127. Miller, M. Mark and Byron Reeves. "Dramatic TV
Content and Children's Sex-Role Stereotypes." Journal of
Broadcasting, 1976, 20(1), pp. 35-50.

sample: one week of prime-time programs broadcast in
1974; 51 programs, 449 major characters.

Women made up only 28 percent of characters overall
and 16 percent of the characters in police/detective
programs. Westerns and action-adventure programs
also were highly skewed in sex distribution. Women
appeared much more often in situation comedies and
family dramas: 45 percent of the characters in these
programs were women. Women usually were not

61

portrayed as doctors, lawyers, or police; they were
found in traditional female occupational roles
(homemaker, teacher, secretary). Some of the more
recent programs had several women in
non-stereotypical jobs (park ranger, high school
principal, police officer).

128. National Organization for Women, National Area
Chapter. "Women in the Wasteland Fight Back: A Report on
the Image of Women Portrayed in TV Programming."
Pittsburgh, Pa.: NOW, Inc., 1972.

sample: a composite week of programming on one
network affiliate; includes commercials, dramatic
programming, quiz programs, talk shows, soap operas,
children's programming, sports, public affairs and
variety programs.

The analyses all point out that women on television
are usually outnumbered by men; the only exceptions
are in soap operas and quiz programs where women make
up more than 40 percent of the total number of
characters/participants. On quiz programs, however,
there were more female than male contestants and no
woman was a program "host." On quiz programs, women
also were frequently patronized (called "honey") and
the target of humorous remarks; the men were not
treated in either of these ways. Women were rarely
found as moderators/narrators and they were only 23
percent of the participants in public affairs
programming. No women were shown participating in
sports.

129. Nolan, John D., Joann Paley Galst, and Mary Alice
White. "Sex Bias on Children's Television Programs."
Journal of Psychology, 1977, 96, pp. 197-204.

sample: characters in network and public TV Saturday
morning programs and commercials broadcast over a
four week period in 1975.

Females made up 26 percent of the sample of
characters in Saturday morning programs. Analysis of
sex differences in verbal approval and disapproval
indicated that males were significantly more likely
than females to give approvals and disapprovals.
Males received significantly more disapprovals than
approvals; the proportion was more balanced for
females. Most of the disapprovals males received
were for destructiveness and noise-making; most of

their approvals were for other-directed and heroic behavior. Females received considerably more approvals than males for resourcefulness and physical appearance; they received more disapprovals than males for other-directed behavior (sharing, helping) and for avoidance behaviors (in responding to frightening situations, accepting responsibilities, etc.).

130. Northcott, Herbert C., John F. Seggar, and James L. Hinton. "Trends in TV Portrayal of Blacks and Women." Journalism Quarterly, 1975, 52(4), pp. 741-744.

sample: characters in occupational roles in three weeks of dramatic programming (excluding westerns) broadcast in 1971 (N=394) and 1973 (N=679).

In regard to visibility, authors found that white women gained between 1971 (five males to one female) and 1973 (four males to one female) while black women lost visibility between 1971 (two males to one female) and 1973 (seven males to one female). Women were still usually found in "non-census" occupations (eg., housewives). White women appeared to be moving gradually into low-level census occupations, while black women were not.

131. O'Donnell, William J. and Karen J. O'Donnell. "Update: Sex-Role Messages in TV Commercials." Journal of Communication, 1978, 28(1), pp. 156-158.

sample: one week of prime-time commercials aired on each of the three networks in 1976; 367 commercials.

Traditional stereotypes were unchanged since earlier studies (Courtney and Whipple, (29); Culley and Bennett, (30); and Dominick and Rauch, (37)). In commercials using voice-overs, 93 percent were done by men. About half of the product representatives were women; this percentage was influenced by the type of product. The association between women and the home remained strong. Women promoted mostly domestic products in a home setting, while men promoted mostly non-domestic products in settings outside the home.

132. O'Kelly, Charlotte G. "Sexism in Children's Television." Journalism Quarterly, 1974, 51(4), pp. 722-724.

63

sample: seven hours of children's shows, including
commercials, broadcast in 1973; 242 characters in
programs, 347 characters in commercials.

Females made up 15 percent of the characters in the
programs and were usually young girls (71 percent of
the females). There were only 25 adult
females: one-quarter of them were
housewives/mothers; 17 percent were in traditional,
low-authority positions; and genies, witches, etc.
made up the remainder. Among male characters, 55
percent were young boys, 6 percent were
husbands/fathers. On the whole, boys were more
active than girls. The sample of characters in
commercials was one-third female. One-third of the
women were housewives/mothers compared to 14 percent
of the men presented as husbands/fathers. Again,
those females depicted in employment were in
traditionally female jobs.

133. O'Kelly, Charlotte G. and Linda Edwards Bloomquist.
"Women and Blacks on TV." Journal of Communication, 1976,
26(4), pp. 179-184.

sample: one month of hour-long segments of network
programs and commercials broadcast throughout the day
in 1973; 2,309 characters.

Females made up 34 percent of the characters in adult
programs and 59 percent of the characters in
commercials aired during adult programs; 12 percent
of the people in the news and 36 percent of the
characters in the commercials aired during the
news; and 15 percent of characters in children's
programs and 33 percent of the characters in
commercials aired during children's programs. The
visibility of females in commercials was a function
of their role as consumer/housewife. In adult
programs, women were more likely than men to be
portrayed as housekeeper/parent. Women also appeared
in only 15 occupations compared to 44 for the men.
Women were underrepresented (except in adult program
commercials) and, when shown, were depicted according
to traditional sex-role stereotypes.

134. Peevers, Barbara Hollands. "Androgyny on the TV
Screen? An Analysis of Sex-Role Portrayal." Sex Roles,
1979, 5(6), pp. 797-809.

sample: 24 regularly scheduled evening network dramatic programs broadcast in 1975 and in 1976; 91 principal adult characters (52 males and 39 females).

The author analyzed sex-role portrayals for the overall sample and compared portrayals in early evening programs (7 to 9 p.m.) to those in late evening programs (9 to 11 p.m.). Since the "family hour" scheduling concept was in effect in 1975, it was expected that the portrayals in the former group of programs (with less sex and violence) would be less stereotyped than portrayals in late evening programs. In the combined sample, women made up 43 percent of the characters. There was more sex-role stereotyping, measured by the Bem Sex-Role Inventory, among male characters: 85 percent of the males were classified as "masculine" while 44 percent of the females were classified as "feminine." Moreover, only 4 percent of the male characters scored in the feminine range while about 28 percent of the females scored in the masculine range. The remaining characters were classified as "androgynous" (exhibiting masculine and feminine traits about equally) -- 11 percent of the males compared to about 28 percent of the females. When analyzed by viewing period, males were more sex-typed on late evening programs and females were more sex-typed on early evening ("family hour") programs in 1975. In 1976, after the "family hour" was discontinued, there was significantly less difference in sex-roles by viewing periods.

135. Petersen, Marilyn. "The Visibility and Image of Old People on Television." Journalism Quarterly, 1973, 50(3), pp. 569-573.

*** see age roles ***

136. Pierce, Chester M., Jean V. Carew, Diane Pierce-Gonzalez, and Deborah Wills. "An Experiment in Racism: TV Commercials." Education and Urban Society, 1977, 10(1), pp. 61-87.

*** see racial-ethnic groups ***

sample: 190 different prime-time network commercials broadcast during a two week period in 1972; 140 were aired during programs with predominantly white characters and 50 during programs with predominantly black characters; 671 characters, 53 blacks.

Females made up 43 percent of the characters in these commercials. The male-female imbalance was greater among white characters. Among black characters, the number of females was about equal to the number of males. Only 6 percent of the commercials had female voice-overs. Females were more likely to touch, while males were more likely to be touched in a positive manner. Family relationships were more overt for females. Females were less likely to work for wages (32 percent) and more likely to do household chores (83 percent).

137. Poulos, Rita Wicks, Susan E. Harvey, and Robert M. Liebert. "Saturday Morning Television: A Profile of the 1974-75 Children's Season." Psychological Reports, 1976, 39, pp. 1047-1057.

sample: one Saturday morning of network, independent, and public programming broadcast in 1974-75; 48 programs, 376 major and minor human characters. (Note: two subsamples were used for comparative analyses - one excluding programs broadcast on the independent stations and one using just programs broadcast on network affiliates.)

Females made up 29 percent of the total sample: 21 percent were white, three percent were black and five percent were of other ethnic groups. Males made up the remainder (71 percent) of the total sample: 54 percent were white, 10 percent were black and 7 percent were other ethnic groups. The characters performed a total of 175 aggressive acts -- 80 percent by males. Almost a quarter of the males were aggressive compared to only seven percent of the females. A quarter of the females were sympathetic and discussed feelings compared to only eight percent of the males.

138. Pyke, S.W. and J.C. Stewart. "This Column Is About Women: Women and Television." Ontario Psychologist, 1974, 6(5), pp. 66-69.

sample: one week of all programs and commercials broadcast on three Canadian stations (including one education channel); 2,653 central characters in programs, 2,662 commercials.

Females made up 28 percent of the total sample of
central characters. There was a greater percentage
of females in afternoon programs and the percentage
of males was highest in prime-time programs. The
educational channel had a larger imbalance of males
and females: females made up only 26 percent of
these characters. Both males and females were
generally depicted as active, capable, good-natured
and intelligent. Males, but not females, were
responsible, dominant, independent, and
work-oriented. Females, but not males, were
understanding, outgoing, practical, and sexy. In the
commercials, males had authoritative roles; female
roles were not employment-oriented. Male voice-overs
predominated (90 percent), but there was a more
equitable distribution of voice-overs on the
educational channel. Females on camera were
accompanied by a male voice-over about one-third of
the time.

139. Ramsdell, M.L. "The Trauma of Television's Troubled
Soap Families." Family Coordinator, 1973, 22, pp. 299-304.

sample: eight soap operas aired on one network
station in 1971-72; 57 leading female roles.

One-third of these women were office and service
workers, or shop owners, 14 percent were
professionals (doctors, nurses, librarians), and the
remainder were affluent housewives. The working
women were beset by misfortunes, were villainous or
unstable while housewives were innocent, victimized,
and referred to as "real women." Older women were
presented as valued advisors. About half of the
couples on these programs were divorced or in the
process of being divorced, in keeping with the
overall orientation toward personal and domestic
crises.

140. Real, Michael R. "Marcus Welby and the Medical
Genre." In Michael Real, Mass Mediated Culture. Englewood
Cliffs, N.J.: Prentice Hall, 1977, pp. 118-139.

*** see health ***

141. Reid, Pamela Trotman. "Racial Stereotyping on
Television: A Comparison of the Behavior of Both Black and
White Television Characters." Journal of Applied
Psychology, 1979, 64(5), pp. 465-471.

sample: 28 episodes of ten situation comedies
stratified by racial composition of the cast
(all-black, all-white, or mixed-race), broadcast in
1977; 110 characters.

Females comprised 40 percent of these characters and
the sex distribution was more equal among black
characters than among whites. Characters were
analyzed to determine sex and racial differences
using twelve behavior variables common in sex-role
research. Sex of character was a significant,
dominant influence in several behaviors/traits.
Females scored higher than males in nurturance, with
the black female highest. Males scored higher than
females in dominance, with the black female higher
than the white female. There was a more complex
interaction in terms of character achievement
(defined as plans or intent to overcome obstacles):
white females scored closest to the high level for
black males, while black females scored the lowest of
the four groups. While sex/race differences for
other variables were not significant, the pattern for
the white female was consistent: she was lowest of
all groups on activity, aggression directed toward
males, dominance, deference, harm avoidance, and
recognition. At the same time, she was high on
nurturance and achievement and highest of all in
autonomy and succorance.

142. Rickel, Annette U. and Linda M. Grant. "Sex-Role
Stereotypes in the Mass Media and Schools: Five Consistent
Themes." International Journal of Women's Studies, 1979,
2(2), pp. 164-179.

Documents consistent findings of sex-role stereotypes
in several media. Women appeared less frequently,
were more likely to be victimized (the target of
jokes, insults, and violent crime as well as engaging
in self-deprecation). Men and women also had
different action/achievement orientations (males were
active and ambitious while females were more
emotional and submissive). Women were generally
trivialized in media -- they were portrayed as a
"special interest group" whereas male activities were
seen as universally relevant and important.

143. Roberts, Elizabeth J. "Television and Sexual Learning in Childhood." In David Pearl, Lorraine Bouthilet, and Joyce Lazar (eds.), Television and Behavior: Ten Years of Scientific Progress and Implications for the Eighties. Washington, D.C.: GPO, 1982, pp. 209-223.

Overall view of television's "sexual curricula" including a summary of several sex-role portrayal studies Busby (16); Lemon (111); Long and Simon (117); McNeil (122); Seggar (148)). Discusses implications of these findings for children's social learning.

144. Scheibe, Cyndy. "Sex Roles in TV Commercials." Journal of Advertising Research, 1979, 19(1), pp. 23-27.

sample: 6,262 commercials broadcast over a five-month period in 1975-76; 10,000 characters.

The number of occupations in which female characters in commercials were portrayed was increasing, although they were still seen in half as many occupations as male characters. While some females were found in traditionally male occupations, the reverse (males in traditionally female occupations) was not found. The activities of males and females did not change: even when employed, females were shown doing housework and not working at their paid job. Compared to census data, professional men and women were overrepresented in commercials, while low level occupations were underrepresented.

145. Schneider, Kenneth C. and Sharon Barick Schneider. "Trends in Sex Roles in Television Commercials." Journal of Marketing, Summer 1979, 43, pp. 79-84. See also Kenneth C. Schneider. "Sex Roles in Television Commercials: New Dimensions for Comparisons." Akron Business and Economic Review, Fall 1978, pp. 20-24.

sample: 287 commercials in 27 hours of prime-time network programming broadcast during October 1976; 252 female characters and 304 male characters.

The results of this analysis were compared with those of an analysis from a sample of commercials broadcast in 1971 (Dominick and Raugh (37)). There were fewer young adults (male and female) in the 1976 sample than the 1971 sample, and more older (over 50) men and women in 1976 than in 1971. Women were still

portrayed as younger than the men. In the 1976
sample men were still more likely than women to be
portrayed as employed, although there was a trend
toward a more even balance of employed men and women.
Television commercials, nevertheless, understated
actual U.S. employment rates. In addition, females
were relatively more likely to be seen in
traditionally male-dominated occupations than were
males in traditionally female-dominated occupations.
Females were also more likely to be presented as a
spouse/parent (but not otherwise employed) than
males. Both married men and women were significantly
underrepresented in the 1976 sample. A trend toward
a more equal utilization of male and female
characters in both indoor and outdoor settings was
also uncovered. Finally, sex-role spokesperson
differences were reduced between 1971 and 1976.
Although in 1976 as in 1971 women were seen in more
narrowly defined roles than men, there had been some
improvement in the portrayal of women.

146. Schuetz, Stephen and Joyce N. Sprafkin. "Portrayal
of Prosocial and Aggressive Behaviors in Children's TV
Commercials." Journal of Broadcasting, 1979, 23(1),
pp. 33-40.

sample: 242 commercials broadcast during network and
independent Saturday morning children's programs in
1974; 2,226 human characters.

Females made up 37 percent of the sample of human
characters. The only prosocial behavior that
occurred with any degree of frequency (N=110 acts)
was altruism (sharing, helping, cooperation) -- a
behavior found most often in public service
announcements and in commercials for non-cereal
foods. Males were significantly more likely than
females to behave altruistically; they performed 78
percent and females performed 22 percent of these
acts. The 113 aggressive acts (use of threat or
force) appeared approximately once every two minutes,
particularly in cereal commercials. All of the
aggressive acts performed by humans (58 percent of
113 acts) were performed by males. Children were
more likely than adults to perform both altruistic
and aggressive acts.

147. Schuetz, Stephen and Joyce N. Sprafkin. "Spot Messages Appearing Within Saturday Morning Television Programs." In Gaye Tuchman, Arlene Kaplan Daniels, and James Benet (eds.), Hearth and Home: Images of Women in the Mass Media. New York: Oxford University Press, 1978, pp. 69-77.

sample: commercials and public service announcements (PSA's) broadcast during network and independent Saturday morning children's programs in 1974; 372 spot messages with 2,226 human characters.

Females made up 37 percent of this sample of characters. Fifteen percent of these spot messages had only female characters while 38 percent had only male characters. Commercials, except those for dolls and miniature appliances, featured fewer females than did PSA's. Representation of nonwhite characters was roughly comparable for males and females: 22 percent of the males were black and 6 percent were nonblack minority members; 16 percent of the females were black and 4 percent were nonblack minority members.

148. Seggar, John F. "Imagery of Women in Television Drama: 1974." Journal of Broadcasting, 1975, 19(3), pp. 273-282. See also "Women's Imagery on TV: Feminist, Fair Maiden, or Maid? Comments on McNeil." Journal of Broadcasting, 1975, 19(3), pp. 289-294.

sample: a stratified random selection (50 percent) of afternoon and evening dramatic and variety programs, excluding westerns and cartoons, broadcast during a five week period in 1974; 946 female characters, including 87 in major roles, and 142 male major characters.

The total sample of female characters was analyzed to determine the types of roles portrayed by women; there were 87 (9 percent) in major roles, 102 (11 percent) in supporting roles, 140 (15 percent) in minor roles, and the remainder (65 percent) in bit parts. Nonwhites comprised 15 percent of the total sample of female characters, but only seven percent of major female characters. When portrayed in an occupation, women were presented in the traditional ones: housewife, secretary, nurse. In the comparison with male major characters, females were more likely to be presented as married (30 percent compared to 16 percent), better off financially, and generally dominated by males during interactions. They were

significantly less likely than males to be depicted
in occupational roles, especially as professionals.

149. Seggar, John F. "Television's Portrayal of
Minorities and Women: 1971-75." Journal of Broadcasting,
1977, 21(4), pp. 435-446.

sample: a stratified random selection of afternoon
and evening dramatic and variety programs, excluding
westerns and cartoons, broadcast during a five week
period in 1971 and 1973 (50 half-hour units) and 1975
(50 percent of programs); 10,794 characters.

Documents a trend of increasing visibility of female
characters: females were 21 percent of the 1971
sample, 26 percent of the 1973 sample, and 31 percent
of the 1975 sample. The proportion of women in
dramatic roles of three or more minutes rose from 32
percent in 1971 to 54 percent in 1973; the
proportion of male characters in similar roles also
rose, but to a lesser degree (from 34 percent in 1971
to 49 percent in 1973). In the 1975 sample, men
outnumbered women by three to one in major roles and
minor roles, by two and a half to one in supporting
roles, and by two to one in bit parts.

150. Seggar, John F., Jeffrey K. Hafen, and Helena
Hannonen-Gladden. "Television's Portrayals of Minorities
and Women in Drama and Comedy Drama, 1971-1980." Journal
of Broadcasting, 1981, 25(3), pp. 277-288.

sample: a stratified random selection of afternoon
and evening dramatic and variety programs, excluding
westerns and cartoons, broadcast during four five
week periods in 1971 and 1973 (50 half-hour units)
and in 1975 and 1980 (50 percent of programs).

Documents an increase in the percent of female
characters: females were 21 percent of the 1971
sample (N=1,942), 26 percent of the 1973 sample
(N=3,278), 31 percent of the 1975 sample (N=5,572),
and 39 percent of the 1980 sample (N=7,132).

151. Seggar, John F. and Penny Wheeler. "World of Work on
TV: Ethnic and Sex Representation in Television Drama."
Journal of Broadcasting, 1973, 17(2), pp. 201-214.

sample: 250 half-hours of afternoon and prime-time drama (excluding westerns and cartoons) and weekend morning programs sampled over a five week period in 1971; 1,830 characters.

Females made up 18 percent of the entire sample, 17 percent of the blacks, 3 percent of the Chicanos, 15 percent of the British and other Europeans, and 44 percent of the Asians. There were no female American Indians. White males were in higher prestige occupations than minority males. Among women, minorities in minor roles were in higher prestige occupations than white females. Overall, there were fewer occupational roles for women than men; employed women generally were service workers and entertainers.

152. Seiter, Ellen. "Men, Sex, and Money in Recent Family Melodrama." Journal of University of Film and Video Association, 1983, 35(1), pp. 17-27.

*** see sexual preference ***

Descriptive study of family melodramas (daytime serials and prime-time programs such as Dynasty and Dallas).

In terms of moral judgments, family melodramas continued to be rather soft on men and extremely harsh on women. Prime-time serials revolved around masculine competetion and intrigue in the business world. While women were affected by and sometimes embroiled in these financial matters, they existed largely as appendages to the men. Often women were prizes to be won by men, rewards for shrewdness and material success. While scenes between two women were prominent on daytime serials, they occurred rarely during the prime-time serials.

153. Shaw, Jeffrey. "Interactions on Television: An Analysis of the Interactions of the Main Characters of All in the Family and The Honeymooners." Small Group Behavior, 1980, 11(4), pp. 411-418.

sample: one week of reruns, broadcast in 1978, of each program.

Coded all main family member reactions using Bale's interaction process analysis. Archie made 102 responses compared to Edith's 48; Ralph made 37

compared to Alice's 22. Archie's responses showed
antagonism, tension, disagreement and information
giving; Edith gave information, showed tension
release, tension and solidarity. Ralph gave
information,and showed tension and antagonism and
Alice gave information, opinions, suggestions, and
showed solidarity. Archie and Edith were
characterized by his creating tension and her
reducing it; Ralph and Alice were characterized by
his creating tension and her remaining "cool."

154. Shinar, Dov, Adrian Tomer, and Ayala Biber. "Images
of Old Age in Television Drama Imported to Israel."
Journal of Communication, 1980, 30(1), pp. 50-55.

*** see age roles ***

sample: seven weeks of programs broadcast in 1976; 46
programs, 562 characters.

The percentage of female characters decreased with
age. Females made up 39 percent of the characters
under 49, 21 percent of the characters between 50 and
59, and 19 percent of the characters 60 and older.

155. Signorielli, Nancy. "Content Analysis: More than
Just Counting Minorities." In In Search of
Diversity: Symposium on Minority Audiences and Programming
Research. Washington, D.C.: Corporation For Public
Broadcasting, 1981, pp. 97-108.

Overview of several analyses of sex- and
minority-role portrayals with a discussion of content
analysis methodology.

156. Signorielli, Nancy. "The Demography of the
Television World." In Gabrielle Melischek, Karl
E. Rosengren, and James Stappers (eds.), Cultural
Indicators: An International Symposium. Vienna,
Austria: The Austrian Academy of Sciences, 1983,
pp. 137-157. Also in Oscar H. Gandy, Jr., Paul Espinosa,
and Janusz A. Ordover (eds.), Proceedings from the Tenth
Annual Telecommunications Policy Research Conference.
Norwood, New Jersey: Ablex Publishing, 1983, pp. 53-73.

sample: annual week-long samples of prime-time and
weekend-daytime network dramatic programming
broadcast between 1969 and 1981;   14,037 prime-time
and 6,243 weekend-daytime characters.

Women on television were usually underrepresented by
a factor of three: for each female character there
were three or more male characters. Women were most
underrepresented in action-adventure programs.
Although situation comedies had the largest
proportion of female characters, women were still
outnumbered by two to one. In weekend-daytime
(children's programming) women were outnumbered by
four or more to one. Trend analysis revealed that
the smallest percentage of female characters appeared
in the 1973 sample (25 percent) and the largest
percentage appeared in the 1980-81 sample (31
percent).

157. Signorielli, Nancy. "Marital Status in Television
Drama: A Case of Reduced Options." Journal of
Broadcasting, 1982, 26(2), pp. 585-597.

sample: annual week-long samples of prime-time
network dramatic programming broadcast between 1975
and 1979; 1,298 major characters, 447 programs.

Television world is stereotyped and traditional.
Males outnumbered females by three to one. Female
characters were less important, played fewer
different types of roles, and were concentrated in
roles best described as "typically female." Women
were usually younger and more attractive than the
men; they were also found in the context of home and
family, were likely to be married, and, if employed,
cast in traditionally female occupations. Women who
were married were not usually employed outside the
home. Six out of ten single women and
formerly-married women were employed outside the
home. Only 12 percent of the women, compared to 33
percent of the men, could not be coded on marital
status. Marital status clearly differentiated female
characters. Only the formerly-married woman was
presented less traditionally; but she fared the least
well of all women in that she was older, less
attractive, somewhat unhappy, less feminine, and
somewhat selfish. She also had children and
performed housekeeping activities for others.

158. Signorielli (Tedesco), Nancy. "Patterns in Prime
Time." Journal of Communication, 1974, 24(2), pp. 119-124.

   sample: annual week-long samples of prime-time
   network dramatic programming broadcast between 1969
   and 1972; 775 major characters.

   Females made up 28 percent of the sample. Only
   one-quarter of the female characters compared to over
   half of the male characters were found in
   action-adventure programs. Only 40 percent of the
   females, compared to 64 percent of the males, were
   employed; males were found in a wider variety of
   occupations. Women were more likely to be married --
   over half of the women as compared to a third of the
   men. While only 20 percent of the female characters
   were involved in violence, three times as many women
   were killed as killed other people. Males, on the
   other hand, killed twice as often as they were
   killed. Female characters were more attractive,
   youthful, sociable, warm, and happy; male characters
   were more powerful, smart, rational, and stable.
   Overall, females were more dependent and had fewer
   adventures than males.

159. Signorielli, Nancy and George Gerbner. "The Image of
the Elderly in Prime-time Network Television Drama."
Generations, Fall, 1978, pp. 10-11.

   sample: major and minor characters in annual
   week-long samples of prime-time network dramatic
   programming broadcast between 1969 and 1976.

   Females made up 28 percent of the sample of major
   characters and 26 percent of the sample of minor
   characters. The percentage of female characters
   decreased with age. Older women had more "bad"
   qualities than older males and younger women; they
   were also the only group more likely to be
   unsuccessful (failing to achieve goals) than
   successful. Women, except elderly women, were more
   likely to be involved in romance than men. Family
   life was especially important to older women.
   Overall, women were less likely to be involved in
   violence; older women were, however, more likely than
   males and younger women to be killed.

160. Signorielli, Nancy and George Gerbner. "Women in Public Broadcasting: A Progress Report." The Annenberg School of Communications, University of Pennsylvania, Philadelphia, Pa., March, 1978.

    sample: one week of programs distributed by PBS in 1977; 28 adult programs and 534 segments from 25 children's programs.

    Update of the 1975 Task Force Report on Women in Public Broadcasting; also provides new information on portrayal of minorities and women in public broadcasting. Women made up 28 percent of the entire sample of characters, an increase from the 1975 study. Women made up 29 percent of the people in general/information programs, 10 percent of those in music and dance programs, 28 percent of the dramatic characters. Three-quarters of the announcers and all of the moderators were men. In children's programming (Sesame Street and The Electric Company), females made up 35 percent of the characters (little change from 1975). Only 25 percent of the characters were seen in an occupational role; of these, 77 percent of the women were in "masculine" jobs.

161. Silverman, L. Theresa, Joyce N. Sprafkin, and Eli Rubinstein. "Physical Contact and Sexual Behavior on Prime-Time TV." Journal of Communication, 1979, 29(1), pp. 33-43.

*** see sexual preference ***

    sample: one week of regularly scheduled prime-time programs including variety, movies, and specials broadcast during the 1977-78 season; 678 characters.

    Females made up 32 percent of the sample. Among blacks, the distribution of men and women was about equal; other racial minorities, however, showed more unbalanced male-female distributions. Females were significantly more likely than males to engage in physical forms of affection (hugging, kissing, affectionate touching), performing 68 percent of this behavior.

162. Silverstein, Arthur J. and Rebecca Silverstein. "The Portrayal of Women in Television Advertising." Federal Communications Bar Journal, 1974, 27, pp. 71-98.

sample: 496 commercials from four days of prime-time network programming broadcast in 1973.

Women made up 50 percent of the primary actors and 52 percent of the secondary actors. The use of women for voice-overs ranged from 4 percent of commercials for neutral products (those used by either sex) to 21 percent of commercials for "female" products. There were somewhat fewer women in commercials for neutral products than in commercials for household products. Although women had somewhat greater visibility in commercials for household products, their portrayal in these ads was more negative. A very small number of commercials contained explicit directives to buy or use a product; all were directed to women. About an equal percentage of male and female actors gave advice; about twice as many females as males were given advice on household products.

163. Singleton, Loy A. and Stephanie L. Cook. "Television Network News Reporting by Female Correspondents: An Update." Journal of Broadcasting, 1982, 26(1), pp. 487-491.

sample: ten weeks of news programs (150 newscasts for each network) broadcast in 1977; 1,247 news reports.

News reports were coded for position in newscast, sex of the correspondent, and topic. Overall, female reporters were 17 percent and male reporters were 83 percent of the sample. Female reporters were well represented in "lead stories;" they filed 16 percent of the first, 15 percent of the second, and 18 percent of the third stories. Women reported proportionately fewer stories than men about foreign affairs, the economy, business, sports, disasters, and "features." Women were significantly over assigned to stories about the U.S. government, the environment, women's issues, and social problems.

164. Smythe, Dallas, W. "Reality as Presented by Television." Public Opinion Quarterly, 1954, 18, pp. 143-156.

sample: one week of dramatic programs broadcast on several New York City stations in 1953; 86 programs, 476 characters.

One-third of the characters were females. The average age of females was 33 compared to an average

age of 38 for males. Villains, especially female villains, were somewhat older than heroes; the average age of female villains was 47. Housewives made up 37 percent of the sample of females; women in other occupations were proportionally more likely to break the law than housewives or employed men.

165. Sternglanz, Sarah Hall and Lisa A. Serbin. "Sex-role Stereotyping in Children's Television Programs." Developmental Psychology, 1974, 10(5), pp. 710-715.

sample: three episodes of each of the 10 most popular commercial children's programs with at least one regularly appearing male and female character broadcast in the 1971-72 season; 147 major and minor characters.

Females made up one-third of this sample. A significantly higher percentage of females than males was classified as "good." Females were less likely than males to be aggressive and make plans. They were more likely than males to be deferent, to be punished for a high level of activity, and to use magic.

166. Stocking, S. Holly, Barry S. Sapolsky, and Dolf Zillman. "Sex Discrimination in Prime-Time Humor." Journal of Broadcasting, 1977, 21(4), pp. 447-455.

sample: ten-minute segments of all prime-time network programs broadcast during one week in 1975; 63 programs and 852 humorous incidents.

Almost two-thirds of the humorous incidents in all program types (comedy, variety, drama) involved a "put-down." Males were significantly more often the source and object of hostile humor. Both males and females were disparaged humorously about as often as they disparaged others humorously. Contrary to the stereotype of women fighting among themselves, females were less often portrayed as "catty" in humorous encounters with other women.

167. Streicher, Helen White. "The Girls in the Cartoons." Journal of Communication, 1974, 24(2), pp. 125-129.

sample: anecdotal account of cartoons and commercials broadcast on Saturday and Sunday mornings and weekday afternoons during a nine week period in 1972.

In the programs, males outnumbered females overall and in leading roles. Females were much less often portrayed in positions of responsibility. Mothers worked only at home, and no males did housework. Males were stereotyped as bumbling husbands and dumb athletes. In the commercials, males outnumbered females on camera and in voice-overs, except in doll and toy appliance ads.

168. Tognoli, Jerome and Judith L. Storch. "Inside and Outside: Setting Locations of Female and Male Characters in Children's Television." EDRA: Environmental Design Research Association, 1980, No. 11, pp. 288-297.

sample: 13 prime-time and weekend programs most watched by children on network, public, and independent stations in 1978 and 1979.

Male characters were depicted about twice as often as female characters. Outdoor settings appeared more frequently than interiors and home settings. In nine of 13 programs, males predominated in outdoor settings; females predominated in outdoor settings in the other four programs. Males were most often seen in stereotypically masculine activities and females in stereotypically feminine activities.

169. Tuchman, Gaye. "The Symbolic Annihilation of Women by the Mass Media." In Gaye Tuchman, Arlene K. Daniels, and James Benet, (eds.), Hearth and Home: Images of Women in the Mass Media. New York: Oxford University Press, 1978, pp. 3-38, esp. pp. 3-17.

Summarizes and synthesizes research on television programming (commercial and public) and commercials from 1950s to mid-1970s and considers the source of sex stereotypes. Concludes, based upon Cantor and Isber's (20,99) examination of public television, that the commercial foundation of network television is not the essential agent, but that the mass media reflect predominant societal beliefs and values.

170. Tuchman, Gaye. "Women's Depiction by the Mass Media." Signs, 1979, 4(3), pp. 528-542.

Discusses communications research with specific reference to image studies and stereotyping. Considers the institutional/economic basis for media

myths and uses this framework to evaluate current
research and theory.

171.   Tuchman, Gaye, Arlene Kaplan Daniels, and James
Benet, (eds.).   Hearth and Home: Images of Women in the
Mass Media.   New York: Oxford University Press, 1978.

An anthology of articles about the portrayal of women
in television, magazines, and newspapers. Includes a
section on possible causes and effects of these
portrayals.

172.   Turow, Joseph.   "Advising and Ordering: Daytime,
Prime Time." Journal of Communication, 1974, 24(2),
pp. 138-141.

sample: advising/ordering interactions between males
and females in twelve hours of adult daytime serials
and twelve hours of prime-time programs;   105
prime-time interactions; 117 daytime-serial
interactions.

In prime-time, females made up 30 percent of the
speaking characters in the sampled programs. The
most frequent category of interaction was "masculine"
topics (business, law, government, crime/danger).
Two-thirds of the males initiated orders/advice on
"masculine" subjects; only 22 percent of the females
initiated similar types of orders/advice. Women,
even those whose occupations related to business,
gave directives related to "feminine" topics (love,
family, home, personal problems);   only 10 percent of
the men gave these types of directives. Females,
however, gave a considerably larger percentage of
"neutral" advice/orders than males. In daytime
serials, the male/female ratio was about equal (54
percent male and 46 percent female) and directives
focused more upon neutral and "feminine" topics.
Women were more likely to advise on "feminine" and
neutral subjects than in prime time; males were also
more likely to give directives about neutral and
"feminine" subjects than they were in prime time.
Although women and traditional feminine concerns were
more central to these programs, women were seldom
given an opportunity to show superior knowledge
except in traditional areas.

173. Turow, Joseph. "Occupation and Personality in
Television Dramas: An Industry View." Communication
Research, 1980, 7(3), pp. 295-318.

    sample: four industry "breakdowns" (character
descriptions/plot summaries used in casting) for each
of 36 prime-time non-comedy network dramatic
series; 144 episodes, 824 characters in non-regular
roles.

    Author examined personality stereotyping among
occupational groups in crime and adventure series.
Women made up 24 percent of the sample of characters.
Females were the largest component of the "other"
occupational category (50 percent female, including
homemakers, students, artists, and other non-census
occupations). Females also comprised 21 percent of
blue collar workers and 19 percent of the white
collar workers. They were only 9 percent of the
criminals and 5 percent of law enforcers.

174. United States Commission on Civil Rights. Window
Dressing on the Set: Women and Minorities in Television.
Washington, D.C.: Government Printing Office, August 1977.

    program sample: annual week-long samples of
prime-time and weekend-daytime network dramatic
programming broadcast from 1969 through 1974; 5,624
characters.

    Females made up 26 percent of the sample. The
sex-racial distribution of the sample was 24 percent
white women, 2 percent nonwhite women, 65 percent
white men and 9 percent nonwhite men. There was a
slight decrease in the number of nonwhite males from
1969 to 1974, but an increase in the number of
nonwhite females. Female characters were generally
younger and as characters aged, the male-female
distribution increasingly favored male
characters; females outnumbered males only in the
21-30 age group. Almost two-thirds of the males were
in serious roles as compared to only half of the
females. Females were less likely than males to be
villains. Females were more likely to be
married: half of the females as compared to only a
third of the males. About 57 percent of the females
had no identifiable occupation (higher for the
nonwhite female), as compared to 31 percent of the
males. Females who could be classified by occupation
usually were found in clerical and service jobs or in
the professions. There were proportionally fewer

82

female professionals than male professionals and
their number decreased from 1969 to 1974.
Females, especially nonwhite females, were less likely
to commit violence but were the most frequent
victims. Overall, sex differences were more
influential than racial-ethnic differences.

news sample: 230 stories from a composite week of
network news broadcast on each of the three networks
in 1974-75.

Women made up 12 percent (N=10) of the 85
correspondents; only one of the first three stories
broadcast each night was reported by a woman. Women
generally covered health, education and welfare, and
other items of special interest to women and/or
minorities. Three out of 230 stories were related to
women; two about a birth control device, and one on
abortion hearings. Out of the 141 identified
newsmakers, only 13 percent were women. While 56
percent of the white males who appeared were
government officials, 56 percent of the white females
were private individuals, generally wives or mothers.
Nonwhite women, except for one congresswoman, were
generally victims of economic deprivation.

175. United States Commission on Civil Rights. Window
Dressing on the Set: An Update. Washington, D.C.,
Government Printing Office, January, 1979.

program sample: five week-long samples of prime-time
and weekend-daytime network dramatic programming
broadcast in 1975, 1976, and 1977 (5,042 characters).

Examines portrayal of women in three additional
samples of programming; compares these findings to
those analyzed in the 1977 report. Females made up
28 percent of the sample and the only significant
gains were made by nonwhite females. Female
characters continued to be younger than male
characters, and the male-female distribution
continued to favor males as characters aged. In
regard to occupations, females continued to be
portrayed in traditional or lower-level occupations
(homemaker, secretary, nurse).

news sample: 330 stories from a composite 5-day week
broadcast by the three networks in 1977.

Less than two percent of the stories related to women
and minorities; a decrease from the 1974-1975

sample. Women were 10 percent of the 90
correspondents; there were no minority female
correspondents. Women began to report stories of
national relevance rather than primarily stories of
concern to women and minorities. Out of 249
newsmakers, 7 percent were women; there was also a
decrease in the number of minority women presented as
newsmakers. Women were still presented as wives,
mothers, and victims.

176. Uselding, Douglas K. "Assessing the Level of
Sex-Role Stereotyping on Children's Preferred Programming."
Technical Report No. 1: Children's Use of Television as a
Source of Social Role Models. University of South Dakota,
Department of Psychology, 1979.

sample: 64 favorite programs of children five to
twelve years old; 174 leading characters.

Rated characters for both "male" and "female"
concepts (eg., achievement orientation vs. pleasing
personality). There was a degree of stereotyping
among programs ranging from excessive to little or
none. Several patterns were found: some programs
presented characters with traditional male and female
stereotypes; others reversed the stereotype for one
group (i.e., all characters were "masculine" or
"feminine"); and some presented the sexes in a
neutral way (reversed stereotypes for both males and
females). Overall, female characters were more
stereotyped and skewed toward the "female" concept.
Animated characters were the most neutral.

177. Verna, Mary Ellen. "The Female Image in Children's
TV Commercials." Journal of Broadcasting, 1975, 19(3),
pp. 301-309.

sample: 173 network commercials broadcast on Saturday
morning in 1973.

Male-oriented/dominated commercials made up 58
percent of the sample, female oriented/dominated
commercials made up 14 percent of the sample, and the
remainder were neutral. Commercials directed toward
or dominated by male characters displayed
significantly more activity than those with a female
orientation. Eight out of ten females appeared in
single person activities and two out of ten in
cooperative activities; no females appeared in
aggressive/competitive activities. The pattern for

males was quite different: 45 percent were in
aggressive/competitive activities, 33 percent in
single person activities, and 23 percent in
cooperative activities. A male voice-over was used
in 94 percent of the ads, including 55 percent of
those oriented toward females. Female-oriented
commercials were more likely to have quiet
backgrounds (77 percent) than male-oriented
commercials (9 percent). There were no loud
female-oriented commercials, while 21 percent of the
male-oriented ads were loud.

178. Volgy, Thomas J. and John E. Schwarz. "TV
Entertainment Programming and Sociopolitical Attitudes."
Journalism Quarterly, 1980, 57(1), pp. 150-154.

sample: themes and central characters in four weeks
of prime-time network entertainment programming,
broadcast in 1975.

Male-female relationships in most programs were
presented according to traditional values and norms.
Only four programs scored as less traditional than
others on Spence and Helmreich's Rejection of
Traditional Sex Roles Scale. Authors report results
of a cultivation analysis based on these content
findngs.

179. Wartella, Ellen. "Children's Impressions of
Television Families." In Herbert S. Dordick (ed.),
Proceedings of the Sixth Annual Telecommunications Policy
Research Conference. Lexington, Mass: Lexington Books,
1978, pp. 57-72.

sample: 11 episodes from ten family/situation comedy
series broadcast during the 1975-76 season.

Behaviors were coded as prosocial (willingness to
work with others) or antisocial (unwillingness to
work with others, and aggressive methods used to
attain goals). Neutral behaviors (nearly two-thirds
of behaviors) were not coded. Series were divided
into two groups based upon expectations of father's
behavior profile as predominently prosocial or
multi-dimensional (displaying antisocial as well as
prosocial behaviors). Mothers were dominant
characters in only three series: Brady Bunch, Good
Times, and Partridge Family. In most series the
father was a dominant character, either standing
alone in his domination of the series -- All in the

Family, Jeffersons, and Swiss Family Robinson -- or
sharing domination with his wife or one of his
children. Only one of the multi-dimensional fathers
performed more prosocial than antisocial behaviors.
Mothers were uniformly portrayed in a positive
manner, with all but two mothers performing at least
70 percent prosocial behaviors. Children also were
likely to be portrayed positively, but with fewer
prosocial elements of behavior as positive fathers or
mothers. Both boys and girls exhibited about
two-thirds prosocial and one-third antisocial
behaviors. Data from content analyses were then used
to examine children's impressions of favorite
television characters.

180. Weibel, Kathryn. Mirror Mirror: Images of Women
Reflected in Popular Culture. New York: Anchor Books,
1977.

Examined major daytime and evening television
formulas to illustrate how television fostered a
dichotomy between the situated woman (housewife) and
the male superhero. Game shows, particularly,
reinforced the image of woman as housewife/consumer
and man as professional/provider. Since daytime
serials were especially geared for the housewife
viewer, the importance of jobs held by both male and
female characters was subordinated to the importance
of personal relationships and family life. The
attitude toward working women on the serials was
generally supportive, so long as these women did not
neglect family responsibilities. Serials also
presented strong dichotomies between good and evil.
More than anything else the daytime serials presented
the image of woman as victim. In evening
programming, situation comedies were the only
programs that portrayed women as the full peers of
men, and occasionally as their superiors. By
contrast, in drama and drama/adventure programs, men
were the heroes and women victims or window dressing.
Females who were not principal characters appeared
more frequently on adventure programs, but they were
cast as victims or criminals. One of television's
most sexist "crimes" was to encourage women to
identify with the victimized while, at the same time,
encouraging men to identify with the victors.

181. Weigel, Russell, H. and James W. Loomis. "Televised Models of Female Achievement Revisited: Some Progress." Journal of Applied Social Psychology, 1981, 11(1), pp. 58-63.

sample: one week of prime-time network dramatic programming broadcast in 1978; 139 characters.

A replication of Manes and Melnyk (123). Males outnumbered females by about two to one (91 males and 48 females). There was no significant change from Manes and Melnyk's data collected in 1972 in regard to the marital status of employed male and female characters (employed females were still less likely than employed males to be married). However, in a departure from earlier findings of employment-happy marriage incompatability, there was a 20 percent decrease in the percentage of unsuccessful marriages among working women and an increase in the percent of unsuccessful marriages among housewives. Authors interpret findings as a reflection of acceptance of expanded options for women.

182. Welch, Renate L., Aletha Huston-Stein, John C. Wright, and Robert Plehal. "Subtle Sex-Role Cues in Children's Commercials." Journal of Communication, 1979, 29(3), pp. 202-209.

sample: 60 commercials for toys aired during morning children's programs in 1977.

The greater level of activity in commercials featuring boys was the result of the specific toys in the commercials. Male-oriented ads contained more "cuts" while female-oriented ads contained more "fades/dissolves." The amount of dialogue in male- and female-oriented ads was about equal, although males talked more in commercials featuring both males and females. Male-oriented commercials were noisier: they featured loud music and sound effects; female-oriented ads, on the other hand, more often had background music. Aggression toward objects and other characters was also frequent in male-oriented commercials. Overall, commercials with both boys and girls were more similar to commercials featuring just girls than those featuring just boys.

183. Wexler, Marvin and Gilbert Levy. "Women on Television: Fairness and the 'Fair Sex'." Yale Review of Law and Social Action, 1971, 2, pp. 59-68.

sample: 600 hours of commercial television monitored in the Washington, D.C. area from October 11-17, 1970.

Women appeared as leading characters in 53 hours (77 programs) of programming; men were leads in 508 hours (655 programs). No women appeared as leads in religious, educational, straight news, daytime serials, sporting events, or cooking programs. Women were seen primarily as maids, nurses, housewives, dizzy teenagers, secretaries, witches, and scatter-brained starletts. Men, by comparison, were seen as ranch owners, doctors, lawyers, engineers, sheriffs, professors, and so on. Thirteen of the 14 continuing dramas with women leads were comedies, while only 14 of the 48 dramas starring men were comedies. No women were M.C.'s on game or quiz shows. Even children's programs were dominated by men. Arguments were presented to the effect that this portrayal of women on television constitutes a controversal issue of public importance.

184. Whipple, Thomas W. and Alice E. Courtney. "Social Consequences of Sex Stereotyping in Advertising." In George Fisk, Johan Arndt, and Kjell Gronhaug (eds.), Future Directions for Marketing. Cambridge, Ma.: Marketing Science Institute, 1978, pp. 332-350.

Overview of content studies on the portrayal of women in advertising. The overwhelming conclusion was that advertising portrays the typical woman in a limited and traditional role. Women's place was seen to be the home and their labor force roles were underrepresented. Women were typically portrayed as housewives and mothers with low intelligence, dependent upon men, subservient, and with other personality problems. Housewives were shown as desperately in need of product benefits to satisfy and serve their husbands and families. In addition, women often were portrayed as sex objects; they had a great need for personal adornment to attract and hold men. In advertising addressed to men, women were used as decorative, attention-getting objects.

185. Winick, Charles, Lorne G. Williamson, Stuart F. Chusmir, and Mariann Pezella Winick. Children's Television Commercials: A Content Analysis. New York: Praeger, 1973.

sample: 236 non-toy commercials obtained from
advertising agencies in 1971.

Young girls appeared in 36 percent of the
commercials, boys in 58 percent; women appeared in 26
percent of the commercials while men appeared in 68
percent. Heroes, usually males, appeared in 18
percent of the commercials: they were explorers,
scientists, police. Females were presented in
traditionally stereotyped ways. Female authority
figures (mother, stewardess, movie star, circus
performer) appeared in 15 percent of the
commercials; male authority figures (father, athlete,
rock star, doctor) appeared in 42 percent of the
commercials.

2.
Racial and Ethnic Minorities

186. Abelman, Robert and Kimberly Neuendorf. "Religion in Broadcasting: Demographics." Cleveland, Ohio: Cleveland State University, 1983.

sample: three episodes of each of the "top 27" religious programs in the U.S.; 81 episodes, 514 characters.

Of all speaking individuals on these programs 86 percent were white, six were black, and the remainder were members of other racial/ethnic groups. Over nine out of ten of these people were born and lived in the U.S. Women made up about a third of both the white and the black people on these programs. Ethnic minorities were typically younger than their white counterparts: about nine out of ten of the elderly, mature adults, and young adults were white, two-thirds of the adolescents and more than half of the children were white. Most of the persons whose occupations could be isolated were white and a significant number of blacks and Hispanics were students. Minorities, because they were younger, were not often married: only one percent of the married persons were black. Racial minorities were also relegated to lower socio-economic status than whites: 25 percent of lower class persons were black, 8 percent were Hispanic and 67 percent were white. The middle class roles were 87 percent white and seven percent black and only three percent of those in the upper class were black.

187. Allen, Richard L. "Communications Research on Black Americans." In In Search of Diversity -- Symposium on Minority Audiences and Programming Research. Washington, D.C.: Corporation for Public Broadcasting, 1981, pp. 47-63.

Brief summary of a decade's research on the portrayal of blacks (1969-1979) in TV news, drama, and

90

advertising. Documents visibility, occupational
levels, and amount of stereotyping as well as use of
the medium by blacks and its possible effects upon
them.

188. Arias, M. Beatriz. "Educational Television: Impact
on the Socialization of the Hispanic Child." In Gordon
L. Berry and Claudia Mitchell-Kernan, (eds.), Television
and the Socialization of the Minority Child. New
York: Academic Press, 1982, pp. 203-214.

Cites findings in communications research that
Hispanics were presented generally as law breakers,
law enforcers, and comic characters (see, for
example, Greenberg and Baptista-Fernandez (242)).
There was some evidence that portrayals varied
according to the specific ethnic group. The author
notes that many educational television series did not
meet the needs of children of Hispanic background,
leading to the development of programs such as
Carrascolendas, Villa Alegre, and Sonidos Mios.
These programs provided the benefit of being
bilingual, presenting positive bi-lingual role
models, and emphasizing Spanish-American culture.

189. Asi, Morad. "Arabs, Israelis, and TV News: A
Time-Series Content Analysis." In William C. Adams,
Television Coverage of the Middle East. Norwood,
N.J.: Ablex Publishing, 1981, pp. 67-75.

sample: 15 weeks of Middle East news coverage
broadcast on ABC, CBS, and NBC (5 weeks in 1973 prior
to the war, 5 weeks in 1976-1977 after the war and
before Sadat's trip, and 5 weeks in 1979 after
Sadat's trip); 183 news stories (69 on ABC, 63 on
CBS, and 53 on NBC).

Most of the stories (9 out of 10) ranked third or
later in the newscast; only 8 were lead stories.
Egypt, Anwar Sadat, and other Egyptian leaders were
depicted progressively more favorably. By 1979 all 8
stories about Sadat were coded as favorable. On the
other hand, Israeli leaders, while getting the best
coverage of Mideast leaders in the early period,
suffered a relative decline in 1979. Conversely, PLO
leaders went from overwhelmingly unfavorable coverage
(94 percent) to only 62 percent unfavorable in 1979.
No strong trends were found in regard to the
treatment of other Arab leaders. Overall Egypt (and
Sadat) received more favorable coverage than Israel

in 1979. Similarly, Palestinians and the PLO made notable gains on network television. These dramatic changes did not extend to other Arab states or leaders.

190. Banks, Cherry McGee. "A Content Analysis of the Treatment of Black Americans on Television." Social Education, 1977, 41(4), pp. 336-339.

sample: three weeks' episodes of six evening network series (both crime and comedy drama) with regularly-appearing black actors broadcast in 1974.

Programs with all black casts presented blacks in more negative, stereotypical ways (e.g., carefree, poorly educated), with low social status, and more beset with personal problems. Programs with racially mixed casts presented black characters with higher social status, exhibiting such socially valued characteristics as cooperation, bravery, and competence. Blacks in these programs were depicted with the positive stereotypes normally associated with whites.

191. Baptista-Fernandez, Pilar and Bradley S. Greenberg. "The Context Characteristics and Communication Behaviors of Blacks on Television." In Bradley S. Greenberg (ed.), Life on Television: Content Analyses of U.S. TV Drama. Norwood, New Jersey: Ablex Publishing, 1980, pp. 13-21.

sample: one week of prime-time and Saturday morning commercial network series (excluding movies) broadcast in 1977; 81 programs, 585 speaking characters.

Blacks (N=101) appeared in 43 out of 81 fictional series episodes. Comparative analyses used 101 randomly selected white characters from the 43 programs with black characters. Half of the black characters, compared to one-fifth of the white characters, appeared in situation comedies. Blacks were generally younger than whites: the average age for black characters was 28 compared to an average age of 35 for white characters. Moreover, 62 percent of the black characters were under 23 compared to 38 percent of the white characters. Blacks were less likely to have an identifiable job (33 percent compared to 50 percent of the whites) and were also less likely to be in professional/managerial positions (10 percent compared to 25 percent of the

whites). The male-female ratio was two to one for
blacks and three to one for whites. While both races
discussed domestic matters most frequently, whites
were significantly more likely to discuss business
and crime than were blacks. There was no significant
difference in dominance, defined as giving or
receiving of advice, information, and orders. While
only one black character was "bad," 14 white
characters were so categorized.

192. Barcus, F. Earle. "Commercial Children's Television
on Weekends and Weekday Afternoons: A Content Analysis of
Children's Programming and Advertising Broadcasting in
October 1977." Newtonville, Mass.: Action for Children's
Television, 1978.

sample: network and independent weekend morning
programming and independent weekday afternoon
programming broadcast in 1977; 228 program segments,
889 characters, and 1,455 announcements.

Nonwhites were seven percent of the characters in the
sample of weekday programs and 15 percent of the
characters in the sample of weekend programs. There
was, however, considerable variation by program type
and type of broadcast: cartoons had the largest
percentage of white characters in both time periods.
Nonwhite characters in both time periods were
somewhat more likely to be children than adults.
Nonwhites were ten percent of the characters in the
sample of commercials. Somewhat more blacks appeared
on commercials broadcast during the weekend.

193. Barcus, F. Earle. Images of Life on Children's
Television. New York: Praeger Publishers, 1983.

sample: network and independent children's programs
broadcast during a weekend (and some weekday
afternoons) in 1981; 235 programs, 1,145 characters.

Only 18 percent of the program segments represented
integrated worlds where both white and black or other
minority characters appeared together. In contrast,
56 percent contained only white characters (or white
animal characters), and two percent had only black
characters. Among racial categories, males dominated
each category, although there was a slightly greater
proportion of females among blacks than among whites
or other minorities. Black ethnics were more often
cast as heroes than as villains, but their

93

proportions in both roles were low. Other ethnics
were more often cast as villains. Blacks and other
minorities were less frequently portrayed as employed
than white characters. When shown as employed, both
black and white characters were most often shown in
professional and managerial jobs, while other
minorities were more likely to be portrayed as
craftsmen, laborers, or service workers. Commercial
television programs avoided racial or ethnic
messages. Cartoon-comedy programs contained the most
blatant ethnic stereotypes. These programs avoided
the portrayal of black characters, and frequently
provided cruel stereotypes of other ethnic
minorities.

194. Barcus, F. Earle. "Saturday Children's Television; a
Report on Television Programming and Advertising on Boston
Commercial Television." Newtonville, Ma.: Action for
Children's Television, 1971.

sample: one Saturday morning (7 a.m. to 1:45 p.m.)
of network and independent programming and
commercials broadcast in 1971; 132 different
commercials.

Almost three-quarters of the 113 commercials with
characters that could be classified by race contained
only white characters. Characters of other
racial/ethnic backgrounds appeared in 23 percent of
these commercials.

195. Barcus, F. Earle. "Television in the After-School
Hours: A Study of Programming and Advertising for Children
on Independent Stations Across the United States."
Newtonville, Ma.: Action for Children's Television, 1975.

sample: three hours of afternoon programming for each
of ten independent stations (located in different
cities) broadcast in 1975; 92 program segments, 405
major characters, and 487 commercials.

Seven out of ten characters could be identified by
racial-ethnic background. In all program types,
about four percent of the characters were categorized
as belonging to a racial minority group. Blacks were
absent, however, in cartoons. Minority males
outnumbered minority females by two to one. Five
percent of the characters in the sample of
commercials were black.

94

196.   Barcus, F. Earle.   "Weekend Commercial Children's
Television -- 1975." Newtonville, Ma.: Action for
Children's Television, 1975.

      sample: one weekend network and independent station
children's programs and commercials broadcast in
1975; 97 program segments, 400 major characters, 403
commercials.

      More than seven out of ten major characters could be
identified by race. Minorities made up 11 percent of
the characters; 7 percent were black. Minorities
were more likely to appear on informational programs
-- 22 percent of the characters in these programs
were minorities. Overall, minority males outnumbered
minority females by five to one in these programs.
Of the characters who could be identified by race in
the sample of commercials, eight percent were black
and one percent were members of other racial
minorities.

197.   Barrera, Aida and Frederick P. Close.   "Minority Role
Models: Hispanics." In Meg Schwarz (ed.), TV and
Teens: Experts Look at the Issues. Reading,
Ma.: Addison-Wesley Publishing Co., 1982, pp. 88-95.

      Cites research revealing that television roles for
Hispanics have been too few and their range too
limited. Hispanics rarely, if ever, were presented
as professionals. In general, the characterizations
reflected commonly-held stereotypes.

Book 198.   Berry, Gordon L.   "Research Perspectives on the
Portrayals of Afro-American Families on Television." In
Anthony W. Jackson (ed.), Black Families and the Medium of
Television. Ann Arbor, Michigan: Bush Program in Child
Development and Social Policy, 1982, pp. 47-59.

      Presents findings from research (Hinton, et al.,
(257); Gerbner and Signorielli, (237); Greenberg et
al., (250)) noting that blacks were underrepresented
on television and that even though their portrayals
have improved, blacks still tend to be relegated to
minor and insignificant roles. Black families were
also misrepresented, they were isolated from whites,
the father role was often missing, and the mother
character typified the dominant, efficient, effective
decision-maker. Suggests that the challenge is to
offer more diversity in portrayals; to have these

portrayals emerge from perspectives black Americans
see as important ingredients of their own experience.

199. Berry, Gordon L.   "Television and
Afro-Americans: Past Legacy and Present Portrayals."   In
Stephen B. Withey and Ronald P. Abels (eds.), _Television
and Social Behavior: Beyond Violence and Children_.
Hillsdale, N.J.: Lawrence Erlbaum Associates, 1980,
pp. 231-248.

> Summarizes findings of scholarly and popular research
> on black image in the mid-70s and outlines three
> stages of portrayal: the stereotypic age (to
> 1965); the period of new awareness (1966-1972) when
> blacks were given very positive traits; and the
> period of stabilization (1973 on) in which blacks
> were presented in a presumably more "realistic"
> manner in black-cast programs. The author warns
> against accepting depictions in this latest phase
> simply because they lacked the blatant, traditional
> stereotypy of the past; newer, more subtle
> stereotypes of the black community and lifestyle
> perpetuated old biases about racial inferiority.
> Among these were the irresponsibility of the black
> male demonstrated by his absence in the black
> family; the aggressiveness of the black woman; the
> lack of positive attributes of the black
> community; the esteem given bad, "flashy" characters
> by the black community; and the use of Black English
> Vernacular as a symbol of moral or educational
> inadequacy of blacks.

200. Berry, Gordon L. and Claudia Mitchell-Kernan.
Television and the Socialization of the Minority Child.
New York: Academic Press, 1982.

> Twelve articles originally presented at an
> invitational conference convened by the Center for
> Afro-American Studies at the University of California
> at Los Angeles. Helps to bridge the gap between the
> vast amount of general literature focusing upon
> television and social behavior and the increased
> attention to the special issues of minority-group
> socialization in a television-oriented culture.

201. Bond, Jean Carey. "The Media Image of Black Women."
Freedomways, 1975, 15, pp. 34-37.

> sample: four prime-time network dramatic programs
> featuring black women.

The author concludes from a thematic interpretation of these programs that increased black visibility since the 1960s is a front for old stereotypes. For example, the latent meaning of The Autobiography of Miss Jane Pittman (white domination of blacks) was coupled with positive images of black women. In Get Christy Love! a competent black woman received sexist treatment and served a cosmetic function in a repressive police force. The myths of the black matriarch and the substandard black man (portrayed as irresponsible and mindlessly defiant) were presented in Good Times and That's My Mama. The author considered such portrayals destructive for black people, if not for black women, and questioned the likelihood of change except on the prevailing white terms.

202. Bush, Ronald F., Paul J. Solomon, and Joseph F. Hair, Jr. "There are More Blacks in TV Commercials." Journal of Advertising Research, 1977, 17(1), pp. 21-25.

sample: two weeks of afternoon and prime-time commercials (product, promotions, and public service announcements) broadcast in 1973 in the West and South; 6,480 commercials.

Blacks were found in 13 percent of these commercials, an increase compared to data collected by Dominick and Greenberg (212). In ads with black characters, blacks were more often in major than minor roles. Commercials with blacks had more characters (average 13 per ad) than commercials without blacks (average 4 per ad); this ratio decreased since the earliest period reported by Dominick and Greenberg (212). Blacks were found in a greater number of commercials for products, and their appearance in public service announcements remained high. Together, these trends indicated improvement in black portrayal in commercials, with some geographical differences in sex distribution, racial distribution, and appearance as major or minor characters.

203. Cheng, Charles W. and Marsha Hirano-Nakanishi. "Minority Role Models: Asian-Americans." In Meg Schwarz (ed.), TV and Teens: Experts Look at the Issues. Reading, Ma.: Addison-Wesley Publishing Co., 1982, pp. 101-103.

The commercial broadcasting industry continued to

convey limited and unsatisfactory images of
Asian-Americans, most of them based on subtle or
blatant forms of racism and ignorance. An important
distinction, usually ignored, was that between Asians
and Asian-Americans.

204. Clark, Cedrick C. "Television and Social
Controls: Some Observations On the Portrayals of Ethnic
Minorities." Television Quarterly, 1969, 8(2), pp. 18-22.

sample: all black starring characters in dramatic
series broadcast in 1968; 15 characters, 13 programs.

Author discusses changing treatment of blacks on
television as a reflection of the social structure.
Negative characterizations served to "vitiate the
self-image of the minority group, while bolstering
the dominant culture's self-image." More recent
portrayals of blacks have reflected a "regulation"
phase -- i.e., portrayed in law enforcement
occupations, upholding and protecting existing values
and institutions. Author questions whether blacks
eventually will be portrayed with genuine respect or
will remain in this phase.

205. Colle, Royal D. "Negro Image in the Mass Media: A
Case Study in Social Change." Journalism Quarterly, 1968,
45, pp. 55-60.

One of the earliest studies of black portrayal
published in an academic journal. The author
documented the almost complete invisibility and
extremely stereotyped portrayals of blacks in the
early days of television, citing the 1964 efforts of
the Committee on Integration of the New York Society
for Ethical Culture to publicize this bias. The
roots of televised portrayal were traced to film and
radio of an earlier period. The predominant focus of
the article, however, was the role of various social
institutions in changing the black media image.

206. Collier, Eugenia. "'Black' Shows for White Viewers."
Freedomways, 1974, 14(3), pp. 209-217.

sample: three dramas with black casts.

Author presents interpretations of three television
dramas with predominantly black casts to demonstrate
the effect of white versus black production staffs,

including writers and actors. The black images in
the popular The Autobiography of Miss Jane Pittman
were diluted to be acceptable to a mass white
audience, and the characters on Sanford and Son were
seen as unauthentic and negative, with the effect of
permitting white audiences to feel justifiably
superior. On the other hand, black participation in
Good Times resulted in portrayals that created
empathy and respect among white viewers for blacks
and their struggle to overcome problems. This author
is almost alone in noting the strength denoted in the
portrayal of a black father who can apologize and
take advice as well as show defiance, and the
portrayal of a black mother who radiates warmth and
good humor. There were some thematic weaknesses,
however, even in this generally positive program --
black characters tended to end up laughing about
their difficult situations, and black militancy was
treated with ridicule.

207. Comer, James. "The Importance of Television Images
of Black Families." In Anthony W. Jackson (ed.), Black
Families and the Medium of Television. Ann Arbor,
Michigan: Bush Program in Child Development and Social
Policy, 1982, pp. 19-26.

The media, especially cinema and television, have
helped perpetuate a stereotypic myth about black
Americans. Minorities have been shown in comedic
positions, in degrading ways, omitted, or distorted.
The portrayals have suggested that minorities are
frivolous and irresponsible, and not able to
participate in the mainstream of society. Television
has been especially powerful in maintaining this
myth. In regard to families, the impression
television supplies is that blacks cannot care for
their families adequately, and that they are not
responsible or competent. Television programming
generally has failed to present the significant and
systematic problems and limitations blacks face in
this society.

208. Culley, James D. and Rex Bennett. "Selling Women,
Selling Blacks." Journal of Communication, 1976, 26(4),
pp. 160-174.

sample: 368 prime-time network commercials, including
station promotions, broadcast over a two week period
in 1974; 770 characters.

One out of ten commercials contained a black
character; only four commercials contained more than
one black. Blacks made up 5.5 percent of this sample
of characters (43 out of 770). Black characters
included a large number of children: 16 out of 43
black characters.

209. DeGooyer, J. and F. Borah. "What's Wrong with this
Picture?: A Look at Working Women on Television."
Washington, D.C. National Commission on Working Women,
1982.

*** see women ***

sample: 25 top rated programs broadcast from 1972 to
1981.

Minorities were generally underrepresented in these
programs. Hispanic women were almost invisible and
black women were underrepresented. Only eight of
these top programs had at least one black character.
In 1977 and 1978 there were no black female
characters.

210. Dohrmann, Rita. "A Gender Profile of Children's
Educational TV." Journal of Communication, 1975, 25(4),
pp. 56-65.

sample: two episodes each of Sesame Street, The
Electric Company, Mister Rogers Neighborhood, and
Captain Kangaroo broadcast in 1974.

Out of 206 racially identifiable characters, 75
percent (N=154) where white, 18 percent (N=37) were
black, and seven percent (N=15) were members of other
racial groups. Women had greater visibility among
the nonwhite racial groups.

211. Dominick, Joseph R. "Crime and Law Enforcement on
Prime-Time Television." Public Opinion Quarterly, 1973,
37(2), pp. 241-250.

sample: one week of prime-time network drama
including comedy but excluding feature films,
broadcast in 1972; 269 speaking characters, 119
crimes.

Nonwhites made up 7 percent of the criminals and 14
percent of the law enforcement agents. Seven percent

of the overall victims of crime and 27 percent of the
murder victims were nonwhite. (According to FBI
Uniform Crime Reports, during this period 30 percent
of criminals and 56 percent of murder victims were
nonwhite.)

212. Dominick, Joseph R. and Bradley S. Greenberg. "Three
Seasons of Blacks on Television." Journal of Advertising
Research, 1970, 10(2), pp. 21-27.

sample: three one-week samples of daytime and evening
programming and commercials broadcast in 1967, 1968,
and 1969 (an average of 60 programs and 900
commercials each year).

Blacks appeared in 25 percent of the daytime programs
(a proportion that was stable over the three-year
period) and their appearance in major roles
increased. In prime time, the appearance of blacks
increased from 34 percent of the programs in 1967 to
52 percent of the programs in 1968. Although the
absolute number of blacks increased in prime time,
their portrayal in major roles decreased. Blacks
generally were presented as similar to whites in both
daytime and prime-time programs, but they were more
likely to be segregated from whites in prime-time
programs. The most frequent occupational fields for
blacks in prime time were law enforcement and
education. In commercials, the percent of blacks in
speaking roles and in overall appearances increased
from 5 percent in 1967 to 11 percent in 1969. Blacks
were more likely to appear in public service
announcements and station promotions than in
commercials for products.

213. Donagher, Patricia C., Rita Wicks Poulos, Robert
M. Liebert, and Emily S. Davidson. "Race, Sex, and Social
Example: An Analysis of Character Portrayals on
Inter-Racial Television Entertainment." Psychological
Reports, 1975, 37, pp. 1023-1034.

sample: one episode of each of nine prime-time
network series broadcast in 1974 (selected on the
basis of at least one regularly appearing black and
males and females of both races).

Nonwhites made up 30 percent of the sample. There
was no significant difference in role significance
among the race/sex groups as defined by average
amount of time on screen. The authors found movement

toward equalization of occupational status, with both
black and white males presented as professionals and
semi-professionals. Black females, however, did not
have as many non-traditional options as white
females, in terms of employment. There was a
significant sex-race interaction in both aggressive
and prosocial behaviors. White males were more
aggressive than black males, and black females were
more aggressive than white females. Blacks,
especially black females, were more likely to
demonstrate and share feelings than white characters.

214. Doolittle, John and Robert Pepper. "Children's TV Ad
Content: 1974." Journal of Broadcasting, 1975, 19(2),
pp. 131-142.

sample: one Saturday morning (9 a.m. to 1 p.m.) of
network commercials broadcast in 1974; 49 different
commercials.

Minority characters appeared in about 20 percent of
the commercials; about half of them appeared in major
roles. Minority children appeared more frequently
than older minority characters.

215. Downing, Mildred H. "Heroine of the Daytime Serial."
Journal of Communication, 1974, 24(2), pp. 130-137.

*** see women ***

sample: 20 episodes of each of 15 serial dramas
broadcast in 1973; 300 episodes, 256 characters.

Nonwhites were 5 percent of the characters in the
serial dramas; less than half of these (42 percent)
were women. Whites in this sample were divided
evenly between men and women.

216. Estep, Rhoda and Patrick T. Macdonald. "How Prime
Time Crime Evolved on TV, 1976-1981." Journalism
Quarterly, 1983, 60(2), pp. 293-300.

*** see women ***

sample: 50 crime programs broadcast in 1976-77, 49
crime programs broadcast in 1978-79, and 30 in
1980-81.

Televised crime continued to overrepresent violent crime (murder, robbery, assault) compared to property crime. There was a persistent trend in overrepresenting middle class, middle-aged whites in suspect and victim roles. There has also been a gradual shift in placing more blacks and young characters in suspect and victim roles.

217. Fife, Marilyn D. "Black Image in American TV: The First Two Decades." Black Scholar, 1974, 6(3), pp. 7-15.

Traces the changes in programming and portrayal from the late forties to the late sixties -- from the infrequent portrayal of blacks as specialized characters (domestics or variety show entertainers) to starring roles (I Spy, Julia), and, finally, to the emergence of black satire and social comment. On the whole, the author sums up black television portrayal over the two decades as "dishonest and unflattering" and relates this to the industry's almost total "whiteness" and its commercially-dictated need to avoid offending white audiences.

218. Fine, Marlene G. and Carolyn Anderson. "Dialectical Features of Black Characters in Situation Comedies on Television." Phylon, 1980, 41(4), pp. 396-409.

sample: three episodes of each of three situation comedies with primarily black casts (Good Times, The Jeffersons, and What's Happening).

An extension of the author's 1979 study (Fine, Anderson and Eckles (219)). Analysis of the use of Black English Vernacular (BEV) in these series revealed that BEV in these programs was used as a form of substandard English characteristic of the lower class rather than as a legitimate and complex dialect. Of ten common BEV syntactic features, only three appeared regularly in the dialogue. There also was little use of BEV across all characters and programs (several characters were more frequent users, particularly in emotionally tense moments). Males were more likely to use BEV than females in all programs, although in certain programs female use of BEV was close to the rate used by male characters. The author speculated that this language homogenization might be the result of a need for commonly-understood expressions in the mass media.

219. Fine, Marlene G., Carolyn Anderson, and Gary Eckles.
"Black English on Black Situation Comedies." Journal of
Communication, 1979, 29(3), pp. 21-29.

    sample: two episodes of each of three situation
    comedies with predominently black casts aired in
    1975-76 (The Jeffersons, Sanford and Son, and Good
    Times).

    Overall, analysis of utterances by black speakers
    revealed that these programs presented an homogenized
    version of Black English and that males "took more
    turns at speaking" than females. Moreover, the
    traditional female role of keeper of the standard
    language was emphasized; each of the women in these
    shows rarely used Black English and rarely got a
    laugh. There was also a tendency for the characters
    in the lowest social positions (eg., escaped
    convicts, maids) to use Black English more
    frequently. Overall, this analysis revealed that the
    language used by black characters was a dialect that
    was "black, but not too black."

220. Friedman, Leslie, J. Sex Role Stereotyping in the
Mass Media: An Annotated Bibliography. New York: Garland
Publishing, Inc., 1977.

    Annotated bibliography on sex role
    stereotyping; includes section on the image of
    minority women in the media.

221. Gerbner, George. "Communication and Social
Environment." Scientific American, September, 1972,
pp. 5-12. Reprinted in Communications: A Scientific
American Book. San Francisco, Ca.: W.H. Freeman and Co.,
1972.

    sample: annual week-long samples of prime-time and
    weekend-daytime network dramatic programming
    broadcast between 1967 and 1971.

    Analysis revealed a "pecking order" in which white
    males were the least likely to be victimized while
    women and minorities were the most likely to be
    victimized.

222. Gerbner, George. "Cultural Indicators: The Case of Violence in Televison Drama." The Annals of the American Academy of Political and Social Science, 1970, 388, pp. 69-81.

> sample: annual week-long samples of prime-time and weekend-daytime network dramatic programming broadcast in the fall of 1967 and 1968.
>
> An examination of characters' involvement in violence on television was discussed in terms of a scenario of power. In general, white males were the most powerful, while nonwhites and women were the least powerful groups of characters. Six out of ten upper and middle class characters, but nine out of ten lower class characters, fell victim to violence. Those who committed violence comprised half of all white American characters, six out of every ten white foreigners, and two-thirds of all nonwhites. The groups were victimized in the same order -- nearly six out of ten whites, but eight out of ten nonwhites fell victim to some violence. Those who both committed and suffered violence included 39 percent of white Americans, 46 percent of white foreigners, and 60 percent of nonwhites. The pattern of fatal victimization showed that while white American killers outnumbered white Americans killed by four to one, and outnumbered white foreigners killed by three to two, the nonwhite ratio was one to one (for each killer, one was killed).

223. Gerbner, George. "Interpreting the TV World." Irish Broadcasting Review, Spring 1980, pp. 7-11.

*** see women ***

224. Gerbner, George. "Television: The American Schoolchild's National Curriculum Day In and Day Out." PTA Today, April 1981, pp. 3-5.

*** see women ***

225. Gerbner, George. "Violence in Television Drama: Trends and Symbolic Functions." In George A. Comstock and Eli A. Rubinstein (eds.), Television and Social Behavior, Vol. I, Media Content and Control. Washington, D.C.: GPO, 1972, pp. 28-127.

sample: annual week-long samples of prime-time and
weekend-daytime network dramatic programming
broadcast in 1967, 1968, and 1969; 762 major
characters.

More than three-quarters of these characters were
white and less than a quarter were nonwhite or their
race could not be identified. The white majority was
82 percent American, while the nonwhite majority was
only 15 percent American. Of those clearly
identified as Americans, 95 percent were white, only
35 percent of the "others" could be identified as
white. Almost three in ten whites but barely one in
ten nonwhites were women; fully half of all
characters were white, American males. Nonwhites
were virtually all male and mostly distant from the
American social setting. Nonwhites were more than
proportionately represented among violents and
especially among victims, but less than
proportionately represented among killers. For every
white killed, 2.3 whites were killers, but a nonwhite
was killed for every nonwhite killer.

226. Gerbner, George and Larry Gross. "Living With
Television: The Violence Profile." Journal of
Communication, 1976, 26(2), pp. 173-199.

*** see women ***

227. Gerbner, George and Larry Gross. "The Violent Face
of Television and Its Lessons." In Edward L. Palmer and
Aimee Dorr (eds.), Children and the Faces of
Television: Teaching, Violence, and Selling. New
York: Academic Press, 1980, pp. 149-162.

*** see women ***

228. Gerbner, George, Larry Gross, Stewart Hoover, Michael
Morgan, Nancy Signorielli, Harry E. Cotugno, and Robert
Wuthnow. "Religion on Television and in the Lives of
Viewers." Report prepared for the Ad Hoc Committee on
Religious Television Research, National Council of the
Churches of Christ, New York, New York, 1984.

sample: one week of local and syndicated religious
television programs broadcast in 1982; 99 programs
and 752 characters.

The demographic distribution of characters in this
sample of local and syndicated religious programming
revealed patterns remarkably similar to those found
on dramatic programs: women made up 34 percent, the
elderly three percent, and blacks ten percent of the
characters. There were fewer women among the black
characters: 27 percent of the blacks as compared to
34 percent of the whites were women. Only 8 percent
of the women as compared to 11 percent of the men
were black. Blacks were somewhat more likely to
appear on local programs than syndicated programs (14
percent of the characters on local programs as
compared to 10 percent of those on syndicated
programs).

229. Gerbner, George, Larry Gross, Marilyn Jackson-Beeck,
Suzanne Jeffries-Fox, and Nancy Signorielli. "Cultural
Indicators: Violence Profile No. 9." Journal of
Communication, 1978, 28(3), pp. 176-207.

sample: annual week-long samples of prime-time and
weekend-daytime network dramatic programming
broadcast between 1967 and 1977; 3,651 major
characters.

More than six out of ten major characters were
involved in some type of violence: nearly seven out
of ten men as compared to less than five out of ten
women. Minority characters were more likely to be
victimized and less likely to be cast as killers than
whites. Women fared worse except that no nonwhite
woman was shown as involved in any killing. Although
foreign women were more likely to be killers than
either U.S. women or foreign men, they also had the
highest rate of overall victimization.

230. Gerbner, George, Larry Gross, Michael Morgan, and
Nancy Signorielli. "Aging with Television
Commercials: Images on Television Commercials and Dramatic
Programming, 1977-1979." Annenberg School of
Communications, University of Pennsylvania, 1981.

sample: commercials in three annual samples of
prime-time and weekend-daytime network dramatic
programming broadcast in 1977, 1978, and 1979 plus
commercials from the evening network news broadcast
during the same week as the 1979 dramatic
sample; 1,949 prime-time, 510 weekend-daytime, and 97
news commercials.

The world of the television commercial is a very
stable world with little change between 1977 and 1979
in terms of the basic dimensions of characterization.
Blacks appeared in one out of five commercials, while
people of other minority groups were rarely seen.
Hispanics were especially invisible -- they appeared
in only 1.6 percent of all prime-time commercials, in
less than one percent of the weekend-daytime
commercials, and in none of the commercials broadcast
during the national evening news. There were also
very few commercials that did not have at least one
white character -- 90 percent of the commercials in
prime-time and news programs and 97 percent of the
commercials in children's programs were cast with
white people. Blacks were the sole actors in less
than 2 percent of the commercials while whites were
the sole actors in more than seven out of ten
commercials. Nonwhite characters were also
underrepresented; they made up 11 percent of the men
and 9 percent of the women in prime-time commercials,
and 10 percent of the men and 7 percent of the women
in weekend-daytime commercials. Blacks make up only
one percent of the older men and 2 percent of the
older women and there were no older Hispanics; among
the younger characters, nonwhites made up between
eight and twelve percent of the characters.

231. Gerbner, George, Larry Gross, Michael Morgan, and
Nancy Signorielli. "Charting the Mainstream: Television's
Contribution to Political Orientations." Journal of
Communication, 1982, 32(2), pp. 100-127.

*** see women ***

232. Gerbner, George, Larry Gross, Michael Morgan, and
Nancy Signorielli. "The 'Mainstreaming' of
America: Violence Profile No. 11." Journal of
Communication, 1980, 30(3), pp. 10-29.

*** see women ***

233. Gerbner, George, Larry Gross, Michael Morgan, and
Nancy Signorielli. "Television Violence, Victimization,
and Power." American Behavioral Scientist, 1980, 23(5),
pp. 705-716.

*** see women ***

234. Gerbner, George, Larry Gross, and Nancy Signorielli.
"The Role of Television Entertainment in Public Education
About Science." Annenberg School of Communications,
University of Pennsylvania, 1985.

*** see health ***

    sample: annual week-long samples of prime-time
network dramatic programming broadcast between 1973
and 1983.

    Minorities were generally underrepresented on
television. About 90 percent of the characters,
major and minor, were white, about 8 percent were
black, and 2 percent were Asians. Scientists were
one of the more prestigious occupational groups in
which minorities were a little more prevalent. Most
of these minority scientists were Asians (10 percent
of all scientists and 5 percent of scientists in
major roles). Three of the fifteen female scientists
were Asians; none, however, was in a major role.
More than 10 percent of the women doctors were Asian.
Asians were rarely cast in any of the other
occupational roles; they made up 2 percent or less
of professionals, white collar workers, blue collar
workers, and the police. There were also very few
blacks among the more prestigious occupational
groups. Blacks were especially underrepresented
among scientists (only 2 percent and they were all
men). Blacks did appear in other occupational roles:
over 10 percent of nurses, police, and blue collar
workers. Hispanics were also rarely seen and they
were especially missing in occupational roles. No
scientists and only two doctors were Hispanic.

235. Gerbner, George, Larry Gross, Nancy Signorielli,
Michael Morgan, and Marilyn Jackson-Beeck. "The
Demonstration of Power: Violence Profile No. 10." Journal
of Communication, 1979, 29(3), pp. 177-196.

*** see women ***

236. Gerbner, George and Nancy Signorielli. "Women and
Minorities in Television Drama, 1969-1978." Annenberg
School of Communications, University of Pennsylvania, 1979.

    sample: annual week-long samples of prime-time and
weekend-daytime network dramatic programming
broadcast between 1969 and 1978; 1,365 programs, over
17,000 characters.

In prime time, nonwhites made up 12 percent of all
characters and 10 percent of major characters.
Nonwhite females were more underrepresented than
white females, especially in major roles. A
comparison of characters with 1973 census figures
revealed that Asians were overrepresented among all
characters and approached parity with census figures
among major characters. American Indians had parity
with census figures among all characters, but were
underrepresented among major characters. The
representation of black characters was nearer parity
than that of Hispanics. Until 1977, there was a very
gradual increase of minority characters, particularly
of blacks and mostly in minor roles; minority
representation decreased after 1977. Minorities
shared, with females, stereotyped casting; they
generally were in non-serious and/or family-centered
roles, limiting their opportunities for action and
diminishing their symbolic power. In weekend-daytime
programs, nonwhites made up nine percent of all
characters and seven percent of major characters. On
these programs ethnic minorities, except Asians, were
very underrepresented.

237. Gerbner, George and Nancy Signorielli. "The World
According to Television." American Demographics, October
1982, pp. 15-17.

sample: annual week-long samples of prime-time
network dramatic programming broadcast between 1969
and 1981; 878 programs and over 14,000 characters.

In practically every type of prime-time program,
minorities were underrepresented in relation to their
numbers in the U.S. Census. Blacks represented only
73 percent of their share in the real world's
population and Hispanics represented only 37 percent
of their share; a disproportionate number of minority
characters played minor rather than major roles.
Asians in minor roles were overrepresented primarily
because of one program -- Hawaii Five-O. The
disproportionate male-female patterns of the entire
television population also held for minority
characters. Marital status was presented differently
for white and nonwhite characters. Among white male
characters, the single life was overrepresented while
marriage was underrepresented. Fewer black male
characters, however, were single. Among women there
was a different pattern: white women were less likely
to be married than black women (in the U.S. the

reverse is true). Formerly married characters, whether white, black, male, or female, were underrepresented despite the growing divorce trend in the U.S.

238. Gerson, Mauricio. "Minority Representation in Network Television Drama, 1970-1976." Mass Communication Review, 1980, 7(3), pp. 10-12.

sample: annual week-long samples of prime-time and weekend-daytime network dramatic programming broadcast between 1970 and 1976.

This sample was 74 percent male, 87 percent white, eight percent black, two percent Hispanic, two percent Asian, and less than one percent American Indian. There was a considerable increase in black characters, especially in the 1975 sample; the other three minority groups remained at about the same level of representation. All groups were more likely to be victimized than to be perpetrators of violence except the American Indians. In regard to fatal violence, blacks and American Indians were more likely to kill than be killed, while whites, Asians and Hispanics were more likely to be killed than kill. In all categories, more females were likely to be killed than to kill. The occupations of minorities were more difficult to code than those of whites; 74 percent of the American Indians, 47 percent of the Hispanics, and 45 percent of the blacks could not be coded on occupational status.

239. Greenberg, Bradley S. Life on Television: Content Analyses of U.S. TV Drama. Norwood, New Jersey: Ablex Publishing, 1980.

An anthology of studies concerning the appearance and treatment of females, racial and ethnic minorities, the elderly, and sexual behavior. Listed under respective authors and titles.

240. Greenberg, Bradley S. "Television and Role Socialization: An Overview." In David Pearl, Lorraine Bouthilet, and Joyce Lazar (eds.), Television and Behavior: Ten Years of Scientific Progress and Implications for the Eighties. Washington, D.C.: GPO, 1982, pp. 179-190.

Concise summary of research (conducted during the
1970s), including that of the author and his
colleagues, focusing upon family, sex, race,
occupation, and age-roles. Notes that although
sex-role stereotyping is relevant to both male and
female portrayals, it is accentuated for females by
their more limited appearance in the medium.
Includes an extensive bibliography.

241. Greenberg, Bradley S. "Three Seasons of Television
Characters: A Demographic Analysis." Journal of
Broadcasting, 1980, 24(1), pp. 49-60.

sample: characters in three composite weeks of
network fictional series broadcast during prime time
and Saturday morning in 1975 (N=1,212), 1976
(N=1,120), and 1977 (N=1,217); 255 episodes.

The proportion of blacks was fairly consistent -- 10
percent of the sample. This approximates the
proportion of blacks reported in the 1970
U.S. Census.

242. Greenberg, Bradley S. and Pilar Baptista-Fernandez.
"Hispanic Americans: The New Minority on Television." In
Bradley S. Greenberg, Life on Television: Content Analyses
of U.S. TV Drama. Norwood, N.J.: Ablex Publishing, 1980,
pp. 3-12.

sample: characters in three composite weeks of
network fictional series broadcast during prime time
and Saturday morning in 1975 (N=1,212), 1976
(N=1,120), and 1977 (N=1,217); 255 episodes.

The entire sample of 3,549 speaking characters
contained 53 Hispanics (1.5 percent) in prime-time
programs and two in Saturday morning programs. There
was a decreasing percentage of Hispanics across the
three seasons; there were only two characters in
programs that appeared in more than one season. Half
of the Hispanic characters appeared in four
programs: Quest, Joe Forrester, Delvecchio, and Popi
(the only program with a regularly appearing Hispanic
cast). The Hispanics included 29 Mexican Americans,
6 Mexicans, 14 Puerto Ricans, 1 Cuban, 3 Uraguayans,
and 1 Spaniard. Women were outnumbered by five to
one (44 males and 9 females). About half of the
characters worked hard and half were lazy. They had
little education and limited aspirations, but family
life was very important to them. Among the Hispanics

the most common occupations were crook (N=12) and law enforcer (N=10).

243. Greenberg, Bradley S., Nadyne Edison, Felipe Korzenny, Carlos Fernandez-Collado, and Charles K. Atkin. "Antisocial and Prosocial Behaviors on Television." In Bradley S. Greenberg, Life on Television: Content Analyses of U.S. TV Drama. Norwood, New Jersey: Ablex Publishing, 1980, pp. 99-128.

> sample: characters in three composite weeks of network fictional series broadcast during prime time and Saturday morning in 1975 (N=1,212), 1976 (N=1,120), and 1977 (N=1,217).
>
> Blacks and whites were equally likely to give and receive each type of antisocial act (physical/verbal aggression and deceit). In regard to prosocial acts, blacks were somewhat less altruistic. They were more concerned than whites about feelings of others but less likely than whites to express their own feelings.

244. Greenberg, Bradley S., David Graef, Carlos Fernandez-Colluado, Felipe Korzenny, and Charles K. Atkin. "Sexual Intimacy on Commercial Television During Prime Time." In Bradley S. Greenberg, Life on Television: Content Analyses of U.S. Television Drama. Norwood, N.J.: Ablex Publishing, 1980, pp. 129-136.

> sample: two weeks of prime-time network series broadcast in 1977 and 1978.
>
> There were 156 agents of intimate sexual references (e.g., references to sexual intercourse, prostitution) and 146 targets of these references in the sample of programs. Black characters, about ten percent of the characters in this viewing period, comprised five percent of the agents and five percent of the targets of these references.

245. Greenberg, Bradley S. and Carrie Heeter. "Television and Social Stereotypes." In Joyce Sprafkin, Carolyn Swift, and Robert Hess (eds.), Rx Television: Enhancing the Preventive Impact of TV. New York: The Haworth Press, 1983, pp. 37-52.

> Summary and review of ongoing research on the portrayal of minorities on television. Since 1968

blacks have made up about 10 percent of the
prime-time characters (close to U.S. Census figures).
Hispanics made up 3 percent, Asians 2.5 percent, and
Native Americans less than one-half of one percent of
prime-time characters. Minorities were very
underrepresented on daytime serials -- less than 3
percent of these characters. Minorities were often
portrayed in a segregated "minority context."
Cross-racial relationships were predominantly
egalitarian and more formal than white-white
relationships; they also were much more likely to be
job-related. Overall, blacks had lower status, lower
job prestige, and were less likely to be employed.

246. Greenberg, Bradley S., Carrie Heeter, David Graef,
Kurt Doctor, Judee K. Burgoon, Michael Burgoon, and Felipe
Korzenny. "Mass Communication and Mexican Americans." In
Bradley S. Greenberg, Michael Burgoon, Judee K. Burgoon,
and Felice Korzenny, Mexican Americans and the Mass Media.
Norwood, N.J.: Ablex Publishing, 1983, pp. 7-35.

Summarizes content studies focusing upon the
portrayal of Hispanics on television. Notes the
consistent finding that Hispanics were very
underrepresented, and that Hispanics were usually
cast in stereotypical roles (crooks, cops, comics).
The best known stereotypes included Desi Arnez (I
Love Lucy), the Chicano gardener (Father Knows Best),
and Sargeant Garcia (Zorro). Half of all Hispanics
appeared on 4 programs and 5 out of 6 were men. In
regard to news programming, research revealed that
minority problems were generally given low priority
and the stories were not often considered important.

247. Greenberg, Bradley S. and Sherrie L. Mazingo.
"Racial Issues in Mass Media Institutions." In Phyllis
A. Katz (ed.), Toward the Elimination of Racism. New
York: Pergamon Press, 1976, pp. 324-328.

sample: one week of prime-time drama and commercials
broadcast in 1973; 30 programs and 366 commercials.

Updates Dominick and Greenberg (212) and Roberts
(282). The 49 blacks made up nine percent of
dramatic characters and appeared in 44 percent of the
programs. About 18 percent of these black characters
appeared in major roles; 30 percent in minor
roles; and about 52 percent were background
characters (a decrease in major roles and an increase

in background roles from earlier analyses). There
was less tokenism in prime-time programs, with a
significant decrease in the percentage of blacks
appearing only with whites. In analyzing dominance,
the authors found that the giving and receiving of
orders was about equally distributed. In
advertisements, about seven percent of the characters
were blacks, appearing in an average of 14 percent of
the commercials (29 percent of the public service
announcements and 13 percent of product commercials).
Most black characters were cast in background roles
with other blacks (18 percent in major roles, 17
percent in minor roles, and 65 percent as background
characters).

248. Greenberg, Bradley S. and Kimberly A. Neuendorf.
"Black Family Interactions on Television." In Bradley
S. Greenberg, Life on Television: Content Analyses of
U.S. TV Drama. Norwood, New Jersey: Ablex Publishing,
1980, pp. 173-181.

sample: 160 families from three composite weeks of
network prime-time and Saturday morning fictional
series broadcast in 1975, 1976, and 1977.

There were 19 black families out of a total of 160
families; some of these families appeared in more
than one season, but with a different family
structure. About half of the black families were
headed by a single parent, compared to about a
quarter of the white families. The nuclear family
(two parents and their children) was the dominant
white family structure; only three of the 19 black
families were nuclear families. Sons had a more
frequent and significant role among black TV
families; they had the larger share of interactions
than any other family role in either racial group.
Most of family interactions for both racial groups
were affiliative. Whites, however, were more likely
than blacks to offer information in these
interactions.

249. Greenberg, Bradley S., Kimberly A. Neuendorf, Nancy
Buerkel-Rothfuss, and Laura Henderson. "The Soaps: What's
On and Who Cares?" Journal of Broadcasting, 1982, 26(2),
pp. 519-536.

sample: three episodes per week of each of 13
afternoon serial dramas broadcast over a two week
period in 1977; 308 speaking characters.

Authors outline demographics of soap opera
characters, comparing them to earlier data provided
by Gade (51), to 1975 U.S. Census figures, and to the
prime-time population described in the author's own
research Greenberg, (241). About three percent of
the characters were nonwhite compared to 13 percent
in real life.

250. Greenberg, Bradley S., Katrina W. Simmons, Linda
Hogan, and Charles K. Atkin. "The Demography of Fictional
TV Characters." In Bradley S. Greenberg, Life on
Television: Content Analyses of U.S. TV Drama. Norwood,
New Jersey: Ablex Publishing, 1980, pp. 35-46.

sample: characters in three composite weeks of
network fictional series broadcast during prime time
and Saturday morning in 1975 (N=1,212), 1976
(N=1,120), and 1977 (N=1,217).

The percentage of blacks was fairly stable: 10
percent in 75-76, 11 percent in 76-77, and 9 percent
in 77-78; this represented parity with the 1970
census. Blacks were significantly more likely to be
found in situation comedies. The proportion of black
males and black females was consistent and
equal: they each made up about ten percent of the
sample. They were more likely to be young (one-third
of the characters under 20); they were
underrepresented among the middle-aged characters.
Blacks were consistently underrepresented in
higher-level jobs. From 1975 to 1977 there was a
drop in the proportion of blacks portrayed as law
breakers.

251. Harvey, Susan E., Joyce N. Sprafkin, and Eli
Rubinstein. "Prime-time TV: A Profile of Aggressive and
Prosocial Behaviors." Journal of Broadcasting, 1979,
23(2), pp. 179-189.

*** see women ***

sample: one week of network prime-time programming
broadcast in 1975-1976; 66 programs, 946 human
characters.

Nonwhites were 17 percent of the sample (11 percent
were black). Black characters were slightly less
aggressive than white characters; nonblack minority

characters, however, were significantly more
aggressive than white characters.

252. Haskell, Deborah. "The Depiction of Women in Leading
Roles in Prime-Time Television." Journal of Broadcasting,
1979, 23(2), pp. 191-196.

*** see women ***

253. Haskins, James. "New Black Image in the Mass
Media: How Educational is Educational TV?" Freedomways,
1974, 14(3), pp. 200-208.

A context of white control of media production and
finance surrounds the author's discussion of the
general impact of Sesame Street, and two PBS programs
aimed specifically at the black audience -- Soul and
Black Journal. The greater impact of blacks on
commercial stations in specific areas must be seen in
juxtaposition with the problem of presenting
"acceptable" black images; i.e., unthreatening images
similar to those characteristic of prevailing white
culture. Author urges, as a practical step toward
resolution, increased participation by blacks in the
business/financial institutions related to the
medium.

254. Head, Sidney W. "Content Analysis of Television
Drama Programs." Quarterly of Film, Radio, and Television,
1954, 9(2), pp. 175-194.

sample: four episodes of each of 64 network dramas
broadcast in 1952; 1,023 major and 740 minor
characters.

Nonwhites made up ten percent of the characters
(N=114) and appeared in 29 percent of the plays.
They were more likely to be cast in service
occupations and small businesses and less likely to
be cast in police/detective and white collar
occupations. There were more nonwhites,
proportionately, categorized as lower class than
whites: 23 percent of nonwhites compared to nine
percent of whites. Approximately the same percentage
of both racial groups was portrayed as criminals: 11
percent of nonwhites and 14 percent of whites. The
proportion of blacks treated unsympathetically was
much lower than that of other racial/ethnic groups or
whites.

255. Heeter, Carrie, Bradley S. Greenberg, Bradley
E. Mendelson, Judee K. Burgoon, Michael Burgoon, and Felipe
Korzenny. "Cross Media Coverage of Local Hispanic American
News." Journal of Broadcasting, 1983, 27(4), pp. 395-402.

>sample: 20 newscasts broadcast in 2 southwest cities
>(20 percent Hispanic population) from a randomly
>constructed composite two week period in September
>1980.

>Hispanic stories were longer than non-Hispanic
>stories (average of 1 minute and 15 seconds compared
>to 56 seconds). Hard news stories predominated and
>there was a substantial proportion of crime news,
>minority issue stories, and feature stories. None of
>the on-camera personnel was Hispanic. Cross media
>(newspaper, radio, TV) coverage of Hispanic news was
>quite similar.

256. Hiemstra, Roger, Maureen Goodman, Mary Ann
Middlemiss, Richard Vosco, and Nancy Ziegler. "How Older
Persons are Portrayed in Television Advertising:
Implications for Educators." Educational Gerontology,
1983, 9, pp. 111-122.

*** see age-roles ***

>sample: 136 commercials broadcast during the summer
>of 1981 on the three major networks.

>There was only one black character over 50 and none
>over 60.

257. Hinton, James L., John F. Seggar, Herbert
C. Northcott, and Brian F. Fontes. "Tokenism and Improving
Imagery of Blacks in TV Drama and Comedy: 1973." Journal
of Broadcasting, 1974, 18(4), pp. 423-432.

>sample: 371 major and minor characters in 133 early
>evening and prime-time network dramas (excluding
>westerns) randomly selected during a six week period
>in 1973. Sampling procedure generated about the same
>number of black and white characters; 149 black
>characters.

>Six percent of the programs featured a black as a
>regular character. Black females were noticeably
>absent as major characters. Blacks were found more
>often in subordinate roles than were white
>characters. They were less often hostile or violent

118

and less likely to engage in immoral or illegal behavior than white males. There was no significant social difference in industriousness, competence, or attractiveness. Overall, television remained a white man's world; analysis supported charges of tokenism in regard to blacks, particularly black females. The data did not support a charge of negative stereotyping, although blacks were portrayed more often in subordinate roles than white characters.

258. Iiyama, Patti and Harry H. L. Kitano. "Asian Americans and the Media." In Gordon L. Berry and Claudia Mitchell-Kernan, Television and the Socialization of the Minority Child. New York: Academic Press, 1982, pp. 151-186.

Summarizes previous research on television portrayals of Asians (Gerbner and Signorielli (236); U.S. Commission on Civil Rights, (301)). Notes exceptions to usual stereotypical presentations: Jack Soo on Barney Miller and Sam, the coroner's assistant, on Quincy. Otherwise, Asian portrayals were very stereotyped and often a result of the program location -- Asians clustered in token background roles for the effect of authenticity (e.g., Hawaii Five-0 and Mash). When Asian women appeared they emphasized the helplessness, dependency, and weakness of the Asian in the Western world. News coverage of events relating to Asians in the U.S. or abroad had been inadequate; and the mass media continued to portray the Chinese as peculiar, quaint, mystifying foreigners. Asian women had been accepted as on-camera reporters in California; while Asian men were still discriminated against in on-camera jobs. Asians in commercials usually were associated with products representative of old stereotypes, such as the Chinese laundryman.

259. Jackson, Anthony W. Black Families and the Medium of Television. Ann Arbor, Michigan: Bush Program in Child Development and Social Policy, 1982.

Papers from a May, 1980 conference, "Black Families and the Medium of Television," sponsored by the Bush Program in Child Development and Social Policy. Notes how television perpetuates the myth of the black American in a comic, distorted, and degrading manner. Participants cited several different reasons for the predominently negative portrayals of blacks on television (racism, power, economic profit).

119

Images of black families were often narrow, negative, stereotypical portrayals.

260. Jeffries-Fox, Suzanne and Nancy Signorielli. "Television and Children's Conceptions of Occupations." In Herbert S. Dordick (ed.), Proceedings of the Sixth Annual Telecommunications Policy Research Conference. Lexington, Mass: Lexington Books, 1978, pp. 21-38.

sample: annual week-long samples of prime-time network dramatic programming broadcast between 1969 and 1976.

Psychiatrists, paramedics, judges, and lawyers were predominently white. The racial distribution of doctors and police was similar to that of the general character population (about 10 percent nonwhite).

261. Kassarjian, Waltraud M. "Blacks as Communicators and Interpretors of Mass Communiation." Journalism Quarterly, 1973, 50(2), pp. 285-291.

Summarizes early racial/ethnic analyses of several media (such as Dominick and Greenberg (212)), including television programming and commercials. Notes that television has a higher percentage of blacks in commercials than magazines and newspapers have in advertisements. Cautions against hasty interpretations of findings about black portrayal: frequency of appearance may increase in commercials because of an increase in the number of commercials. Further, phases of portrayals (see Clark, (204)) may pertain to all television characters, not only blacks.

262. Kaufman, Lois. "Prime Time Nutrition." Journal of Communication, 1980, 30(3), pp. 37-46.

sample: first 30 minutes of the top 10 regularly scheduled series, including commercials, broadcast in 1977; 20 programs, 108 commercials, 537 characters (50 overweight and 10 obese).

Nine out of ten television characters were white; consequently most of the overweight characters were white. There were important racial differences. A disproportionate number of blacks (16 percent) were represented among the overweight and 90 percent of the obese characters were black. A number of Asians were also depicted as overweight.

263. Lemon, Judith. "Dominant or Dominated? Women on Prime-Time Television." In Gaye Tuchman, Arlene Kaplan, and James Benet (eds.), Hearth and Home: Images of Women in the Mass Media. New York: Oxford University Press, 1978, pp. 51-68.

*** see women ***

sample: characters in occupational interactions in a sample of situation comedy and crime drama (stratified for significance of female roles) broadcast in 1975; 274 males and 84 females.

Analysis of dominance/equality in male-female verbal and nonverbal interactions, looking at occupational status as an intervening variable. Race influenced dominance patterns for women, although sex was the more influential variable. Black females were more dominant in family situations than white females. White females, however, were given more latitude in non-family related appearances.

264. Lemon, Judith. "Women and Blacks on Prime-Time Television." Journal of Communication, 1977, 27(4), pp. 70-79.

sample: 93 interactions between blacks and whites chosen randomly from 8 crime dramas and 11 situation comedies (stratified for significance of black roles) broadcast during prime time in 1975; about two-thirds of the interactions were in crime dramas.

An analysis of dominance/equality in black-white verbal and nonverbal interactions. Program type had a significant effect on dominance/equality. Whites were more dominant than blacks in crime drama, dominating in 41 percent of interactions compared to ten percent for blacks. On the other hand, blacks were more dominant than whites in situation comedy, dominating in 34 percent of interactions compared to 18 percent for whites. There were more equal interactions in situation comedy (55 percent) than in crime drama (41 percent). In general, sex was a stronger determinant of dominance than race, with considerable interaction between the two variables.

265. Lichter, Linda S. and S. Robert Lichter. "Criminals
and Law Enforcers in TV Entertainment." Prime Time Crime,
Washington, D.C.: The Media Institute, 1983.

    sample: all programs from a six week sample of
    prime-time programs broadcast in 1980-81 in which at
    least one crime was committed or a law enforcer
    appeared: 263 programs, 250 criminals committing 417
    crimes.

    By the late 1960s the proportion of black characters
    on television was roughly equal to the proportion of
    blacks in the population (10 to 12 percent).
    Nonwhites, mostly blacks, were 12 percent of all TV
    criminals; they committed 10 percent of the violent
    crimes and 3 percent of the murders. Fifteen percent
    of law enforcement officials, portrayed in this
    sample, were blacks.

266. Lichter, S. Robert and Linda Lichter.
"Italian-American Characters in Television Entertainment."
Prepared for The Commission for Social Justice, May 1982.

    sample: 263 episodes from a six week sample of the
    1980-81 television season that contained at least one
    Italian-American; 96 Italian-American characters.

    Most Italian-American characters were males; only one
    in six was a woman. Negative portrayals of
    Italian-Americans outnumbered positive portrayals by
    a margin of nearly two to one. Almost half of the
    Italian-American characters were shown in a negative
    light; only one in four was portrayed positively.
    One Italian-American character out of six engaged in
    criminal activities. Among the villains, the largest
    number were criminals. Most Italian-American
    characters held low status jobs; only one in seven
    worked as an executive, manager, or professional.
    The majority of Italian-American characters did not
    speak proper English. Other bad types included
    characters who were malevolent, greedy, or merely
    foolish. The good Italian-Americans were usually
    friendly people rather than heroes.

267. Liebert, Robert M., John M. Neale, and Emily
S. Davidson (eds.). The Early Window: Effects of
Television on Children and Youth. New York: Pergamon
Press, Inc., 1973, pp. 18-22.

Brief summary of studies dealing with the portrayal
of television characters (DeFleur (32); Gerbner
(58); Head (94); and Smythe (164)) in regard to
racial/ethnic and sex-role stereotypes.

268.   Liebmann-Smith, Joan and Sharon L. Rosen.   "The
Presentation of Illness on Television."   In Charles Winick
(ed.), Deviance and Mass Media.   Beverly Hills, Ca.: Sage
Publications, 1978, pp. 79-93.

*** see health ***

sample: 50 episodes of Marcus Welby, M.D. plus a
qualitative analysis of other medical programs.

There was a trend in casting more women and racial
minorities as both physicians and paraprofessionals
in medical programs.   The patients in this sample of
Marcus Welby, M.D. were 94 percent white and 6
percent black or Chicano.

269.   MacDonald, J. Fred.   Blacks and White
TV: Afro-Americans in Television Since 1948.
Chicago: Nelson-Hall Publishers, 1983.

Extensive review/description of blacks in television
drawn from private film and tape collections,
extensive viewing, publications such as Variety and
TV Guide, interviews, and discussions.   Wherever
possible, citations from actual programs were used.

The relationship between blacks and television was
ambivalent.   While there was a genuine effort to
treat blacks as talented and equal, to employ them
fairly, and to depict them honestly, there was also
persistent stereotyping, a reluctance to develop
and/or star black talent, and an exclusion of
minorities from the production side of the industry.

270.   Mendelson, Gilbert and Morissa Young.   A Content
Analysis of Black and Minority Treatment on Children's
Television.   Boston, Ma.: Action for Children's Television,
1972.

sample: Saturday morning network programs broadcast
in 1971 (47 program segments; 14.5 hours; 440
characters).

Blacks were 7 percent and other ethnic groups 2 percent of the characters. Minorities appeared in 17 program segments and whites appeared in 40 segments; 25 segments had only white characters and there were no segments with only black or other minority characters. Blacks and other minorities rarely appeared as major characters: only one black and one other minority were so cast. While there were no black villains there were ten programs with white villains; three programs had black heroes and five programs had white heroes. While blacks were depicted more often than whites with predominantly positive traits, other minority characters were generally depicted in a derogatory manner (especially Asians, American Indians).

271. Monroe, William B. "Television: The Chosen Instrument of the Revolution." In Paul L. Fisher and Ralph L. Lowenstein (eds.), Race and the News Media. New York: Frederick A. Praeger, Inc., 1967, pp. 83-93.

The news director of a southern television station during the racial unrest of the 1960s recounts how the medium advanced the cause of racial equality by news accounts of black unrest and by raising the aspirations of the disadvantaged with images of the relative affluence of white society. The author discusses the political and psychological obstacles these images created for Southern conservatives, who charged that media served as instigators of the turbulence rather than as a vanguard of change in society. Author refutes this charge.

272. Northcott, Herbert C., John F. Seggar, and James L. Hinton. "Trends in TV Portrayal of Blacks and Women." Journalism Quarterly, 1975, 52(4), pp. 741-744.

sample: characters in occupational role portrayals (lasting three minutes or longer) in three weeks of dramatic programming (excluding westerns) broadcast in 1971 (N=394) and 1973 (N=679).

Blacks appeared in 12 percent of the occupational roles in 1971 and in 9 percent of the occupational roles in 1973. In 1971 proportionately more blacks were in high status jobs (38 percent) than whites (30 percent); in 1973, the percentage of both blacks and whites in high status jobs dropped considerably. At the same time, depiction of blacks in service jobs (includes police) increased from 13 percent to 64 percent. While white women appeared to be moving gradually from "non-census" occupations (e.g., housewife) into low-level census occupations, black women did not.

273. O'Kelly, Charlotte G. and Linda E. Bloomquist. "Women and Blacks on TV." Journal of Communication, 1976, 26(4), pp. 179-184.

sample: one month of randomly selected hour-long segments of network programming and commercials broadcast throughout the day in 1973; 2,309 characters.

Minorities made up 7 percent of characters in adult programs and 3 percent of characters in the commercials broadcast during these programs; six percent of people on the news and five percent of characters in news commercials; and two percent of characters on children's programs and four percent of characters in children's commercials. Although nonwhites were underrepresented, there were no apparent differences in the roles of whites and nonwhites.

274. Paik, Irvin. "A Look at the Caricatures of the Asian as Sketched by American Movies." In A. Tachiki, E. Wong, and F. Odo (eds.), Roots: An Asian-American Reader. Los Angeles, Ca: UCLA, Asian-American Studies Center, 1971, pp. 30-36.

A qualitataive analysis of themes, casting, characterizations in films and television from World War I to 1970.

Asians have been used stereotypically for background "flavor" or in major roles as villains who employ physical and/or mental torture (the Fu Manchu stereotype, for example, dates from World War I). Asians and whites were rarely involved romantically on the screen for fear of offending the white, middle class audience (taboo against miscegenation). More recently, Asian females have been portrayed in romantic relationships with white males, but relationships between Asian males and white females have not been portrayed. The author states that movies and television ignore the achievements of Asian-Americans and that the dehumanization inherent in stereotypes sets up ethnic groups as targets of political aggression.

275. Pierce, Chester M. "Social Trace
Contaminants: Subtle Indicators of Racism in TV." In
Stephen B. Withey and Ronald P. Abeles (eds.), Television
and Social Behavior: Beyond Violence and Children.
Hillsdale, N.J.: Lawrence Erlbaum Associates, 1980,
pp. 249-257.

This author describes and gives examples of subtle
"micro-aggressions" of commission and omission in
white-black relations in televised sports, news,
advertising, and adventure programs. Whites' time,
space, and energy are given priority at the expense
of blacks'. For example, although black players may
dominate the action at a particular moment in a
sports contest, most of the positive commentary will
be directed at whites. In drama, blacks have been
typically portrayed as helpers, frequently
over-emotional, and in need of direction by whites.

276. Pierce, Chester M., Jean V. Carew, Diane
Pierce-Gonzalez, and Deborah Wills. "An Experiment in
Racism: TV Commercials." Education and Urban Society,
1977, 10(1), pp. 61-87.

sample: 190 different prime-time network commercials
broadcast during a two week period in 1972; 140 were
aired during programs with predominantly white
characters and 50 during programs with predominantly
black characters; 671 characters, 53 blacks.

Blacks made up eight percent of this sample and there
was an approximately equal distribution of males and
females. Of those characters shown working for
wages, only 28 percent were black (interpreted as an
index of dependence or subservience). Although
relatively small numbers of characters were depicted
dispensing goods or favors or grooming, these
behaviors were exhibited exclusively by whites.

277. Poulos, Rita Wicks, Susan E. Harvey, and Robert
M. Liebert. "Saturday Morning Television: A Profile of the
1974-75 Children's Season." Psychological Reports, 1976,
39, pp. 1047-1057.

sample: one Saturday morning of network, independent,
and public programming broadcast in 1974-75; 48
programs, 376 major and minor characters. (Note: two
subsamples were used for comparative analyses -- one

excluding programs broadcast on the independent
stations and one using just programs broadcast on
network affiliates.)

Half of these programs had all-white casts and two
had all-black casts. Blacks made up 13 percent and
other racial minorites made up 12 percent of the
primary sample. A regrouped sample and a secondary
sample indicated that these percentages dropped when
programs on independent stations, and particularly
public stations, were excluded. Of the 376
characters, 17 percent were minority males and 8
percent were minority females. There were no
significant differences in the proportion of minority
characters engaging in at least one prosocial act
such as altruism or expressing sympathy. While 21
percent of the white characters demonstrated
aggressive behavior, 14 percent of the nonblack
minority characters and only two percent of the black
characters were aggressive.

278. Pride, Richard A. and Daniel H. Clarke. "Race
Relations in Television News -- Content Analysis of
Networks." Journalism Quarterly, 1973, 50(2), pp. 319-328.

sample: race relations stories in one early-evening
network news program broadcast each week between
August 1968 and April 1970 (source: Vanderbilt
Television News Archive); 3,011 sentences.

An examination of the accuracy of accusations of bias
and irresponsibility leveled at television news in
its coverage of racial issues. While significant
differences were found for emphasis given race
relations stories (measured by placement of the story
within the broadcast) by the three networks, these
differences were minor after January 1970.
Extremists of both races were generally treated
unfavorably, but black militants received more
negative comments (65 percent) than white racists (46
percent). Blacks, as a group, received fewer
negative comments (29 percent) than white society (48
percent). The authors concluded that the criticism
of the medium both by blacks (for unfavorable bias)
and by government spokesmen (for "subversive"
balance) was unjustified.

279. Rainville, Raymond E. and Edward McCormick. "Extent
of Covert Racial Prejudice in Pro Football Announcers'
Speech." Journalism Quarterly, 1977, 54(1), pp. 20-26.

sample: 66 "protocols" (everything said about a
player) from twelve national football league
games; biracial pairs of players were matched for the
analysis.

Whites received more play-related praise and more
comments on the execution of aggressive plays.
Blacks were the subject of more unfavorable
comparisons to other players; all eleven references
to negative non-professional past achievements
(eg. poor scholastic record) were to black players.
Blacks also received significantly more recipient of
aggression and unfavorable comparison ratings.
Overall, announcers covertly built a positive
reputation for white players and a comparatively
negative reputation for black players.

280. Ramsdell, M. L. "The Trauma of Television's Troubled
Soap Families." Family Coordinator, 1973, 22, pp. 299-304.

*** see women ***

sample: eight soap operas aired on one network
station in 1971-72; 57 leading female roles.

Blacks made token appearances in the soaps and were
generally given middle class characteristics; none
was unemployed or on welfare.

281. Reid, Pamela Trotman. "Racial Stereotyping on
Television: A Comparison of the Behavior of Both Black and
White Television Characters." Journal of Applied
Psychology, 1979, 64(5), pp. 465-471.

sample: 28 episodes of ten situation comedies
stratified by racial composition of the cast
(all-black, all-white, or mixed-race), broadcast in
1977; 110 characters.

Characters were rated on twelve behavior variables
used in sex-role research to determine racial and sex
differences. There was no significant difference for
several variables (e.g., activity, deference,
aggression, autonomy). Black and white males were
not significantly different from each other; black
females, however, demonstrated the most nurturance
and more dominance than white females. While black
males scored highest on achievement (plans or intent
to overcome obstacles), black females scored the

128

lowest on this behavior. Analysis of the effect of the racial composition of the cast on these behavioral variables revealed that whites on black shows were significantly more deferent and were portrayed more negatively than whites on mixed- or white-cast programs.

282. Roberts, Churchill. "The Portrayal of Blacks on Network Television." Journal of Broadcasting, 1970-1971, 15(1), pp. 45-53.

sample: characters in occupational roles of three minutes (or more) duration in one week of network prime-time regular series and specials (excluding westerns) and 588 commercials broadcast in 1970.

The increasing visibility of blacks in major roles and in commercials was noted. At least one black character appeared in about half of the regular programs. There were 45 black characters in all roles: 29 met the criterion for occupational portrayal and 13 were in major roles. Blacks were most frequently found in law- and entertainment-related occupations and were often found in glamorous settings (author notes the difference between this image and the negative one often found in news programs). Blacks appeared in ten percent of the commercials, most frequently in ads for toiletries.

283. Roberts, Churchill. "The Presentation of Blacks in Television Network Newscasts." Journalism Quarterly, 1975, 52(1), pp. 50-55.

sample: one three-week period of early evening network news in 1972 and 1973; 874 segments presenting someone other than the regular news commentator.

Blacks appeared in 23 percent of the segments, most frequently in a non-speaking capacity in stories relating to school busing, the civil rights movement, and crime. Skilled and unskilled blue collar workers were the most frequently presented occupational group. Each network broadcast segments dealing with black accomplishments and stories in which race was not the relevant factor.

284.   Schuetz, Stephen and Joyce N. Sprafkin.   "Portrayal
of Prosocial and Aggressive Behaviors in Children's TV
Commercials."   Journal of Broadcasting, 1979, 23(1),
pp. 33-40.

> sample: 242 commercials broadcast during network and
> independent Saturday morning children's programs in
> 1974; 2,226 human characters.

> Nonwhites made up 24 percent of the human characters.
> The characters, regardless of race, were about
> equally likely to behave altruistically in these
> commercials. Nonwhites performed 17 percent of the
> prosocial acts (altruism) and four percent of the
> aggressive acts. White characters were portrayed as
> more aggressive than minority characters. Nonwhites
> demonstrated only four percent of the aggressive
> behavior.

285.   Schuetz, Stephen and Joyce N. Sprafkin.   "Spot
Messages Appearing Within Saturday Morning Television
Programs."   In Gaye Tuchman, Arlene Kaplan, and James Benet
(eds.), Hearth and Home: Images of Women in the Mass Media.
New York: Oxford University Press, 1978, pp. 69-77.

> sample: commercials and public service announcements
> broadcast during network and independent Saturday
> morning programs in 1974; 372 spot messages, 2,226
> characters.

> Nonwhites made up 25 percent of the sample (20
> percent were blacks and 5 percent were nonblack
> minorities). The majority of nonblacks were
> Hispanics (64 percent), followed by Asians (19
> percent), and American Indians (8 percent). The
> remaining nine percent were of unidentifiable
> racial/ethnic origin. Nonblack minority characters
> were found in only 10 percent and blacks in 38
> percent of spot messages with human characters; only
> 4 percent of these spots contained no white
> characters. Representation of nonwhite characters
> was comparable for males and females: 22 percent of
> the males were black and 6 percent were nonblack
> minority members; 16 percent of the females were
> black and 4 percent were nonblack minority members.

286. Seggar, John F. "Imagery of Women in Television
Drama: 1974." Journal of Broadcasting, 1975, 19(3),
pp. 273-282. See also, "Women's Imagery on TV: Feminist,
Fair Maiden, or Maid?" Journal of Broadcasting, 1975,
19(3), pp. 289-294.

   sample: a stratified random selection (50 percent) of
   afternoon and evening dramatic and variety programs,
   excluding westerns and cartoons, broadcast during a
   five week period in 1974; 946 female characters,
   including 87 in major roles and 142 male major
   characters.

   Minority women made up 15 percent of the total sample
   of female characters, 12 percent of the women in
   speaking roles, and 7 percent of female major roles.
   Blacks made up 9 percent of females in all roles, 9
   percent of females in speaking roles, and 6 percent
   of females in major roles. Only 27 percent of
   minority women compared to 36 percent of white women
   were cast in speaking roles.

287. Seggar, John F. "Television's Portrayal of
Minorities and Women: 1971-75." Journal of Broadcasting,
1977, 21(4), pp. 435-446.

   sample: a stratified random selection of afternoon
   and evening dramatic and variety programs, excluding
   westerns and cartoons, broadcast during a five week
   period in 1971 and 1973 (50 half-hour units) and 1975
   (50 percent of programs); 10,794 characters.

   Analysis revealed an increase in black visibility at
   the expense of other minority groups from 1971 to
   1975. In 1971, 6 percent of the sample were blacks
   and 12 percent were other minorities; in 1973, 5
   percent of the sample were blacks and 9 percent other
   minorities; in 1975, 9 percent of the sample were
   blacks and 4 percent were other minorities. While
   white males and females were equally likely to be
   cast in major or supporting roles, black and other
   minority females were considerably less likely than
   black and other minority males to be cast in these
   types of roles. Black females were the most likely
   of all to be cast in bit parts.

288. Seggar, John F., Jeffrey K. Hafen, and Helena
Hannonen-Gladden. "Television's Portrayals of Minorities
and Women in Drama and Comedy Drama, 1971-1980." Journal
of Broadcasting, 1981, 25(3), 277-288.

sample: a stratified random selection of afternoon
and evening dramatic and variety programs, excluding
westerns and cartoons, broadcast during five week
periods in 1971 and 1973 (50 half-hour units) and in
1975 and 1980 (50 percent of programs); 1,942
characters in 1971, 3,278 in 1973, 5,572 in 1975 and
7,132 in 1980.

Blacks made up between 6 to 8 percent of these
samples of television programs (compared to 12
percent of the U.S. population). Other minorities
were virtually excluded from proportional
representation even though they made up 8 to 9
percent of the national population. The proportion
of white males and females in major roles has
increased from 1971 while the proportion of black
males and females in major roles has decreased.
Among major roles, other minority males have
increased their representation and other minority
females have decreased their representation since
1971.

289. Seggar, John F. and Penny Wheeler. "World of Work on
TV: Ethnic and Sex Representation in Television Drama."
Journal of Broadcasting, 1973, 17(2), pp. 201-214.

sample: 250 half-hours of afternoon and prime-time
drama (excluding westerns and cartoons) and weekend
morning programs sampled over a five week period in
1971; 1,830 characters.

The racial/ethnic distribution of the sample was as
follows: 75 percent white American, 12 percent
British and other European, 6 percent black American,
3 percent Chicano, 2 percent Asian, 1 percent
Hawaiian, 0.3 percent Russian, and 0.1 percent
American Indian. Minorities, especially Chicanos,
were less likely than whites to have roles of more
than three minutes; but this pattern was influenced
by the sex of the character. A comparison of
occupational portrayals revealed that the percentage
of blacks in the professional/technical category
approximated that of whites (about 37 percent); but
service worker was a larger category for blacks and
Chicanos (33 percent and 44 percent, respectively)
than for whites (24 percent). Among women, however,
minorities in minor roles were in higher-prestige
occupations than were white females.

290. Shaheen, Jack G. "The Arab Image in American Mass Media." In Edmund Ghareeh, Split Vision: The Portrayal of Arabs in the American Media. Washington, D.C.: American-Arab Affairs Council, 1983, pp. 327-336.

A qualitative description of the pervasive negative image and stereotype of Arabs on television. Notes how this negative image has been reinforced by television news programs as well as some recent openness to change.

291. Shaheen, Jack G. "Images of Saudies and Palestinians: A Review of Major Documentaries." In Willian C. Adams, Television Coverage of the Middle East. Norwood, N.J.: Ablex Publishing, 1981, pp. 89-105.

Qualitative analysis of television documentaries (60 Minutes, The Saudies -- CBS Special Report, CBS's The Palestinians, and ABC's Terror in the Promised Land).

Notes existing stereotypes and the apparent lack of discussion with Saudies and others in some programs. Nevertheless, the documentaries present an alternative and more balanced perspective than the image of the greedy oil sheik found in many entertainment programs. Overall, documentaries provided important opportunities for a more thorough and more accurate examination of Arab nations.

292. Shaheen, Jack G. The TV Arab. Bowling Green, Ohio: Bowling Green State University Popular Press, 1984.

Qualitative description of the image of Arabs on television entertainment and news programming.

The negative stereotype of Arabs remained omnipresent, appearing in both new programs and dated reruns. Presents numerous examples of stereotypes from children's programs, prime-time drama and documentaries. Discusses ways this stereotype could be dispelled and that viewers should see balanced presentations. Arabs should not be portrayed only as billionaires, bombers, or belly dancers. Urges producers to eliminate the current stereotype of Arabs as other derogatory stereotypes (black domestic, savage Indian, cunning Asian, and Italian mobster) have been eliminated.

293. Signorielli, Nancy. "Content Analysis: More Than Just Counting Minorities." In In Search of Diversity -- Symposium on Minority Audiences and Programming Research. Washington, D.C.: Corporation For Public Broadcasting, 1981, pp. 97-108.

Concise summary of major findings of several analyses of the portrayal of racial-ethnic minorities on television. Describes, in detail, the methodology of content analyses and the problems often encountered in this research.

294. Signorielli, Nancy. "The Demography of the Television World." In Gabrielle Melischek, Karl E. Rosengren, and James Stappers (eds.), Cultural Indicators: An International Symposium. Vienna, Austria: The Austrian Academy of Sciences, 1983, pp. 137-157. Also in Oscar H. Gandy, Jr., Paul Espinosa, and Janusz A. Ordover (eds.), Proceedings from the Tenth Annual Telecommunications Policy Research Conference. Norwood, New Jersey: Ablex Publishing, 1983, pp. 53-73.

sample: annual week-long samples of prime-time and weekend-daytime network dramatic programming broadcast between 1969 and 1981; 14,037 prime-time and 6,243 weekend-daytime characters.

Racial distributions indicated that in practically every program type minorities were underrepresented in relation to their numbers in the U.S. Census. The only exceptions were the overrepresentation of Asian-Pacific peoples (due, primarily, to one program -- Hawaii Five-0) and the overrepresentation of blacks, especially black men, in situation comedies. Because of the large numbers of animals, most races were underrepresented in children's programs. For white characters there was a slight negative year-to-year trend, with several fluctuations, while for nonwhite characters there was a slight positive year-to-year trend, again with several fluctuations. For the most part, television continued to overrepresent white men at the expense of nonwhite men and women of all races.

295. Signorielli, Nancy. "Marital Status in Television Drama: A Case of Reduced Options." Journal of Broadcasting, 1982, 26(2), pp. 585-597.

sample: annual week-long samples of prime-time
network dramatic programming broadcast between 1975
and 1979; 1,298 major characters in 447 programs.

Sex and race were important variables in determining
marital status and other aspects of characterization.
While 47 percent of white women were single and 25
percent were married, the reverse was true for
nonwhite women -- 24 percent were single and 41
percent were married. Slightly more nonwhite women
than white women were widowed, divorced, or
separated. The marital status of nonwhite men was
more often apparent than the marital status of white
men: 34.8 percent of white men could not be coded on
marital status as compared to 18.3 percent of the
nonwhite men. White men were also less likely to be
married (19.3 percent) than black men (26.8 percent).

296. Signorielli, Nancy, and George Gerbner. "The Image
of the Elderly in Prime-Time Network Television Drama."
Generations, 1978, 3(2), pp. 10-11.

sample: annual week-long samples of prime-time
network dramatic programming broadcast between 1969
and 1976; 1,898 major and 7,233 minor characters.

Among elderly characters, nonwhites were
proportionally more visible than among younger
characters: 17 percent of the elderly characters were
nonwhite as compared to 8 percent of the middle-aged
and 13 percent of young adult characters.

297. Signorielli, Nancy and George Gerbner. "Women in
Public Broadcasting: A Progress Report." The Annenberg
School of Communications, University of Pennsylvania,
Philadelphia, Pa., March, 1978.

sample: one week of programs distributed by PBS in
1977; 28 adult programs and 534 segments from 25
children's programs.

Nonwhites made up 13 percent of those appearing in
general (information) programs, 10 percent of
dramatic characters, and 2 percent of people in music
programs. Blacks were the most frequently appearing
minority group. There were no minority major
characters in dramatic programs. Nonwhites were more
likely to have supporting rather than major roles in
general programming. The theme of racial rights
appeared in 11 percent of the general programs; it

ranked eighth of eight possible topic areas. In
children's programs, 38 percent of the characters
were members of minority groups, although one-quarter
of the characters could not be categorized by race.
About a fifth of the male characters and a fifth of
the female characters were black while almost half of
the females and only a third of the males were
white; more than a quarter of the males compared to
less than one-tenth of the females could not be
classified by race. Three-quarters of the characters
had no discernable occupation; those who did work,
especially blacks, were found in "masculine"
occupations. Blacks and Hispanics were somewhat less
likely than whites and Asians were somewhat more
likely than whites to be seen working.

298. Silverman, L. Theresa, Joyce N. Sprafkin, and Eli
A. Rubinstein. "Physical Contact and Sexual Behavior on
Prime-Time TV." Journal of Communication, 1979, 29(1),
pp. 33-43.

sample: one week of regularly scheduled prime-time
programs, including variety, movies, and specials,
broadcast during 1977-78 season; 678 characters.

Nonwhites made up 17 percent of the characters in
this sample. Black characters demonstrated a
disproportionate amount of nonsexual verbal
aggression (black males), and non-aggressive child
contact (black females); they also performed
physically intimate behaviors, such as hugging and
kissing, less frequently.

299. Smythe, Dallas W. "Reality as Presented by
Television." Public Opinion Quarterly, 1954, 18,
pp. 143-156.

sample: one week of dramatic programs broadcast on
seven New York stations in 1953; 86 programs and 476
characters.

Nonwhites were 20 percent of this sample; two percent
were blacks. Other ethnic groups (mostly Europeans)
comprised 24 percent of the villains, but only ten
percent of the heroes. Foreign white heroes were
less potent than American white heroes; foreign
heroines were more potent than American white
heroines.

300. Turow, Joseph. "Occupation and Personality in Television Dramas: An Industry View." Communication Research, 1980, 7(3), pp. 295-318.

sample: four industry "breakdowns" (character descriptions/plot summaries used in casting) for each of 36 prime-time non-comedy network dramatic series; 144 episodes, 824 characters in non-regular roles.

Race was unspecified in the vast majority of the breakdowns (over 90 percent). While the distribution of blacks in occupational categories approximated the distribution of characters whose race was unspecified, blacks were somewhat more likely to be found in blue collar jobs. Asians appeared more frequently in criminal and law agent categories than in any other occupational group; they were also rarely found as white collar workers. Ethnic groups, other than blacks and Asians, appeared predominantly in the "other" occupational category.

301. United States Commission on Civil Rights. Window Dressing on the Set: Women and Minorities in Television. Washington, D.C.: Government Printing Office, August 1977.

program sample: annual week-long samples of prime-time and weekend-daytime network dramatic programming broadcast from 1969 through 1974; 5,624 characters.

Nonwhites made up 11 percent of the sample; they increased from 7 percent of the sample in 1969 to 13 percent in 1974. Male characters accounted for most of the increase. Blacks comprised 68 percent of the nonwhite characters, Asian Americans were 21 percent, characters of Spanish origin were 7 percent, and 4 percent were Native Americans. The sex-racial distribution of the sample was 24 percent white women, 2 percent nonwhite women, 65 percent white men, and 9 percent nonwhite men. There was a slight decrease in the number of nonwhite males from 1969 to 1974, but an increase in the number of nonwhite females. Overall sex differences were more influential than racial-ethnic differences. Nonwhites were younger than whites, especially among males. There were no significant racial differences in the proportion of characters in serious/comic classifications. Nonwhite males and females were, however, more likely than white males and females to be depicted as heroes and were less likely to be portrayed as villains. Nonwhite males and females were less likely than white males and females to be portrayed as married. There were no significant racial/sex differences in occupational status except that fewer nonwhites were in managerial jobs and more nonwhites were in service-related jobs. Most nonwhite females could not be classified by occupation. In regard to crime and violence, there were minor racial differences for males and, among female characters, nonwhite females were less likely to commit violence than white females but were the most likely of all characters to be victims of violence.

news sample: a composite week of network news broadcast on each of the three networks in 1974-75; 230 stories.

Nine of 230 stories related to minorities and 5 out of 85 correspondents were nonwhites (four blacks and one Asian American). Stories presented by minority newscasters generally dealt with minority problems rather than political, economic, social problems or events in general. Nonwhites were 11 percent of the newsmakers, they were mostly black with several Hispanics. Nonwhite males appeared most frequently as criminals and public figures; nonwhite females were usually private individuals who were in some type of economic deprivation.

302. United States Commission on Civil Rights. Window Dressing on the Set: An Update. Washington, D.C., Government Printing Office, January, 1979.

program sample: five week-long samples of prime-time and weekend-daytime network dramatic programming broadcast in 1975, 1976, and 1977; 5,042 characters.

Update of 1977 report indicated that stereotyping continued in both news and dramatic programming. Nonwhites made up 13 percent of the sample of characters. Nonwhite females made the only gain in frequency of appearance. Minority males were somewhat more likely to appear in comic roles and minorities were overrepresented in younger age groups. The number of whites in professional occupations increased relative to the number of nonwhites in these occupations; nonwhites also continued to be portrayed more often than expected in service-related occupations. Dimensions of

characterization were similar to those presented in
the first report.

news sample: a composite 5-day week broadcast by the
three networks in 1977; 330 stories.

This sample of news stories revealed a decrease in
the number of stories focusing upon minorities and
women; less than 2 percent of the 330 stories.
Minorities made up 8 percent of the correspondents (a
stable representation). In this sample, minorities
reported more national/informational stories than
stories relating to minorities; nonwhites also
reported stories that were more prominent in the
broadcasts. There was, however, a decrease (to five
percent) in the proportion of minority newsmakers
(due primarily to the decrease in minority criminals
-- the 1977 report covered the Cuban Watergate
burglars).

303. United States National Advisory Commission on Civil
Disorders (Kerner Commission). Report.
Washington: D.C.: GPO, 1968; also New York: Bantam Books,
1968.

sample: six days of TV news coverage of "riots" in
each of 15 cities (3 days before and after each
incident); 955 sequences.

The media failed to give adequate attention to racial
problems, ignoring the difficulties of ghetto life
and the grievances it creates. The Commission found
that newscasts did not itensify the turbulence,
although the focus was often on black-white
confrontations rather than on black reaction to
slums. There were twice as many calm as emotional
sequences at both local and network levels, with
stories focusing on control by law enforcement
personnel, rather than upon the disturbance itself.
There were numerous interviews with whites, even
though the areas affected by riots were populated
mostly by blacks. Coverage dropped off sharply after
the first day of rioting, except in Detroit.
Finally, black leaders did not appear very
frequently, moderate leaders appeared on local
programs, and militant leaders rarely appeared.

304. Volgy, Thomas J. and John E. Schwarz. "TV
Entertainment Programming and Sociopolitical Attitudes."
Journalism Quarterly, 1980, 57(1), pp. 150-154.

sample: themes and central characters in four weeks
of prime-time network entertainment programming aired
in 1975.

Suggests that more air time is being given to blacks
than had been given previously. Television programs
did not discuss or portray racial
discrimination/bigotry, or severe economic
disadvantages. Authors report results of a
cultivation analysis based on these content findings.

305. Weigel, Russell, H. and Paul W. Howes. "Race
Relations on Children's Television." Journal of
Psychology, 1982, 3(1), pp. 109-112.

sample: five hours of children's network dramatic
programming broadcast between 8 a.m. and 1 p.m. on
each of three consecutive Saturdays in 1979.

There was a minimal opportunity for interracial
contact because blacks appeared in only 6.6 percent
of the program time. Almost half of this time was on
one program; 85 percent of appearance time was in
five shows.

306. Weigel, Russel H., James W. Loomis, and Matthew
J. Soja. "Race Relations on Prime-Time Television."
Journal of Personality and Social Psychology, 1980, 39(5),
pp. 884-893.

sample: one week of network, prime-time drama
broadcast in 1978; 63 hours, 91 cross-racial
interactions, 980 commercials.

There were a total of 91 cross-racial interactions
(45 in situation comedies and 46 in dramatic
programs). Blacks appeared in 52 percent of the
situation comedies and in 59 percent of the dramas.
Examination of the total amount of appearance time
revealed that 77 percent of the appearance time of
black characters took place in 18 percent of the
programs (dramatic and comic). Black-white
encounters were rare; a qualitative analysis of
cross-racial interactions revealed that only 2
percent of human appearance time in drama and 4
percent of human appearance time in comedy involved
cross-racial interactions. Cross-racial interactions
were more often formal than friendly; the majority
(70 percent) took place within institutional settings
in which some black characters had comparable levels

of authority or expertise and 13 percent reflected
friendliness and mutual respect. As compared to
white-black interactions, white-white interactions
were more intimate, more multi-faceted, and more
likely to involve shared decision making. Whites
appeared in 95 percent and blacks appeared in less
than 20 percent of the commercials. Two percent of
the commercials had just black characters while 77
percent had only white characters.

307. Winick, Charles, Lorne G. Williamson, Stuart
F. Chusmir, and Mariann Pezella Winnick. Children's
Television Commercials: A Content Analysis. New
York: Praeger, 1973.

sample: 236 non-toy commercials obtained from
advertising agencies in 1971.

About a quarter of the commercials contained a
minority character, usually a close-up shot.
Positive interactions between minority and majority
figures were found in 13 percent of the commercials.

3.
Aging and Age-Roles

308. Abelman, Robert and Kimberly Neuendorf. "Religion in
Broadcasting: Demographics." Cleveland, Ohio: Cleveland
State University, 1983.

> sample: three episodes of each of the "top 27"
> religious programs in the U.S.; 81 episodes, 514
> characters.

> Almost half of the people in this sample were mature
> adults and 37 percent were young adults. Children
> were only 7 percent, adolescents were 4 percent and
> the elderly were only 5 percent of this sample. The
> average age of the people in religious programs was
> 38. Females were the majority among adolescents (57
> percent) and the most underrepresented among mature
> adults (22 percent). Ethnic minorities were younger
> than their white counterparts; over nine out of ten
> of the elderly, mature adults, and young adults were
> white while two-thirds of the adolescents and more
> than half of the children were white.

309. Aronoff, Craig. "Old Age in Prime Time." Journal of
Communication, 1974, 24(4), pp. 86-87.

> sample: three annual week-long samples of prime-time
> network drama aired from 1969 to 1971; 2,741 major
> characters.

> Only five percent of all major characters were
> classified as elderly; this percentage was similar
> for males and females. Among the elderly, males
> outnumbered females by about two to one. Fewer than
> half of the older characters were portrayed as
> successful, happy, or good. For males, increasing
> age was associated with being a "bad" character; for
> females, increasing age was associated with decreased
> chances of succeeding (achieving goals). Moreover,
> elderly females were the only characters who were

more likely to fail than to succeed in achieving goals.

310. Atkin, Charles K. "Mass Media and the Aging." In Herbert J. Oyer and E. Jane Oyer (eds.), Aging and Communication. Baltimore, Md.: University Park Press, 1976, pp. 99-118.

A broad summary of portrayal, use, and effect in relation to television and the elderly. Summarizes several portrayal studies including Aronoff (309); Francher (320); and Peterson (349).

311. Barcus, F. Earle. "Commercial Children's Television on Weekends and Weekday Afternoons: A Content Analysis of Children's Programming and Advertising Broadcasting in October 1977." Newtonville, Ma.: Action for Children's Television, 1978.

*** see women ***

sample: network and independent weekend morning programming and independent weekday afternoon programming broadcast in 1977; 228 program segments, 899 characters, and 1,022 commercial announcements.

Of 224 program segments, 20 related to aging, some of which were minor references. A few of the segments referred to the fear of aging and several had an elderly character as a counselor. Depictions in cartoons were one-dimensional and stereotyped.

312. Barcus, F. Earle. Images of Life on Children's Television. New York: Praeger Publishers, 1983.

sample: one weekend and several weekday afternoons of network and independent children's programming broadcast in 1981; 235 program segments, 1,145 characters.

Although males outnumbered females in all age categories, there were greater proportions of female teenagers and young adults; females were 39 percent of the elderly characters. The middle-aged female was the most underrepresented. There was no great concern for the elderly, who appeared in only three out of 20 segments.

313. Beck, Kay. "Television and the Older Woman."
Television Quarterly, 1978, 15(2), pp. 47-49.

sample: no information given.

Content analysis revealed that the older woman had no
clearly defined role on television and was generally
underrepresented. She made up less than 5 percent of
all female characters. Most women in TV drama were
between 25 and 29 while most men fell into the 35-45
age group. Men were seen in terms of power, women in
terms of sexual attractiveness. Men were always
older and wiser than women. The average woman was
about ten years younger than her male partner. As
she aged she became decreasingly important to the
plot. The aging male, on the other hand, took on
added importance. While men became problem solvers,
women became nags or adoring attendants. The older
man's handsome and weathered face revealed that he
had lived, loved, suffered, and learned. The older
woman had to hide her age lines, dye her hair, and
stay trim lest the world discover that she too had
lived, loved, suffered, and learned.

314. Bishop, James M. and Daniel R. Krause. "Depictions
of Aging and Old Age on Saturday Morning Television."
Gerontologist, 1984, 24(1), pp. 91-94.

sample: cartoons broadcast on commercial networks
between 7 a.m. and 11 a.m. during a six week period
in October and November, 1981; 106 cartoons and 378
characters in 24 hours of programming.

Aging was not a dominant feature of Saturday morning
network programming. Only one in five programs made
some reference to aging or old age, usually negative.
Only 25 (7 percent) of the 378 primary characters
were categorized as "old;" of the 101 negative
characters, 11 percent were old. Old characters,
however, were not portrayed more negatively than
adults in general. In these programs a
disproportionate share of the positive characters
were young. Aging appeared as a major theme in only
one program. In general, cartoons did not portray
old age as healthy, attractive, or good.

315. Cassata, Mary B., Patricia A. Anderson, and Thomas
D. Skill. "The Older Adult in Daytime Serial Drama."
Journal of Communication, 1980, 30(1), pp. 48-49. See
also, "Images of Old Age on Daytime." In Mary Cassata and
Thomas Skill (eds.), Life on Daytime Television: Tuning-In
American Serial Drama. Norwood, N.J.: Ablex Publishing
Corp., 1983, pp. 37-44.

> sample: ten consecutive episodes of each of thirteen
> daytime network serial dramas broadcast in 1978; 365
> characters, 58 aged 55 or older.

> Characters aged 55 and above were 16 percent of the
> total sample. Somewhat more than half of these older
> characters were in their sixties; the remainder were
> in their fifties. One character was 80 years old.
> Men and women were about equally represented among
> the elderly and 90 percent were healthy. Only three
> characters were retired. Most elderly characters,
> especially the men, were classified as upper-middle
> class or wealthy and 75 percent lived in their own
> homes. In general, elderly characters in daytime
> serial dramas were presented quite positively -- they
> were attractive, healthy, economically independent,
> and important.

316. Davis, Richard H. Television and the Aging Audience.
Los Angeles, Ca.: The Ethel Percy Andrus Gerontology
Center, 1980.

> Summarizes research that revealed, contrary to
> U.S. Census figures, that older men outnumbered older
> women in television commercials. Men were permitted
> to look older so long as the image of virility and
> sexual appeal was maintained. Older women were
> seldom seen in commercials; when they appeared they
> often played less than attractive characters. In
> dramatic programs, older men were more likely to be
> presented as bad or evil; they often were victims
> and suffered fatal punishment. Women over the age of
> 30 were less likely to be seen on screen and were
> rarely presented as romantic partners. Older women
> in lead roles were shown in mid-life. The older male
> was more interesting; he gained in power and
> experience.

317. Davis, Richard H. and Robert W. Kubey. "Growing Old
on Television and With Television." In David Pearl,
Lorraine Bouthilet, and Joyce Lazar (eds.), Television and
Behavior: Ten Years of Scientific Progress and Implications
for the Eighties. Washington, D.C.: GPO, 1982,
pp. 201-208.

    Review of research on aging and television, noting
    especially underrepresentation and the reinforcement
    of negative stereotypes of the elderly. Includes an
    extensive bibliography.

318. Dominick, Joseph R. "Crime and Law Enforcement on
Prime-Time Television." Public Opinion Quarterly, 1973,
37(2), pp. 241-250.

    sample: one week of prime-time network drama,
    including comedy and excluding feature films,
    broadcast in 1972; 51 programs, 269 speaking
    characters, 119 crimes.

    Compares the demographics and circumstances of crime
    on television with U.S. crime statistics. Out of 96
    criminals, eight percent were between 51 and 65 and
    one percent was over 65 (approximate parity with real
    life data). Among 26 murder victims in this sample,
    none was over 50. (In real life, 20 percent of
    murder victims are over age 50.) Among overall crime
    victims, 84 percent were between 20 and 50 years old.

319. Downing, Mildred H. "Heroine of the Daytime Serial."
Journal of Communication, 1974, 24(2), pp. 130-137.

*** see women ***

320. Francher, J. Scott. "'It's the Pepsi
Generation'...Accelerated Aging and the Television
Commercial." International Journal of Aging and Human
Development, 1973, 4(3), pp. 245-255.

    sample: 100 television commercials aired throughout
    the day (no year given).

    Fifty-seven percent of these commercials were
    oriented toward youthful appearance and/or energy and
    one-third featured youthful females. Older people
    were less likely to sell personal products, were more
    likely to be in humorous commercials, and more likely

to be isolated characters in the commercial; i.e., not appearing with other characters.

321. Gerbner, George. "Children and Power on Television: The Other Side of the Picture." In George Gerbner, Catherine J. Ross, and Edward Zigler (eds.), Child Abuse: An Agenda for Action. New York: Oxford University Press, 1980, pp. 239-248.

> sample: annual week-long samples of prime-time and weekend-daytime network dramatic programming broadcast between 1969 and 1978; 14,973 major and minor characters.

> The world of television ignored children, underplayed adolescents in prime-time and overplayed them in children's programs. Youngsters were a more interracial group than older characters: more white females and black males were cast as children and adolescents than as older characters. The class structure of age portrayals showed more children and adolescents, especially nonwhites, coming from lower socioeconomic backgrounds than members of other age groups. Seven percent of prime-time white youngsters were lower class. Fully one-third of all nonwhite youngsters were lower class. More than six out of ten boys were involved in violence and their victimization ratio was 17:10 (for every 17 boys who inflicted violence, ten were victimized). Only half of the girls were involved in violence and their victimization ratio was 13:10. Young boys were the most underrepresented and the most racially mixed group. Young girls started out underrepresented but became more numerous, more desirable, less happy, and much more vulnerable as they matured. The Index to the Vanderbilt Television News Archives revealed that children and youth were found in an average of 63 news stories each year.

322. Gerbner, George. "Violence in Television Drama: Trends and Symbolic Functions." In George A. Comstock and Eli A. Rubinstein (eds.), Television and Social Behavior, Vol. I, Media Content and Control. Washington, D.C.: GPO, 1972, pp. 28-187.

> sample: annual week-long samples of prime-time and weekend-daytime network dramatic programming broadcast in the fall of 1967, 1968, and 1969; 762 major characters.

More than three-quarters of the characters were male,
American, middle and upper class, unmarried, and in
the prime of life. Children, adolescents, and old
people together accounted for only about ten percent
of the total fictional population. Nearly half of
all females were concentrated in the most sexually
eligible young adult population, to which only
one-fifth of males were assigned; women were also
disproportionately represented among the very young
and old. An average of six in ten children, nearly
seven in ten young adults, over six in ten
middle-aged, and over five in ten old characters were
involved in some violence.

323. Gerbner, George, Larry Gross, Stewart Hoover, Michael
Morgan, Nancy Signorielli, Harry E. Cotugno, and Robert
Wuthnow. "Religion on Television and in the Lives of
Viewers." Report prepared for the Ad Hoc Committee on
Religious Television Research, National Council of the
Churches of Christ, New York, New York, 1984.

sample: one week of local and syndicated religious
television programs broadcast in 1982; 99 programs
and 752 characters.

The demographic distribution of characters in this
sample of local and syndicated religious programming
revealed patterns remarkably similar to those found
on dramatic programs: women made up 34 percent, the
elderly 3 percent, and blacks 10 percent of the
characters. Four out of ten children and
adolescents, almost half of the young adults, and
more than half of the elderly characters were women.

324. Gerbner, George, Larry Gross, Marilyn Jackson-Beeck,
Suzanne Jeffries-Fox, and Nancy Signorielli. "Cultural
Indicators: Violence Profile No. 9." Journal of
Communication, 1978, 28(3), pp. 176-207.

sample: annual week-long samples of prime-time and
weekend-daytime network dramatic programming
broadcast between 1969 and 1977; 3,651 major
characters.

More than six out of ten major characters were
involved in some type of violence. Children and
adolescents of both sexes were heavily involved in
violence and absorbed considerable punishment. With
increasing age, the male's risk of general
victimization declined. Old men had the only

positive victimization ratio (i.e., they inflicted more violence than they suffered) of the four age groups of males. For women, increasing age meant increasing risks of both being hurt and being killed. Young (and generally unmarried) women had an even higher victimization ratio than boys. Old women, unlike old men, were three times as likely to get hurt as to hurt others. Old women got killed but, in this nine year sample, not one was a killer.

325. Gerbner, George, Larry Gross, Michael Morgan, and Nancy Signorielli. "Aging with Television: What Viewers See and What They Say." Report for the U.S. House of Representatives Select Committee on Aging, Claude Pepper, Chairman, Los Angeles hearing - April 26, 1980.

sample: annual week-long samples of prime-time and weekend-daytime network dramatic programming broadcast from 1969-1979.

Both the elderly and children were underrepresented in prime-time and weekend-daytime dramatic programs. Television's population curve reflected the world of consumer spending, bulging in the middle years. Individuals under 20, who number one-third of the U.S. population, made up only 11 percent of the fictional population. Those over 65, comprising about 11 percent of the real population, made up 2 percent of the fictional population. These were consistent findings; characters coded as 65 or older never exceeded 3 percent of the total dramatic population. The age distribution of females, compared to that of males, favored young girls and women under 35. Women actually outnumbered men in the early twenties, but then their numbers fell to four or five times below the number of men. The pattern in children's programs was even more skewed: over half of all females but only 28 percent of all males were under 21. More older characters were treated with disrespect, were not held in high esteem, and were not treated courteously; older characters were also more likely than younger characters to be presented as eccentric or foolish.

326. Gerbner, George, Larry Gross, Michael Morgan, and Nancy Signorielli. "Aging with Television Commercials: Images on Television Commercials and Dramatic Programming, 1977-1979." Annenberg School of Communications, University of Pennsylvania, 1981.

149

sample: commercials in three annual samples of
prime-time and weekend-daytime network dramatic
programming broadcast in 1977, 1978, and 1979 plus
commercials from the evening network news broadcast
during the same week as the 1979 dramatic
sample; 1949 prime-time, 510 weekend-daytime, and 97
news commercials.

The world of television commercials, like the world
of dramatic programming, was a very stable world with
little change between 1977 and 1979. Older adults
appeared infrequently in commercials; they appeared
in nine percent of the prime-time commercials, and in
five percent of the commercials aired during
weekend-daytime and news programs. Older adults
rarely appeared alone in commercials -- they were the
only people in less than one percent of the
prime-time commercials and were never the only people
in children's commercials. Children ranked toward
the top in terms of overall appearances in
commercials: they appeared in 25 percent of
prime-time and news commercials and in more than 80
percent of weekend-daytime commercials. Older people
were underrepresented (2 percent of the characters),
while children were overrepresented in prime-time
commercials (22 percent). In weekend-daytime
commercials, children between 5 and 15 were greatly
overrepresented while every other age group was
underrepresented. Blacks made up only one percent of
the older men and two percent of the older women and
there were no older Hispanics; among the younger
characters, nonwhites made up between eight and
twelve percent of the characters. Children were
usually found in commercials for toys and food or
restaurants. Older characters were found in
commercials for food and drink-related products as
well as those for home and cleaning aids; they were
not in commercials for personal hygiene products.
While practically none of the characters in the
commercials was overweight, 15 percent of those
characters who were overweight were old.

327. Gerbner, George, Larry Gross, Michael Morgan, and
Nancy Signorielli. "Media and the Family: Images and
Impact." Paper for the National Research Forum on Family
Issues, White House Conference on Families, April, 1980.

sample: annual week-long samples of prime-time and
weekend-daytime network dramatic programming
broadcast between 1969 and 1978.

Examination of image of the family in several media,
including television. Home and family were important
for all age groups except young adults. In each age
group, the proportion of married characters was
greater among women; the married included 20 percent
of the young women and 8 percent of the young men; 33
percent of middle-aged men as compared to half of the
middle-aged women; and 62 percent of the older men as
compared to 71 percent of older women. Older
characters were the least likely to be portrayed as
involved in a romantic relationship -- from 1973 to
1978 only one older woman and three older men had
romantic relationships. Marriage was the domain of
older characters but was devoid of romance: older
characters were married but were not involved
romantically, while younger characters were involved
romantically but were not married.

328. Gerbner, George, Larry Gross, and Nancy Signorielli.
"The Role of Television Entertainment in Public Education
About Science." Annenberg School of Communications,
University of Pennsylvania, 1985.

*** see health ***

sample: annual week-long samples of prime-time
network dramatic programming broadcast between 1973
and 1983.

Most characters in prime-time drama were in their
30's or 40's and the women were somewhat younger than
the men. Scientists were one of the older groups of
characters: the average age for male scientists was
44 and the average age for female scientists was 36.
Among major characters, male scientsts were a bit
older (45) and female scientists were somewhat
younger (31). The average age for male doctors was
42 while the average age for female doctors was 38.

329. Gerbner, George, Larry Gross, Nancy Signorielli, and
Michael Morgan. "Aging with Television: Images on
Television Drama and Conceptions of Social Reality."
Journal of Communication, 1980, 30(1), pp. 37-47.

sample: annual week-long samples of prime-time and
weekend-daytime network dramatic programming
broadcast between 1969 and 1978; 1,365 programs,
3,700 major and 13,000 minor characters.

Older characters were very underrepresented: two
percent of the sample of characters in prime-time
drama and one percent of the sample of characters in
weekend-daytime drama were categorized as elderly.
Older characters were less likely to be portrayed as
"good" and as characters aged their chances of being
presented as "bad" increased. Old age on television
also meant less success in achieving goals or in
dealing with obstacles, especially for women. Older
characters were more likely than younger characters
to be treated with disrespect, and older women were
particularly more likely to be portrayed as eccentric
or foolish. Elderly male characters were more likely
than any other age-related group to appear in comic
roles.

330. Gerbner George and Nancy Signorielli. "The World
According to Television." American Demographics, 1982,
4(9), pp. 14-17.

sample: major and minor characters in 14 annual
week-long samples of prime-time network dramatic
programming broadcast from 1969 to 1981; 14,037
characters in 878 programs.

Both the very young and the elderly were
underrepresented on television: characters over 65,
who make up 11 percent of the U.S. population,
comprised only two percent of the characters in
prime-time network dramatic programming. Women were
also concentrated in the younger age groups. White
males dominated television's age of dramatic
authority, between 35 and 50; nonwhite males and
white women were concentrated, with half of their
numbers between the ages of 25 and 40; nonwhite women
were even younger, concentrated between the ages of
20 and 34. Although proportionately more women than
men were young, women "aged" faster: over 90 percent
of the women over 65 were categorized as "elderly" as
compared to only 77 percent of the men in this age
group.

331. Greenberg, Bradley S. Life on Television: Content
Analyses of U.S. TV Drama. Norwood, N.J.: Ablex
Publishing, 1980.

An anthology of studies concerning the appearance and
treatment of women, racial and ethnic minorities, the
elderly, and sexual behavior.

332. Greenberg, Bradley S. "Television and Role Socialization: An Overview." In David Pearl, Lorraine Bouthilet, and Joyce Lazar (eds.), Television and Behavior: Ten Years of Scientific Progress and Implications for the Eighties. Washington, D.C.: GPO, 1982, pp. 179-190.

     Concise summary of research conducted during the 1970s, including that of the author and his colleagues, focusing upon family, sex, race, occupation, and age-roles. Includes an extensive bibliography.

333. Greenberg, Bradley S. "Three Seasons of Television Characters: A Demographic Analysis." Journal of Broadcasting, 1980, 24(1), pp. 49-60.

     sample: characters in three composite weeks of network fictional series broadcast during prime time and Saturday morning in 1975 (N=1,212), 1976 (N=1,120), and 1977 (N=1,217).

     Characters in their 20s, 30s, and 40s made up two-thirds of the television population compared to only one-third of the U.S. population. Moreover, adults of retirement age were substantially underrepresented and their representation decreased over the three years of the study.

334. Greenberg, Bradley S., Nadyne Edison, Felipe Korzenny, Carlos Fernandez-Collado, and Charles K. Atkin. "Antisocial and Prosocial Behaviors on Television." In Bradley S. Greenberg, Life on Television: Content Analyses of U.S. TV Drama. Norwood, N.J.: Ablex Publishing, 1980, pp. 99-128.

     sample: characters in three composite weeks of network fictional series broadcast during prime time and Saturday morning in 1975 (N=1,212), 1976 (N=1,120), and 1977 (N=1,217); approximately 2,500 prosocial and antisocial acts per sample year.

     Verbal aggression was the most common antisocial behavior, followed by physical aggression. Altruism was the most common prosocial behavior. Characters 50 and older had the lowest rate of physical aggression (both as initiators and as receivers) while characters between 35 and 49 had the highest

153

rates. The initiation of verbal aggression increased
with age and was highest for characters 50 and older
(being a recipient of verbal aggression was
comparable across age groups). Older characters were
less deceitful than younger characters. In regard to
prosocial behavior, characters 50 and older were no
different from younger characters in altruism,
expression of their own feelings, or expressing
concern for others' feelings. Increasing age,
however, corresponded to decreasing displays of
affection. Characters between 20 and 34 were most
likely to exhibit displays of affection.

335. Greenberg, Bradley S., David Graef, Carlos
Fernandez-Colluado, Felipe Korzenny, and Charles K. Atkin.
"Sexual Intimacy on Commercial Television During Prime
Time." In Bradley S. Greenberg, Life on
Television: Content Analyses of U.S. TV Drama. Norwood,
N.J.: Ablex Publishing, 1980, pp. 129-136.

sample: two weeks of prime-time network series aired
in 1977 and 1978.

There were 156 initiators of intimate sexual
references (e.g., references to sexual intercourse,
prostitution) and 146 targets of these references in
the sample. Characters aged 50 to 64 comprised 15
percent of the agents and the targets of these
references (comparable to their appearance in these
programs). On the other hand, characters aged 65 and
older were neither agents nor targets of intimate
sexual references.

336. Greenberg, Bradley S. and Carrie Heeter. "Television
and Social Stereotypes." In Joyce Sprafkin, Carolyn Swift,
and Robert Hess (eds.), Rx Television: Enhancing the
Preventive Impact of TV. New York: The Haworth Press,
1983, pp. 37-52.

Summary and review of ongoing research on the
portrayal of age-roles on television. Television is
a world of young adults -- both young children and
the elderly have been continually underrepresented,
especially on Saturday morning cartoons. Characters
in daytime serials, however, were somewhat older: 47
percent were mature adults, 47 percent young adults
and 4 percent teens and preteens. The elderly were
less attractive and independent than characters of
other ages on prime time.

337. Greenberg, Bradley S., Felipe Korzenny, and Charles K. Atkin. "Trends in Portrayal of the Elderly." In Bradley S. Greenberg, Life on Television: Content Analyses of U.S. TV Drama. Norwood, N.J.: Ablex Publishing, 1980, pp. 23-33. Also see "The Portrayal of the Aging: Trends on Commercial Television." Research on Aging, 1979, 1(3), pp. 319-334.

sample: characters in three composite weeks of network fictional series broadcast during prime time and Saturday morning in 1975 (N=1,212), 1976 (N=1,120), and 1977 (N=1,217).

Characters between 50 and 64 made up 17 percent of the 1975-76 sample, 11 percent of the 1976-77 sample, and 14 percent of the 1977-78 sample (parity with U.S. Census data). Characters 65 and older made up only 4 percent of the 1975-76 sample, 3 percent of the 1976-77 sample, and 2 percent of the 1977-78 sample (considerably less than U.S. Census figures). Characters over 60 appeared somewhat more frequently in programs broadcast between 9 and 11 p.m. EST. Older characters appeared somewhat more frequently than younger characters in situation comedies and less frequently in crime programs. More than 80 percent of older and elderly characters were white and about 25 percent were women. Approximately 30 percent were upper class and about 20 percent were lower class. Among the elderly, the percentage of upper class characters was somewhat smaller and the percentage of lower class characters was somewhat greater than the percentage of younger characters in these social class groups.

338. Greenberg, Bradley S., Katrina W. Simmons, Linda Hogan, and Charles K. Atkin. "The Demography of Fictional TV Characters." In Bradley S. Greenberg, Life on Television: Content Analyses of U.S. TV Drama. Norwood, N.J.: Ablex Publishing, 1980, pp. 35-46.

sample: characters in three composite weeks of network fictional series broadcast during prime time and Saturday morning in 1975 (N=1,212), 1976 (N=1,120), and 1977 (N=1,217).

Characters over the age of 50 comprised 21 percent of the 1975-75 sample, 14 percent of the 1976-77 sample, and 16 percent of the 1977-78 sample. This percentage varied with sex and race: while 19 percent of all male characters were 50 or older, only 8 percent of all female characters were in this age

group and while 17 percent of all white characters
were 50 or older, only 6 percent of all black
characters were in this age group. Characters over
age 50 were about equally distributed,
proportionally, among different program types (crime,
situation comedy, family drama). About a quarter of
characters in professional occupations, a third of
those in managerial positions, and more than one in
ten of those in service occupations were age 50 or
older.

339. Harris, Adella J. and Jonathan F. Feinberg.
"Television and Aging: Is What You See What You Get?" The
Gerontologist, 1977, 17(5), part 1, pp. 464-468.

sample: six weeks of randomly selected units of daily
network programs (excluding cartoons) and
commercials; 312 speaking characters, including 26
aged 60 or more and 80 commercials with 198
characters, including 22 over the age of 60.

In the programs, almost eight percent of the
characters were 60 to 70 years old and less than one
percent were over 70 (people above the age of 60
comprise about ten percent of the U.S. population).
These older characters appeared somewhat more
frequently in comedy-drama, news/talk shows, and
children's programs than in game shows and serious
drama, including soap operas. Authority and esteem
by others increasesd for males over the age of 40,
but decreased for females in this age group. Men
comprised 92 percent of the authority-holders in the
50-to-60 age group, appearing mostly in news and talk
shows. The great majority (84 percent) of characters
who were romantically involved were under thirty.
There was one instance of positive romantic
involvement by a character in the 50-to-60 age
group; and no instance of involvement by characters
over 60 (perpetuating the image of the "sexless,
boring oldster". The percentage of characters with
health problems increased with age: nine percent of
all characters, 14 percent of 50-to-60 year olds, and
25 percent of the 60-to-70 year olds. In
commercials, 11 percent of the characters were over
60. There was a higher percentage of men in this age
group compared to younger groups. The percentage of
men presented as authority figures increased with
age, but the presentation of women as authority
figures decreased with age. Health problems
increased with age: while about 13 percent of all
characters in commercials had health problems, 35

percent of characters in the 60-to-70 age group had
health problems. Health aids, in fact, were the
largest category of commercials featuring older
characters (22 percent).

340. Harvey, Susan E., Joyce N. Sprafkin, and Eli
Rubinstein. "Prime-Time TV: A Profile of Aggressive and
Prosocial Behaviors." Journal of Broadcasting, 1979,
23(2), pp. 179-189.

*** see women ***

341. Hiemstra, Roger, Maureen Goodman, Mary Ann
Middlemiss, Richard Vosco, and Nancy Ziegler. "How Older
Persons are Portrayed in Television Advertising:
Implications for Educators." Educational Gerontology,
1983, 9, pp. 111-122.

sample: 136 commercials broadcast during the summer
of 1981 on the three major networks.

Of the 136 commercials, only 32 (24 percent) had one
or more characters 50 years of age or older; only 11
(8 percent) included characters 60 or older. Only 12
percent of the characters were 50 or older and 3
percent were 60 or older. Older women were
especially underrepresented: less than 1 percent of
the characters were women over the age of 59. The
majority of older people were portrayed as
"young-old." There was a noticeable absence of very
old looking people. Moreover, few bald or balding
and few people with wrinkled skin were observed.
Older people had no observable family ties and were
most likely found in commercials dealing with health
products. They were least likely to be found in ads
for toys, games, recreation, appliances, cars, or
personal products. In general, the main characters
in commercials were healthy, sexy or macho-looking,
and in their early thirties. Two-thirds of all
central characters were categorized as under 40.
Overall, television commercials did not acknowledge
the existence of the older person.

342. Jeffries-Fox, Suzanne and Nancy Signorielli.
"Television and Children's Conceptions of Occupations." In
Herbert S. Dordick (ed.), Proceedings of the Sixth Annual
Telecommunications Policy Research Conference. Lexington,
Mass: Lexington Books, 1978, pp. 21-38.

sample: annual week-long samples of prime-time
network dramatic progamming broadcast between 1969
and 1976.

Psychiatrists were younger than most
characters; their mean age was 30. Judges were
usually old: one-fifth were classified as "elderly or
old" and their average age was 53. Doctors,
paramedics, lawyers, and police were all about 40
years old.

343. Kaufman, Lois. "Prime-Time Nutrition." Journal of
Communication, 1980, 30(3), pp. 37-46.

*** see health ***

sample: first 30 minutes of the top ten regularly
scheduled series, including commercials, broadcast in
1977; 20 programs, 108 commercials.

Few young people on television were either overweight
or obese. Weight problems were found almost entirely
among middle-aged or older characters.

344. Kubey, Robert W. "Television and Aging: Past,
Present, and Future." The Gerontologist, 1980, 20(1),
pp. 16-35, esp. pp. 21-3.

Comprehensive article spanning several areas relating
to television and the elderly: viewing habits,
portrayal, and potential impact. The section on
portrayal summarizes a number of content analyses.
Notes that reverse stereotype (e.g., older character
riding a motorcycle or references to prolific sex
life) are often interpreted as comical, thus
reinforcing existing negative stereotypes. Includes
an extensive bibliography.

345. Levinson, Richard M. "From Olive Oyl to Sweet Polly
Purebread: Sex Role Stereotypes and Televised Cartoons."
Journal of Popular Culture, 1973, 9, pp. 561-572.

*** see women ***

346. Lichter, Linda S. and S. Robert Lichter. "Criminals
and Law Enforcers in TV Entertainment." Prime Time Crime.
Washington, D.C.: The Media Institute, 1983.

sample: six weeks of prime-time programs broadcast in 1980-81 in which at least one crime was committed or a law enforcer appeared; 263 programs, 250 criminals committing 417 crimes.

In real life, the majority of all arrests involve people under age 30. In television drama 25 percent of criminals were under the age of 30 and the vast majority were between 30 and 50; only 20 percent were over 50 years of age.

347. National Organization for Women, National Area Chapter. "Women in the Wasteland Fight Back: A Report on the Image of Women Portrayed in TV Programming." Pittsburgh, Pa.: NOW, Inc., 1972.

*** see women ***

sample: a composite week of programming on one network affiliate; includes commercials, dramatic programming, quiz programs, talk shows, soap operas, children's programming, sports, public affairs, and variety programs.

Women were younger than the men in these programs. For example, on quiz programs, 71 percent of the under-30 participants were women while 67 percent of those over-45 were men. On the soap operas, the average age for men was 40, while the average age for women was 32. In dramatic programs, only 15 percent of the women compared to 40 percent of the men were over 40.

348. Northcott, Herbert C. "Too Young, Too Old - Age in the World of Television". The Gerontologist, 1975, 15(2), pp. 184-6.

sample: one week of prime-time network drama, excluding westerns, broadcast in 1974; 41 programs, 464 major and minor characters, including seven characters aged 64 or more.

Elderly characters comprised 1.5 percent of all characters (the 1973 U.S. Census figures for this age group was ten percent). Five of these seven characters appeared in minor roles. Women appeared more youthful than men. Older characters were not more likely than younger ones to live alone. Some of the elderly characters were healthy and active and some had physical disabilities; the programs did not emphasize senility, poverty, or poor health. Age was rarely the theme or topic of discussion in these dramas, but when it was, it was considered in a generally negative tone. The overall focus of the dramas was the competence of adult males, emphasizing their vigor, attractiveness, and competence. Older characters were portrayed as depending on these younger men to solve their problems.

349. Petersen, Marilyn. "The Visibility and Image of Old People on Television." Journalism Quarterly, 1973, 50(3), pp. 569-73.

sample: 30 randomly selected half-hour periods broadcast during one week of prime-time commercial network programming in 1972; 247 characters, 32 older characters.

Older characters comprised 13 percent of this sample (compared to ten percent of the U.S. population). Older men, however, were overrepresented on television (12 percent of the television population compared to 4 percent of the U.S. population), while older women were underrepresented (1 percent of the television population compared to 6 percent of the U.S. population). Females made up only 9 percent of the older characters on television. Images of old people were generally positive. Positive elements of portrayal (59 percent) included activity, health, and independence. Unfavorable ratings (18 percent) frequently involved friendliness and esteem by other characters.

350. Ramsdell, M. L. "The Trauma of TV's Troubled Soap Families." Family Coordinator, 1973, 22, pp. 299-304.

*** see women ***

sample: eight soap operas aired on one network station in 1971-72; 57 leading female roles.

Older women were valued advisors in these programs.

351. Rubin, Alan M. "Directions in Television and Aging Research." Journal of Broadcasting, 1982, 26(2), pp. 537-551.

Reviews studies about television's portrayal of the aged (Arnonoff (309); Francher (320); Gerbner et al.

(329); Harris et al. (339); Northcott (348); and
Petersen (349)) as well as literature about
television's uses and gratification functions.
Discusses methodological problems (such as adequate
definitions for "old" and "aging", validity, and
reliability of measurement) and suggests future
research possibilities.

352. Schneider, Kenneth C. and Sharon Barick Schneider.
"Trends in Sex Roles in Television Commercials." Journal
of Marketing, Summer 1979, 43, pp. 79-84.

*** see sex-roles ***

sample: 287 commercials from 27 hours of prime-time
network programming broadcast by three networks
during October 1976; 252 women and 304 men.

Results of this analysis were compared with those
reported for a sample of commercials broadcast in
1971 (Dominick & Raugh (37)). The 1976 sample
contained fewer young adults (males and females) and
more older (over 50) men and women than the 1971
sample. Women were, however, still portrayed as
younger than the men.

353. Shinar, Dov, Adrian Tomar, and Ayala Biber. "Images
of Old Age in Television Drama Imported to Israel."
Journal of Communication, 1980, 30(1), pp. 50-55.

sample: 562 characters from 46 programs (imported
primarily from the United States) aired in 1977.

This sample had a greater percentage of old
characters than similar studies of programs broadcast
in the U.S.: ten percent of all characters were 60 or
older, 32 percent were 50 to 59 years of age, 38
percent were 30 to 49, and only 20 percent were 15 to
29. Older characters were considerably less likely
than younger characters to be in major roles (24
percent of those 60 and older, 32 percent of the 50
to 59 year olds, and 49 percent of the younger
characters). The proportion of women decreased with
age: from about 40 percent of younger characters to
about 20 percent of those over 50 years of age.
Older characters were somewhat more likely than
expected to appear as leaders, independent,
constructive, and functional within the family.
Characters over 50 were significantly more likely
than younger characters to receive negative

personality ratings. Older characters were rated
negatively on pleasantness, liberalism,
attractiveness, and sexual functionality. Younger
characters, by comparison, received mostly positive
personality ratings. Negative ratings of younger
characters were for family functionality, conformity,
leadership, and honesty.

354. Signorielli, Nancy. "Content Analysis: More than
Just Counting Minorities." In In Search of
Diversity: Symposium on Minority Audiences and Programming
Research. Washington, D.C.: Corporation for Public
Broadcasting, 1981, pp. 97-108.

Overview of several analyses of sex-, minority- and
age-role portrayals with a discussion of content
analysis methodology.

355. Signorielli, Nancy. "The Demography of the
Television World." In Gabrielle Melischek, Karl
E. Rosengren, and James Stappers (eds.), Cultural
Indicators: An International Symposium. Vienna,
Austria: The Austrian Academy of Sciences, 1983, pp.
137-157. Also in in Oscar H. Gandy, Jr., Paul Espinosa,
and Janusz A. Ordover (eds.), Proceedings from the Tenth
Annual Telecommunications Policy Research Conference. New
Jersey: Ablex Publishing Corp, 1983, pp. 53-73.

sample: annual week-long samples of prime-time and
weekend-daytime network dramatic programming
broadcast from 1969 to 1981; 14,037 characters.

Both the very young and elderly were underrepresented
while those in the middle years were overrepresented,
a distribution that resembled the profile of
expendable consumer income. Women were concentrated
in the younger age groups, a third of their total
number were between 20 and 29; men were concentrated,
also with a third of their number, in the 35-to-50
age group. While the age distributions of both white
and nonwhite men and women bulged in the middle,
there were sex and racial differences. White men
dominated the age of "dramatic authority" between 35
and 50; nonwhite men and white women were
concentrated between 25 and 40; and nonwhite women
were concentrated between 20 and 34. Among major
characters, however, the women "aged" faster than the
men. Over 90 percent of the women over 65 were
categorized as elderly, as compared to only 77
percent of the men in this age group.

356. Signorielli, Nancy. "Health, Prevention and
Television: Images of the Elderly and Perceptions of Social
Reality." Prevention in Human Services, 1983, 3(1),
pp. 97-117.

sample: annual week-long samples of prime-time
dramatic programming broadcast from 1969 to 1981; 878
programs and 14,037 characters.

The elderly made up about two percent of the
prime-time characters as compared to 11 percent of
the U.S. population. Female characters were most
concentrated, with a third of their total number in
the 20-to-29 age group, while men were most
concentrated, also with a third of their numbers, in
the 30-to-40 age group. White men dominated the age
of dramatic authority between 35 and 50, while
nonwhite men were concentrated between the ages of 25
and 40. Nonwhite women were even more concentrated
in the younger age groups -- about half were between
20 and 34. Among major characters, women "aged"
faster than men: among characters 65 and older over
90 percent of the women were categorized as "elderly"
as compared to only 76.7 percent of the men. Older
characters were also somewhat less likely to be
presented as "good." More elderly women were
categorized as unsuccessful than successful (failing
to achieve goals). Older men were much more likely
than younger men to be cast in a comic role. Older
characters, especially older women, were more likely
to be portrayed as formerly married or widowed (36
percent) than married (27 percent). They were also
quite likely to have children (55 percent as compared
to 32 percent of middle-aged women) but were
considerably less likely to be involved in a romantic
relationship (nine percent as compared to 60 percent
of young women and 50 percent of middle-aged women).
Older men were also more likely to be portrayed as
formerly married or widowed (39 percent) than married
(18 percent). Older men and especially older women
were less likely to be involved in violence. When
involved, old men were the only group more likely to
commit violence than to be a victim of it and more
likely to kill than be killed. Old women, on the
other hand, were six times as likely to be hurt or
killed than to hurt or kill others. In fact, old
women were only victims of lethal violence -- they
never killed anyone.

357. Signorielli, Nancy, and George Gerbner. "The Image of the Elderly in Prime-Time Network Television Drama." Generations, 1978, 3(2), pp. 10-11.

> sample: annual week-long samples of prime-time and weekend-daytime network dramatic programming broadcast between 1969 and 1976; 1,898 major and 7,233 minor characters.

> Descriptive and comparative analyses of elderly characters, including sex-role differences. The elderly had an average age of 63 and comprised approximately four percent of both major and minor character samples. Elderly characters were more likely than younger characters to be nonwhite (17 percent of elderly versus eight percent of settled adults). Almost 19 percent of elderly characters were upper class, the largest percentage of any age group; only ten percent of middle-aged characters were categorized as upper class. Older women were the only group of characters more likely to be unsuccessful than successful in solving problems and achieving goals. The elderly were more likely to be cast in comic roles. They were rated less positively than other adults in terms of attractiveness, rationality, efficiency, and happiness, but were more peaceful and supportive. Family life was an important aspect of elderly portrayal, but there was very little romantic involvement, particularly for women.

358. Turow, Joseph. "Occupation and Personality in Television Dramas: An Industry View." Communication Research, 1980, 7(3), pp. 295-318.

> sample: four industry "breakdowns" (character descriptions/plot synopses used in casting) for each of 36 prime-time non-comedy dramatic newtork series; 144 episodes, 824 characters in non-regular roles.

> Age was unspecified in 44 percent of the breakdowns. Among the characters for whom age was specified, adults aged 30-45 were distributed about equally among occupational categories--criminals, law agents, white collar and blue collar workers, and "others" (non-census occupations)--but were the largest age group among criminals. Middle-aged adults (45-65) appeared more frequently than expected as white collar workers. Older characters appeared most

frequently in the "other" occupational category,
which included retired people and homemakers.

359. United States Congress, House of Representatives,
Select Committee on Aging. "Age Stereotyping and
Television." Washington, D. C.: Government Printing
Office, 1977. See also "Media Portrayal of the Elderly"
(1980 hearings).

Summarizes several media portrayal studies of the
elderly, compares demographic and crime statistics
with those of real life, and calls attention to the
inherent usefulness of stereotypical images in mass
media.

4.
Sexual Behavior
and Orientations

360. Arlis, Laurie, Mary Cassata, and Thomas Skill.
"Dyadic Interaction on the Daytime Serials: How Men and
Women Vie for Power." In Mary Cassata and Thomas Skill
(eds.), Life on Daytime Television: Tuning-In American
Serial Drama. Norwood, N.J.: Ablex Publishing, 1983,
pp. 147-156.

   sample: 316 dyadic transactions from two months'
   episodes of daytime serial drama (One Life to Live,
   Another World, and Guiding Light) broadcast in
   1981-1982; 97 characters.

   Twenty-one percent of 197 male-female dyads were of a
   romantic nature; there were no romantic dyads
   involving characters of the same sex.

361. Fernandez-Collado, Carlos and Bradley S. Greenberg
with Felipe Korzenny and Charles K. Atkin. "Sexual
Intimacy and Drug Use in TV Series." Journal of
Communication, 1978, 28(3), pp. 30-37.

   sample: one week of prime-time and Saturday morning
   regular fictional series, excluding movies, broadcast
   in the 1976-77 season; 77 programs, 100 intimate
   sexual behaviors.

   The modal behavior in these programs was implied
   sexual intercourse between unmarried, heterosexual
   partners. Of the 100 intimate sexual behaviors, the
   vast majority involved heterosexual relationships,
   including 28 percent related to prostitution. Seven
   percent involved homosexual relationships. All seven
   homosexual acts occurred during the early evening
   viewing period; the overall frequency of homosexual
   behaviors in programs with large audiences of
   children was four percent.

362. Fine, Marlene G. "Soap Opera Conversations: The Talk
That Binds." Journal of Communication, 1981, 31(3),
pp. 97-107.

*** see women ***

sample: random samples of five episodes of each of
four soap operas broadcast in 1977; 20 episodes, 232
dyadic conversations.

Romantic involvement reflected a completely
heterosexual pattern of relationships.

363. Franzblau, Susan, Joyce N. Sprafkin, and Eli
Rubinstein. "Sex on TV: A Content Analysis." Journal of
Communication, 1977, 27(2), pp. 164-170.

sample: one week of prime-time network variety and
drama, excluding movies and specials, broadcast in
1975; 61 programs.

This analysis of physically intimate behaviors, such
as kissing, intercourse, embracing, touching, etc.,
revealed no homosexual behavior. In comparison, the
hourly frequency of verbal reference to heterosexual
intercourse was .04 acts per hour. The hourly
frequency of kissing was 3.74; of embracing,
2.68; and flirting, 1.38. These behaviors were
generally casual rather than intense. Kissing and
embracing were most frequent in situation comedies.
The references to heterosexual intercourse appeared
in drama and crime/adventure programs only. Hourly
rates of other intimate behaviors were comparatively
low.

364. Gerbner, George. "Sex on Television and What Viewers
Learn From It." Comments prepared for the National
Association of Television Program Executives Annual
Conference, San Francisco, Ca., February 19, 1980.

sample: annual week-long samples of prime-time
network dramatic programming broadcast in 1977 and
1978.

Examines changes in portrayal of sexual topics in
prime-time drama between 1977 and 1978. References
to homosexual or bisexual behavior increased from 7
percent of the programs in 1977 to 10 percent of the
programs in 1978. Comic treatment of sex decreased
from 57 percent to 44 percent of the programs, while

serious treatment increased correspondingly.
Publicly acceptable sexual behavior such as kissing
and embracing became more explicit as well as more
frequent. More controversial matters such as
premarital and extramarital sex just became more
frequent, with references to such behavior rising
from 21 percent of prime-time programs in 1977 to 43
percent in 1978.

365. Greenberg, Bradley S., Robert Abelman, and Kimberly
Neuendorf. "Sex on the Soap Operas: An Afternoon Delight."
Journal of Communication, 1981, 31(3), pp. 83-89.

sample: 65 hours of approximately 12 soap operas
broadcast in 1976, 1979, and 1980.

Homosexuality did not appear at all in these
programs; rape and prostitution also rarely occurred.
The most common sexual activity in daytime serials
was explicit petting. In prime-time programs the
most common sex-related activity was reference, often
comic, to intercourse (see Fernandez-Collado et al.
(361) and Greenberg et al. (366)). On both
prime-time programs and the daytime serials, partners
in sexual intercourse were not likely to be married
to each other. In daytime serials, sexual acts and
references occurred at least twice each hour; they
occurred about once each hour in prime-time programs.

366. Greenberg, Bradley S., David Graef, Carlos
Fernandez-Collado, Felipe Korzenny, and Charles K. Atkin.
"Sexual Intimacy on Commercial Television During Prime
Time." In Bradley S. Greenberg, Life on
Television: Content Analyses of U.S. TV Drama. Norwood,
N.J.: Ablex Publishing, 1980, pp. 129-136.

sample: two weeks of prime-time network series,
including some movies, broadcast in 1977 and 1978.

Compares data for 1977 and 1976 with data collected
for the 1976 sample (see, Fernandez-Collado et al.
(361)). Reference to homosexual behavior was rare.
The hourly rate of homosexual reference/behavior
dropped from .16 in 1976 to .06 in 1977 and .07 in
1978. The modal intimate behavior was reference to
heterosexual intercourse among unmarried partners, in
programs broadcast after 9 p.m. The only other
significant categories of references were
prostitution and "other intimacies" (such as petting
and unusual sexual behavior).

367.   Gross, Larry.   "The Cultivation of Intolerance:
Television, Blacks and Gays."   In Gabrielle Melischek, Karl
E. Rosengren, and James Stappers (eds.), Symposium on
Cultural Indicators for the Comparative Study of Culture.
Vienna, Austria, 1983, pp. 345-363.

> For the most part homosexuals were invisible in the
> media.   In their rare appearances, gays were
> ridiculed or stereotyped as victims of violence or as
> villains.   Portrayals which countered or broadened
> the narrow and negative stereotypes of homosexuals
> were seldom seen.   Almost never shown in the media
> were gays as ordinary people in roles which did not
> center on their sexual deviance as a threat to the
> moral order.   Typically, media characterizations used
> popular stereotypes as a code which would be readily
> understood by the audience.   Television drama,
> particularly, reflected the deliberate use of cliched
> casting strategies.

368.   Lopate, Carol.   "Daytime Television: You'll Never
Want to Leave Home."   Feminist Studies, 1976, 3(3/4),
pp. 69-82.

> Qualitative description of daytime serials, game
> shows, and their commercials.

> The game shows, daytime serials, and their
> commercials eroticize the family and everyday life
> but "infantilize" family members.   The focus of both
> the eroticism and the "infantilization" in game shows
> is the M.C., with his power to bestow goods.   The
> daytime serials eroticize and "infantilize" with
> commodities at a background level.   The world
> presented by the daytime serials offers the intimacy,
> protection, and lack of separateness that most people
> missed as children -- with the added attraction of
> also stirring up and meeting sexual desire.   The
> commercials fall between the game shows and the
> serials.   In this genre the romantic dramas are
> played out, but the solution to the sexual or
> familial plot is accepting the suggestions for goods
> made by the voice over.

369.   Lowry, Dennis T., Gail Love, and Malcolm Kirby.   "Sex
on the Soap Operas: Patterns of Intimacy."   Journal of
Communication, 1981, 31(3), pp. 90-96.

sample: composite week of 12 randomly-selected
network soap operas broadcast in 1979; 50 hours, 329
sexual acts.

Sexual acts occurred at the rate of 6.58 per
hour; the largest category was erotic touching with
an hourly rate of 2.86 acts. Such behaviors
generally took place between unmarried partners.
References to sexual intercourse between unmarried
partners occurred about twice as often as between
spouses. There was a complete absence of reference
to homosexuality in this sample of daytime serials.

370. Roberts, Elizabeth J. "Television and Sexual
Learning in Childhood." In David Pearl, Lorraine
Bouthilet, and Joyce Lazar (eds.), Television and
Behavior: Ten Years of Scientific Progress and Implications
for the Eighties. Washington, D.C.: GPO, 1982,
pp. 209-223.

Reviews research on gender roles; body
images; affection, love, and intimacy; marriage and
family life; and erotic conduct. Notes that
sexuality on television encompasses more than a
special on adolescent pregnancy, the double entendre
of a variety show, or the VD theme of a situation
comedy. Programs and characters provide insight on
what it means to be a man and woman in our society,
how affection and intimacy are expressed, and how
erotic conduct fits into daily life. Human sexuality
on television often was equated with sexiness,
cloaked in humor, or accompanied by violence.
Homosexuality has not been depicted to any noticeable
degree on television.

371. Seiter, Ellen. "Men, Sex, and Money in Recent Family
Melodrama." Journal of University of Film and Video
Association, 1983, 35(1), pp. 17-27.

*** see sex-roles ***

Descriptive study of family melodramas (daytime
serials and prime-time programs such as Dynasty and
Dallas).

There was an obsession with sexual relationships
(usually complicated) in both daytime and prime-time
serials. Prime-time serials were steamier than
daytime serials and the characters were more sexually
active. Like daytime serials, however, this

prime-time genre was deeply sentimental about
marriage -- the greatest esteem was awarded to
monogamous individuals. Homosexuality was, for the
most part, avoided. On daytime serials it was
introduced rarely and hastily dropped. It has
appeared recently in prime-time serials and again,
treated in a negative way. In the family melodrama
good sexuality must always be directed toward
marriage and children, thus homosexuality must either
be associated with villainy and neuroses, or banished
altogether.

372. Silverman, L. Theresa, Joyce N. Sprafkin, and Eli
A. Rubinstein. "Physical Contact and Sexual Behavior on
Prime-Time TV." Journal of Communication, 1979, 29(1),
pp. 33-43.

sample: one week of regularly-scheduled prime-time
programs, including variety, movies, and specials,
broadcast during the 1977-78 season; 678 characters.

This analysis revealed an increase in the televised
depiction of sexual behavior since Franzblau's (363)
analysis of data collected in 1975. Affectionate
touching, suggestiveness, kissing, and hugging were
more frequently observed acts. Although there were
no explicit depictions of sexual intercourse,
references to intercourse were more likely to involve
heterosexual partners. The rates for heterosexual
intercourse were .10 verbal references per hour and
.24 implied acts per hour. Homosexuality, classified
as a discouraged sexual practice, occurred at a rate
of .20 acts per hour, usually involving indirect
innuendos in a few programs aired between 9 and 11
p.m.

373. Sprafkin, Joyce N. and L. Theresa Silverman.
"Update: Physically Intimate and Sexual Behavior on
Prime-Time Television, 1978-79." Journal of Communication,
1981, 31(1), pp. 34-40.

sample: composite week of prime-time network drama,
including movies and variety shows, broadcast during
the 1978-79 season; 68 programs.

Documents increasing depiction of various intimate
and sexual acts, both overt and implied. Sexual
innuendo increased to 11 acts per hour. In relation
to less intimate behaviors, hugging increased to
about five acts per hour, and kissing to seven acts

per hour. Verbal reference to and implied
heterosexual intercourse increased to 1.3 acts per
hour. Several categories of "discouraged sexual
practices" also increased in frequency. There were
more references to prostitution (1.4 acts per hour),
aggressive sexual contact (.5 acts per hour), and
homosexuality (.3 acts per hour). Allusions to
homosexuality generally occurred in situation
comedies.

5.
Health and Handicaps

374. Alley, Robert S. "Media, Medicine and Morality." In
Richard P. Adler (ed.), Understanding Television: Essays on
Television as a Social and Cultural Force. New
York: Praeger Publishers, 1981, pp. 231-246.

> A qualitative review of dramatic medical programs
> tracing the development of the genre since the
> "Medic" series in 1954.

375. Barcus, F. Earle. "Commercial Children's Television
on Weekends and Weekday Afternoons: A Content Analysis of
Children's Programming and Advertising Broadcasting in
October 1977." Newtonville, Mass.: Action for Children's
Television, 1978.

> sample: network and independent weekend morning
> programming and independent weekday afternoon
> programming broadcast in 1977; 228 program segments,
> 889 characters, and 1,022 commercial announcements.

> Nine segments dealt with the handicapped. Four were
> about Mr. Magoo, who was badly nearsighted; two about
> speech impediments (one involved Porky Pig); and one
> about a character who pretended to be physically
> handicapped and used a wheelchair. There was one
> interview in which the problems of the handicapped
> were discussed in a serious manner.

376. Barcus, F. Earle. Images of Life on Children's
Television. New York: Praeger Publishers, 1983.

> sample: one weekend and several weekday afternoons of
> network and independent children's programming
> broadcast in 1981; 235 program segments, 1,145
> characters.

The programs in this sample rarely included or focused upon handicapped persons.

377. Barcus, F. Earle and Susan M. Jankowski. "Drugs and the Mass Media." The Annals of the American Academy of Political and Social Science, 1975, 417, pp. 86-100. See also F. Earle Barcus et al. "Drug Advertising on Television." In National Commission on Marihuana and Drug Abuse: Drug Use, pp. 623-668, and Richard Heffner, Assocs. Inc. "Over the Counter Drug Commercials: Network Television, Spring, 1971." In National Commission on Marihuana and Drug Abuse: Drug Use, pp. 669-697.

sample: 132 commercials for over-the-counter drugs in 126 hours of commercial television broadcast in Boston, Ma. (Barcus); 465 drug commercials broadcast during 250 hours of network programming (Heffner).

Drug commercials made up 5.5 percent of all commercials in the Barcus study and 13.4 percent of all ads in the Heffner study. Internal analgesics such as aspirin were the most prominent (25 percent), followed by antihistamine preparations, antacids, laxatives, vitamin and mineral preparations, sleeping aids, etc. In both studies 80 to 90 percent of the commercials made reference to specific ailments, conditions, or symptoms for which the drug was intended. The ads offered not only specific relief but also relaxation, general well-being ("look better", "feel younger"), or the maintenance of one's overall health. Psychological well-being and mood changes were also indicated (frowns turned to smiles).

378. Breed, Warren J. and James R. DeFoe. "Drinking on Television: A Comparison of Alcohol Use to the Use of Coffee, Tea, Soft Drinks, Water, and Cigarettes." The Bottom Line, 1979, 2(1), pp. 28-29.

sample: 225 episodes of the top 30 prime-time television programs broadcast during the 1976-1977 season.

There were 701 alcohol-related acts (consumption and preparation) compared to 329 for coffee and tea, 40 for soft drinks, 45 for water, and 72 for cigarettes. Alcohol was consumed in 76 percent of the programs at a rate of 3.1 drinks per program and 4.7 drinks per hour. "Good guys" were involved in 52 percent, "bad guys" in 10 percent, and "weak" characters in 38 percent of the drinking incidents.

379. Breed, Warren J. and James R. DeFoe. "Mass Media,
Alcohol, and Drugs: A New Trend." Journal of Drug
Education, 1980, 10(2), pp. 135-143.

> sample: prime-time programs broadcast in the
> 1976-1977, 1977-1978, and 1978-1979 television
> seasons.

> Analysis of situation comedies revealed an approval
> of alcohol and a disapproval of illegal drugs. In
> the last couple of years, however, marihuana has been
> portrayed as a relatively harmless escape from care
> and boredom. Overall on prime time, drinking
> occurred at least four times each hour while smoking
> was seen about once every four hours.

380. Breed, Warren J. and James R. DeFoe. "The Portrayal
of the Drinking Process on Prime-Time Television." Journal
of Communication, 1981, 31(1) pp. 58-67.

> sample: 14 weeks of both the top 15 situation
> comedies and dramas broadcast during the 1976-1977
> season; 225 episodes, 396 characters in 233 scenes
> involving alcohol.

> Of 226 characters who were depicted as drinkers, 18
> percent were chronic drinkers (another 125 characters
> expressed disapproval of drinking). Crisis-related
> situations accounted for 61 percent of all drinking
> incidents; these incidents usually involved men,
> those in middle-age, and poor people. Regular
> characters were involved in serious drinking as often
> as guest characters, but were less subject to both
> disapproval and negative consequences.

381. Cassata, Mary, Thomas D. Skill, and Samuel O. Boadu.
"In Sickness and in Health." Journal of Communication,
1979, 29(4), pp. 73-80.

> sample: summaries (from Soap Opera Digest) of
> thirteen daytime serial dramas broadcast in 1977; 341
> characters, 191 health-related occurrences involving
> 144 characters.

> Health-related occurrences included accidents and
> violence and involved 68 male and 76 female
> characters (the distribution of males and females in
> the overall sample was equal). Cardiovascular

disease was the only prominent serious physical
disease, afflicting 21 characters. Psychiatric
disorders were somewhat more common, afflicting 25
characters (18 of these were women between the ages
of 22 and 45). Three of these women attempted
suicide. Only two cases of cancer, the second
leading cause of death in the U.S., appeared; neither
ended in death. Prognosis was generally good for
"good" characters, while "bad" characters received
less sympathetic treatment.

382. Cassata, Mary, Thomas Skill, and Samuel O. Boadu.
"Life and Death in the Daytime Television Serial: A Content
Analysis." In Mary Cassata and Thomas Skill (eds.), Life
on Daytime Television: Tuning-In American Serial Drama.
Norwood, N.J.: Ablex Publishing, 1983, pp. 47-70.

sample: summaries (from Soap Opera Digest) of
thirteen daytime serial dramas broadcast in 1977; 341
characters, 191 health related occurrances involving
144 characters.

Illness, along with accidents, violence, and death,
formed an important story element in daytime serials.
Health-related occurrences included accidents and
violence (41 percent) and involved 68 male and 76
female characters. Health-related disorders also
included illnesses of a psychiatric nature (13
percent), cardiovascular disease (11 percent),
symptomatic disorders (9 percent), pregnancy (10
percent), homicides (8 percent), and suicides (7
percent). Deaths were most often associated with
accidents and/or violence: eight out of every 100
characters died because of an accident or violence.
Men and women were equally likely to suffer accidents
or violence; women were, however, twice as likely to
commit suicide as men. The frequency of disease was
also evenly dispersed among men and women; but again
women were more likely to die than men.

383. DeFoe, James R., Warren Breed, Lawrence A. Breed.
"Drinking on Television: A Five-Year Study." Journal of
Drug Education, 1983, 13(1), pp. 25-38. See also, Warren
Breed, James R. DeFoe, and Lawrence Wallack. "Drinking in
the Mass Media: A Nine-Year Project." Journal of Drug
Issues, 1984, 15.

sample: 5 seasons of top-rated prime-time programs
(1976-1977 to 1981-1982); 615.5 hours.

The preferred drink on prime-time television was
alcohol. The number of alcohol-related acts per hour
increased from under 5 in 1976-1977 to over 8 in
1981-1982; the increase was primarily in
drink-preparation acts. To a lesser degree, similar
trends were isolated for non-alcoholic beverages.
Overall, non-alcoholic beverages were drunk much less
frequently than alcohol. All types of characters,
except children and adolescents, were involved in
drinking alcohol. The consequences of drinking as
well as other character's reactions to drinking
abuses were not shown very often. Cigarette use was
sparce -- the rate was less than once every three
hours. This rate also decreased over the 5 seasons
of programming. Illegal drug use was virtually
absent, although there were several incidents of
joking about the use of marijuana. The study also
found that drinking was often used as a way to deal
with stress, that drinking was generally glamorized,
that characters did not usually refuse drinks when
offered, and that there was a considerable amount of
heavy drinking with no presentation of the possible
hazards or consequences.

384. Derry, Charles. "TV Soap Opera: Incest, Bigamy, and
Fatal Disease." Journal of the University of Film and
Video Association, 1983, 35(1), pp. 4-16.

Descriptive/qualitative study of daytime serials.

Hospitals were an important interior of the daytime
serials allowing this genre to deal with the theme of
life and death. There was an emphasis upon taboos
and fate as well as an obsession with birth and
death. Most pregnancies were not normal and birth
was portrayed as dangerous and traumatic. There also
was a focus upon pre-death states of
semi-consciousness and coma and concerns with mercy
killing and suicide. The conventional health-related
plots included slow and drawn out death, sudden and
unexpected accidents or illnesses, and amnesia.

385. Donaldson, Joy. "The Visibility and Image of
Handicapped People on Television." Exceptional Children,
1981, 47(6), pp. 413-16.

sample: 85 randomly selected half-hour periods of
prime-time network programming broadcast in 1979; 387
major, 542 minor, and 13 handicapped characters.

Three percent of major characters and one percent of both major and minor characters were handicapped. By comparison, 15 to 20 percent of the U.S. population are handicapped. The disabilities of handicapped characters usually were central to their lives. Conspicuously absent were positive portrayals in which the disability was secondary and unimportant. Handicapped persons were seldom shown engaged in social or professional interaction with other characters and were never seen among the many "background" characters (shoppers, spectators, workers, etc.). About half of the segments dealing with the handicapped were positive (i.e., the handicapped as a "developing person"). Handicapped persons were also seen in extremely negative roles: as evil or menacing, sick or pitiful. The author notes that prime-time television is not influential in shaping positive societal attitudes towards handicapped people or in facilitating comfortable relationships between handicapped and non-handicapped people.

386. Dorn, Nicholas and Nigel South. _Message in a Bottle: Theoretical Overview and Annotated Bibliography on the Mass Media and Alcohol_. Great Britain: Gower Publishing, 1983.

Theoretical overview focuses upon the United Kingdom; the annotated bibliography covers research conducted in a number of countries.

387. Fernandez-Collado, Carlos F., Bradley S. Greenberg, Felipe Korzenny, and Charles K. Atkin. "Sexual Intimacy and Drug Use in TV Series." _Journal of Communication_, 1978, 28(3), pp. 30-37.

sample: one episode of each prime-time and Saturday morning dramatic series (excluding movies) broadcast in the 1976-77 season; 77 programs.

Out of a total of 181 incidents of alcohol, drug and tobacco use on television, 127 acts (70 percent) were for alcohol consumption. Alcohol was consumed at a rate of 2.19 incidents per hour. More incidents related to alcohol consumption occurred between 9 and 11 p.m. (3.5 incidents per hour) than from 8 to 9 p.m. (1.8 incidents per hour). Analysis of a subset of these programs (those most often viewed by children) revealed that the rate of alcohol consumption between 9 and 11 p.m. was comparable to the 8 to 9 p.m. hour rate. Overall, smoking and the use of illicit drugs was rare; drug use appeared about once in five hours of programming. These behaviors rarely occurred on Saturday morning programs.

388. Garlington, Warren K. "Drinking on Television: A Preliminary Study with Emphasis on Method." Journal of Studies on Alcohol, 1977, 38(11), pp. 2199-2205.

sample: all daytime serials and game shows broadcast on the three major networks during July and August in 1975 in Spokane, Washington; 79 half-hour periods of daytime serials and 60 half-hour periods of game shows.

Recorded in one-minute intervals of the program any reference to or drinking of an alcoholic beverage, events referring to nonalcoholic drinks, verbal references, drinking scenes, and background drinking. There were 236 alcohol related events on the daytime serials (3 per program) and 18 on game shows (0.3 per program). There were 205 soft drink related events on the serials (2.6 per program) and 9 on game shows (0.2 per program). Alcohol related events were rarely found in commercials aired during the serials (N=11) or game shows (N=8). Commercials for soft drinks appeared much more frequently during both serials (N=146) and game shows (N=127). Actual drinking scenes made up more than half of the drinking-related events. The remainder of the events were either background drinking or verbal references to drinking.

389. Gerbner, George. "Dreams That Hurt: Mental Illness in the Mass Media." In Richard C. Baron, Irvin D. Rutman, and Barbara Klaczynska (eds.), The Community Imperative. Philadelphia, Pa.: Horizon House Institute, 1980, pp. 19-23.

sample: 12 annual week-long samples of prime-time network dramatic programming broadcast between 1969 and 1978.

Data from the Cultural Indicators project revealed that about ten percent of prime-time programs regularly involved some depiction or theme of mental illness and about two percent of the major characters were identified as mentally ill, mental patients, ex-mental patients, etc. There was serious violence in four out of ten dramatic programs overall, but in

two-thirds of the programs with mental illness. The
mentally ill were the group most likely to commit
violence and to be victimized. Forty-five percent of
all "normal" characters as compared to 70 percent of
mentally ill characters were violent; 54 percent of
the "normals" but 80 percent of the mentally ill were
victims of violence. Overall, female characters were
significantly less violent than men. Being cast as
mentally ill tended to equalize chances of inflicting
violence: one-quarter of all female characters
compared to two-thirds of mentally ill female
characters were violent. Six out of ten normal
characters were "good" compared to two out of ten
mentally ill characters. Upper and lower class
characters were more likely to be portrayed as
mentally ill than the large group of middle class
characters. Clerical and sales workers, manual
laborers, criminals, and scientists were the most
likely of all characters in occupations to be
mentally ill; the least prone were proprietors,
police, farmers, and ministers.

390. Gerbner, George. "Mental Illness on Television: A
Study of Censorship." Journal of Broadcasting, Fall 1959,
pp. 293-303.

sample: synopses of TV films, documentary films, and
feature films broadcast between 1948 and 1958 and
censors' remarks as reported in the network film
clearance file.

The number of television films with mental illness
themes increased from 27 in 1954 to a high of 170
films in 1957 and decreased to 73 in 1958. During
this time mental illness became recognized as a
censorship "problem;" references to mental illness
noted by censors increased more rapidly than the
incidence of mental illness themes indicated by the
synopses. Thus, as mental illness themes and
references increased in number, the proportion of
films subjected to censorship increased.

391. Gerbner, George. "Regulation of Mental Illness
Content in Motion Pictures and Television." Gazette, 1960,
6(4), pp. 365-385.

sample: synopses of TV films, documentary films, and
feature films broadcast between 1948 and 1958 and
censors' remarks as reported in the network film
clearance file.

The number of films screened and cut by the censors
increased between 1951 and 1957; it declined in 1958.
Comedies were the most likely films censored because
of references to mental illness; they were followed
by westerns, mysteries, and dramas. Mental illness
themes or mentally ill characters appeared more
frequently in TV productions than in theatrical
feature films. In addition, while such themes in TV
films occurred most often in dramatic programs,
mental illness themes in theatrical feature films
occurred more frequently in horror and mystery films.
This contrast points up a tendency to associate
mental illness with the more bizarre aspects of human
behavior in feature films; TV emphasized mental
illness for "dramatic" purposes.

392. Gerbner, George, Larry Gross, Michael Morgan, and
Nancy Signorielli. "Health and Medicine on Television."
New England Journal of Medicine, 1981, 305(15),
pp. 901-904.

    sample: annual week-long samples of prime-time and
    weekend-daytime network dramatic programming
    (1969-1979).

    Analyses revealed that about 17 percent of prime-time
    programs involved a depiction of mental illness.
    About three percent of major characters were
    identified as mentally ill, as mental patients, or as
    former mental patients. In the late evening, when
    violent programs were more numerous, the percentage
    doubled. The mentally ill characters were the most
    likely both to commit violence and to be victimized.
    Among all prime-time dramatic characters, 40 percent
    of those characterized as "normal" were violent; but
    73 percent of those characterized as "mentally ill"
    were violent. Forty-four percent of the normal
    characters, but 81 percent of the mentally ill, were
    victims. Although only 24 percent of all prime-time
    female characters were violent, 71 percent of
    mentally ill prime-time female characters were
    violent. For every 19 normal male victims of
    violence there were 17 mentally ill male victims; for
    every ten normal female victims of violence, there
    were 25 mentally ill female victims. While ten
    percent of the normal characters were killers and
    five percent were killed, 23 percent of the mentally
    ill were killers and 23 percent were killed.

393. Gerbner, George, Larry Gross, Michael Morgan, and Nancy Signorielli. "What Television Teaches About Physicians and Health." Mobius: A Journal for Continuing Education Professionals in Health Sciences, April, 1982, pp. 44-51.

sample: annual week-long samples of prime-time and weekend-daytime network dramatic programming.

Analyses revealed that about 17 percent of prime-time programs involved some significant depiction or theme of mental illness. About three percent of major characters were identified as mentally ill, as mental patients, ex-mental patients, and so on. In the late evening, with more violent programming, the percentage was twice as high. The mentally ill were likely to be portrayed as both perpetrators of violence and as victims. Out of all prime-time characters, 40 percent of normal characters were violent, but 73 percent of those characterized as mentally ill were violent. Forty-four percent of normal characters, compared to 81 percent of the mentally ill, were victims of violence.

394. Gerbner, George, Larry Gross, and Nancy Signorielli. "The Role of Television Entertainment in Public Education About Science." Annenberg School of Communications, University of Pennsylvania, 1985.

sample: annual week-long samples of prime-time network dramatic programming broadcast between 1973 and 1983.

Themes relating to medicine appeared quite frequently in these programs. Disease was found in about a quarter of these programs and usually presented in a negative way. The harmful effects of drugs were found in 30 percent of these programs and again, practically all of these presentations were negative. Medical technology also appeared in 30 percent of the programs and most of the presentations were positive. Scientists were rather rare -- they were seen by the typical viewer only once a week and were cast in major roles even less frequently. They were, except for women scientists, very underrepresented in relation to their actual numbers in the U.S. labor force. A number of scientists were Asians and foreigners. They also were likely to work alone, be very involved in their work, but also had problems with their work. Although more scientists were portrayed in a positive than in a negative way, among the small number of scientists on prime time, fewer were youthful and involved in romance or family while more were presented as dangerous and headed for ultimate failure. Those in the medical professions and the general character population had an almost across the board, positive portrayal. Scientists' personality traits were generally positive. Compared to health professionals they were relatively less attractive, fair, sociable, warm, rational, stable, efficient and supportive. They were, however, stronger and more violent than doctors. Both doctors and scientists were quite powerful and smart.

395. Gerbner, George, Michael Morgan, and Nancy Signorielli. "Programming Health Portrayals: What Viewers See, Say and Do." In David Pearl, Lorraine Bouthilet, and Joyce Lazar (eds.), Television and Behavior: Ten Years of Scientific Progress and Implications for the Eighties. Rockville, Md.: National Institute of Mental Health, 1982, pp. 291-307.

sample: annual week-long samples of prime-time and weekend-daytime network dramatic programming broadcast between 1969 and 1979; over 5,000 major and 14,000 minor characters.

Summarizes health-related findings from a number of studies (Cassata et al. (381); Katzman (408); and Nunnally (413)). Data from the authors' research, Cultural Indicators, revealed that only three percent of the major characters were mentally ill. Mental illness was associated both with committing and suffering violence: 23 percent of the mentally ill characters, as compared to only 10 percent of normal characters, were killers; and 23 percent of mentally ill characters, as compared to 5 percent of normal characters, were killed. This pattern was accentuated for female characters. In relation to other disabilities, two percent of the major characters had physical handicaps. These characters were older, more likely to be victimized, and less positively portrayed.

396. Greenberg, Bradley S. "Smoking, Drugging, and Drinking in Top Rated TV Series." Journal of Drug Education, 1981, 11(3), pp. 227-233.

sample: 4 episodes of each of the top ten prime-time fictional series broadcast during the 1979-1980 television season and 8 episodes of each of the two top rated daytime serials.

The analysis revealed a near absence of smoking and illicit drug use but considerably more offering/consuming of alcoholic beverages. The incidence of alcohol consumption ranged from 3 to 16.5 incidents per prime-time program hour. A similar analysis of two top rated daytime serials revealed a lower drinking rate and a similar absence of smoking and illicit drug use. The rate of drinking in the top-ten prime-time programs was considerably higher than the rate found in previous analyses of all prime-time programs.

397. Greenberg, Bradley S. and Charles K. Atkin. "The Portrayal of Driving on Television, 1975-1980." Journal of Communication, 1983, 33(2), pp. 44-55.

sample: one week of prime-time commercial programs broadcast in the fall of 1975, 1976, 1977, and 1979; 223 programs, 174.5 hours.

The analysis yielded 784 driving scenes of 5 seconds or longer in duration; 3.5 scenes per program and 4.5 per program hour. Half of the programs contained one or more driving scenes; the average rate for this group was 6.8 per program and 7.2 per program hour. Most driving occurred in action/crime programs (31 percent in urban streets, 21 percent in off-road areas) and was uncomplicated driving on flat terrain, with light traffic, and normal weather conditions. While most scenes were routine business, there were a substantial number of chase and escape scenes (19 percent). The most frequently appearing vehicles were sedans and police cars. Irregular driving also appeared frequently; 25 percent of the scenes had quick braking, 24 percent squealing brakes, 23 percent screeching tires, 20 percent speeding, and 19 percent quick acceleration. While driving acts that endangered people appeared 0.7 times per hour, death and injury were relatively rare (a total of 14 deaths and 24 injuries). Physical damage was somewhat more frequent. Legal penalties for bad driving were also rare. There were a total of 869 drivers: 87 percent were men, 93 percent were white, and 72 percent were in their twenties or thirties. The 479 passengers had similar demographic profiles. Only 4 drivers fastened a seat belt and only 3 drivers and 3 passengers wore seat belts. None of the 5 child passengers wore a seat belt.

398. Greenberg, Bradley S., Carlos Fernandez-Collado, David Graef, Felipe Korzenny, and Charles K. Atkin. "Trends in Use of Alcohol and Other Substances on Television." In Bradley S. Greenberg, Life on Television: Content Analyses of U.S. TV Drama. Norwood, N.J.: Ablex Publishing, 1980, pp. 137-146. See also Journal of Drug Education, 1979, 9(3), pp. 243-253.

sample: two composite weeks of prime-time and Saturday morning network fictional series (excluding movies) broadcast during the 1976-77 and 1977-78 seasons.

Alcohol consumption appeared at the rate of 2.19 acts per hour during 1976-77 and 2.66 acts per hour during 1977-78; tobacco use at the rate of .7 acts per hour during 1976-77 and .48 acts per hour during 1977-78; and illicit drugs at the rate of .22 acts per hour during 1976-77 and .83 acts per hour during 1977-78. Overall, alcohol consumption did not appear on Saturday morning programs, occurred less often between 8 and 9 p.m. and was quite frequent (over 3 acts per hour) from 9 to 11 p.m. Alcohol consumption was also more likely to take place in crime programs. In situation comedies the consumption rate increased from 1.4 acts per hour in the first season to 4.7 acts per hour in the second season. Males consumed alcohol at the rate of 2.04 acts per hour while females consumed at the rate of 1.85 acts per hour; the rate for characters between 20 and 34 was higher (2.35 acts per hour) than the rate for both younger and older characters (average 1.89 acts per hour).

399. Greenberg, Bradley S., Kimberly A. Neuendorf, Nancy Buerkel-Rothfuss, and Laura Henderson. "The Soaps: What's On and Who Cares?" Journal of Broadcasting, 1982, 26(2), pp. 519-536.

sample: three episodes per week of each of 13 afternoon serial dramas for a two week period in 1977; 308 speaking characters.

Updates Katzman's (408) findings concerning medical content in afternoon serials. Medical problems were significant in soap operas, comprising 16 percent of problems (the majority of problems involved personal relationships). Mental illness was more prominent in 1977 than previously noted. Among the more serious mental aberrations: schizophrenia, catatonia, and hysterical blindness.

400. Gussow, Joan. "Counternutritional Messages of Television Ads Aimed at Children." Journal of Nutrition Education, 1972, 4, pp. 48-54.

sample: 388 commercials broadcast by ABC, CBS, and NBC during 29 hours of Saturday morning children's programming.

Food, drink, candy, gum, or vitamin pills made up 82 percent of the 388 Saturday morning commercials. In 5 hours of programming, NBC ran 44 ads, 75 percent for edible products. In the same time period ABC ran 112 commercials, 87 percent for food, drinks, or vitamins. In 6 hours that same Saturday morning, CBS ran 126 commercials, 87 percent for edible products. The 319 food-related ads were distributed in the following product categories: breakfast cereals (38.5 percent), cookies, candy, snacks (17 percent), vitamins (15 percent), beverages and mixes (8 percent), frozen waffles and pop tarts (7.5 percent), canned pasta (5 percent), and other foods (9 percent). Overall, the nutrition-specialist monitors found the total impact blatantly antinutritional.

401. Hanneman, Gerhard J. and William J. McEwen. "The Use and Abuse of Drugs: An Analysis of Mass Media Content." In Ronald E. Ostman (ed.), Communication Research and Drug Education. Beverly Hills, Ca.: Sage Publications, 1976, pp. 65-88. See also William J. McEwen and Gerhard J. Hanneman. "The Depiction of Drug Use in Television Programming." Journal of Drug Education, 1974, 4(3), pp. 281-293.

sample: 101 hours of evening network and local programming, including news, talk shows, and commercials, broadcast during a two week period in 1973.

Public service announcements concerning drug abuse were very rare and did not include any prosocial messages produced to help combat this problem. In the first week there were 40 public service announcements (16 minutes out of 80 hours). Eight of these (20 percent) dealt with social problems, including alcoholism. During the second week, there

186

was one alcohol-related PSA in 21 hours. One-third of the PSAs were broadcast during prime time.

In contrast, commercials for chemical agents were fairly common during prime time: 127 during the first week and 27 in the second, shorter period. Authors noted that while use is not the same as abuse, commercials devoted little time to warnings of abuse.

In dramatic programming, there was a general neglect of the potential for abuse of chemical agents and a lack of consideration for the causes and consequences of abuse. The majority of references were to alcohol; most were positive or neutral and about 30 percent were humorous. Although illicit drugs appeared infrequently, they were shown in a "context of abuse" and evoked unfavorable reactions. Drug abuse was often followed by arrest (a legal, rather than a physical or psychological consequence). These references occurred more often in dramas than in comedy or variety programs.

402. Head, Sidney W. "Content Analysis of Television Drama Programs." Quarterly of Film, Radio, and Television, 1954, 9(2), pp. 175-94.

*** see women ***

sample: 1,023 major and 740 minor characters from four episodes of each of 64 network dramatic programs broadcast in 1952.

Of all the major characters, only one had a serious physical illness and 12 had serious mental illnesses.

403. Kalisch, Beatrice J., Philip A. Kalisch, and Margaret Scobey. "Reflections on a Television Image: The Nurses, 1962-1965." Nursing and Health Care, May 1981, pp. 248-255.

sample: 20 percent random sample of each prime-time series with nurse characters broadcast between 1950 and 1980.

Describes one series, The Nurses, broadcast between 1962 and 1965 and compares the image of nurses in this program with the image found in doctor-oriented programs. The authors concluded that The Nurses was good nursing drama; its stories concerned moral or ethical issues such as racism, child abuse, abortion,

and alcoholism. In physician-based drama, nurses
were often presented as powerless, problem-prone
women who could not solve their own problems. They
often stood by the bedsides of patients watching the
doctors do the important tasks of patient care and
provided the needed emotional support. The Nurses,
however, provided a more realistic view of the
profession -- its nurses were problem solvers who did
not have to sit by and wait for doctors. They helped
each other with personal and professional
difficulties. The classic virtues of nursing --
compassion, patience, self-sacrifice -- were
frequently demonstrated, but not to the exclusion of
qualities such as intelligence, objectivity, and
articulate speech.

404. Kalisch, Philip A. and Beatrice J. Kalisch. "Nurses
on Prime Time Television." American Journal of Nursing,
1982, 82, pp. 264-270.

sample: 20 percent random sample of each of the 28
series with a regular nurse character broadcast
between 1950 and 1980.

Nurses generally received stereotyped treatment on
television. They usually were presented as hand
maidens to the medical profession; doctor-nurse
interactions usually showed the nurse taking orders.
Doctors, usually men, were portrayed with more
ambition, intelligence, risk-taking, rationality,
adeptness, aggression, self-confidence, and
sophistication. They also were more sincere,
altruistic, honest, and perceptive than nurses.
Nurses were presented as more obedient, and showed
more permissiveness, conformity, and flexibility than
doctors. Doctors and nurses, however, did not differ
in efficiency, organization, or discipline. In the
1950s nurses projected a wholesome girl-next-door
image or benign motherly traits; rarely were they
seen as professional; they quit work upon marriage,
and remained subordinate to physicians. The overall
image of nursing was, nevertheless, generally
positive and respectful of the profession. In the
1960s there was less focus on nurses and more upon
doctors. Any gains made in the 1960s, however, were
lost in the 1970s when nurses were often presented as
sexual mascots for groups of men (usually
physicians). Most programs broadcast during this
decade focused upon the omnipotent doctor to the
detriment of the nurse.

405. Kalisch, Philip A. and Beatrice J. Kalisch. "Sex
Role Stereotyping of Nurses and Physicians on Prime Time
Television: A Dichotomy of Occupational Portrayals." Sex
Roles, 1984, 10(7/8), pp. 533-553.

    sample: 20 percent sample of all series with nurses
    and physicians in major roles broadcast between 1950
    and 1980; 28 series, 320 episodes, 240 nurses, 287
    physicians.

    These programs presented extreme levels of both
    sexual and occupational stereotyping. Television
    nurses were 99 percent female and television doctors
    were 95 percent male. The cluster of sex and
    occupational role characteristics, personality
    attributes, primary values, career orientations,
    professional competencies, and the tone of
    nurse-physician relationships produced an image of
    the female professional nurse as totally dependent on
    and subservient to male physicians. Television
    nurses were most likely to be white (95 percent),
    under 35 (44 percent), single (82 percent), and
    childless (95 percent). There was no change in this
    image over 30 years. Exceptions were unfavorable;
    older nurses were less attractive, more sadistic, and
    reprimanding toward patients. There was only a small
    increase in the number of women physicians: none in
    the 1950s, 2 (8 percent) in the 1960s, and 13 (7
    percent) in the 1970s.

406. Kalisch, Philip A., Beatrice J. Kalisch, and
Jacqueline Clinton. "The World of Nursing on Prime Time
Television, 1950-1980." Nursing Research, 1982, 31(6),
pp. 358-363.

    sample: 320 episodes from 28 different series
    broadcast from 1950 to 1980; 240 nurses.

    The majority of nurses on television worked in
    hospitals (82 percent) and conveyed the attitude that
    nursing was an important part of their lives (84
    percent). Nurses were also often characterized as
    women who had entered nursing for altruistic reasons.
    The favorable image of the professional work of
    nurses in entertainment programming reached its apex
    in the 1960s. When nurses were shown in their true
    professional role, they were helpful to patients,
    nurturant, and committed to their work. In later
    years these depictions were rather rare. Nurses who
    exhibited leadership behaviors were also portrayed
    with negative attributes. Administrators were

presented as powerful, intelligent, and competent but also cold and rigid. In the 1970s the image of nursing fell to an all-time low: nurses were found primarily in series highlighting physicians who were presented as demigods. On these programs nurses were consistently made second in importance and their major function was to carry out the doctor's orders. In the more recent programs, these depictions have become rather rare.

407. Kalisch, Philip A., Beatrice J. Kalisch, and Margaret Scobey. Image of Nurses on Television. New York: Springer Publishing Co., 1983.

sample: survey of all television shows that have ever featured nurses.

Study analyzed the development of the image of nurses and nursing on television. Noted television's consistent misrepresentation of the world of medicine and health care -- especially the stereotypes of nurses and the all-encompassing paternal care often provided by television doctors. The most common stereotype was the nurse as the all-around doctor's helper; the nurse who devoted her life to the service of a single physician. Another stereotype was the presentation of nursing as an outlet for maternal feelings. The basic impresion of the hospital nurse was that their value was in their ability to carry out doctor's orders. These stereotypes have persisted: what was televised in 1980 was similar to what was seen in 1950, including uniforms. The image of the office nurse was also static, serving mainly as secretary/receptionist. One change did occur: the transformation of the nurse from a sweet and innocent girlfriend/wife to promiscuous young woman more interested in love affairs than marriage. Overall, the television nurse could be categorized in one of four groups: the nonentity (doctor shows), the good nurse, the nurturing nurse, and the professional nurse.

408. Katzman, Natan. "Television Soap Operas: What's Been Going on Anyway?" Public Opinion Quarterly, 1972, 36(2), pp. 200-12.

*** see women ***

sample: one episode per week of each of 14 soap operas broadcast for four weeks in 1970; 371 characters, 884 conversations.

There were two cases of mental illness, five cases of physical disability, and four cases of psychosomatic illness.

409.   Kaufman, Lois.   "Prime-Time Nutrition."   Journal of Communication, 1980, 30(3), pp. 37-46.

sample: first 30 minutes of the top 10 regularly scheduled series, including commercials, broadcast in 1977; 20 programs, 108 commercials.

This study described and analyzed television messages relating to food, eating behavior, and ideal body image and compared them to the standards set forth by expert nutritionists. More references to food (two or three per program) were found in the sample of programs than in the sample of commercials. Program references focused upon beverages (especially alcoholic) and sweets; commercial references were more evenly distributed over the seven different food categories. Non-nutritious foods predominated in both programs and commercials. Television characters were usually happy when around food, rarely dined alone, and often snacked. Food was never explicitly used to satisfy hunger; rather it was used for social and emotional purposes. There were 50 overweight and ten obese characters in these programs and commercials. Women and blacks appeared disproportionately among the obese, while white males predominated among the less seriously overweight.

410.   Lowery, Shearon A.   "Soap and Booze in the Afternoon: An Analysis of the Portrayal of Alcohol Use in Daytime Serials."   Journal of Studies on Alcohol, 1980, 41, pp. 829-828.

sample: 14 daytime serials broadcast daily during a four week period in March 1977; 172 program hours, 520 incidents of alcohol use.

Drinking was a regular, frequent occurrence in the daytime serial. The average frequency of alcohol consumption was 1.5 drinks per half-hour. There were three drinking patterns: social facilitation (47 percent of incidents), crisis management (23 percent), and escape from reality (30 percent).

Seven out of ten drinking incidents were reinforced or had no consequences. When punishment occurred it was most often for escape from reality drinking but had few long-range effects. Overall, the author noted that the portrayal of alcohol use on daytime serials encouraged drinking for social facilitation and crisis management and that escape from reality drinking, while not encouraged, was not strongly discouraged.

411. Lowry, Dennis T. "Alcohol Consumption Patterns and Consequences in Prime-Time Network TV." Journalism Quarterly, 1981, 58(1), pp. 3-8.

sample: 14 evenings for each network of randomly-selected programming broadcast in 1979; 120 hours, 406 drinking incidents.

Speaking characters made references to alcohol in 64 percent of the programs. No programs dealt with alcohol abuse and treatment. There were 406 drinking incidents: 293 by men and 113 by women. Most of the incidents (201) involved hard liquor, followed by wine (136) and beer (68). There were also 64 attempts to have a drink that were unsuccessful. Overall there were 3.38 incidents per hour (3.92 per hour including drinking attempts): 1.75 incidents per hour from 8 to 9 p.m. and 4.26 incidents per hour from 9 to 11 p.m. Drinking usually accompanied relaxing, dining, and business discussions. The negative consequences of drinking were rarely presented and, if presented, were usually comic.

412. MacDonald, Patrick T. "The 'Dope' on Soaps." Journal of Drug Education, 1983, 13(4), pp. 359-368.

Survey of 165 daytime serial viewers to determine the portrayal of alcohol and drugs in this genre of programming.

Alcohol was the most frequently mentioned "drug"; 54 percent of 299 mentions were negative, and 42 percent were positive. Contrary to statistics on the U.S. population, on daytime serials women were more frequently portrayed as alcoholics or problem drinkers than men and most of the alcoholics were upper-middle class rather than working class. Finally, the portrayal of only whites as alcoholics greatly distorted the racial composition of the alcoholic population in the U.S. There were 140 mentions of tranquilizer use: 45 percent were negative, 34 percent were positive, and 21 percent neutral. Most tranquilizers were prescribed by doctors to overcome emotional stress or to induce sleep. There were 126 mentions of tobacco use: 42 percent neutral, 36 percent negative, and 22 percent positive. Illicit drugs (amphetamines, marijuana, LSD, cocaine, heroin) were reported less frequently by these viewers but when seen they were usually presented negatively. The author hypothesized the potential importance of these images, especially the overrepresentation of women as alcoholics and tranquilizer abusers.

413. Nunnally, Jum C. "The Communication of Mental Health Information: A Comparison of the Opinion of Experts and the Public with Mass Media Presentations." Behavioral Science, 1957, 2(3), pp. 200-230. See also, "Mental Illness: What the Media Present." In Stanley Cohen and Jock Young (eds.), The Manufacture of News: A Reader. Beverly Hills, Ca.: Sage Publications, 1973, pp. 136-45.

sample: all programs aired during one week on one independent VHF television station in 1955.

References to mental health occurred incidentally rather than systematically (only three percent of the programs referred to major mental health problems). In comparison, physical disorders were referred to four to ten times more frequently. There were wide gaps between expert and media viewpoints, with public opinion falling between the two, generally nearer the expert viewpoint. The media emphasized the "bizarre symptoms" of mental disturbance such as unusual physical appearance and behavior. Cause was typically linked to traumatic, sudden environmental, or physical factors rather than long-term experience. Help was provided by a strong, encouraging, and supporting person (a health professional or an acquaintance). Media and public conceptions about neurotics and psychotics were similar, considering them ignorant, dirty, unkind, unpredictable, and dangerous.

414. Ramsdell, M. L. "The Trauma of Television's Troubled Soap Families." Family Coordinator, 1973, 22, pp. 299-304.

*** see women ***

sample: eight soap operas aired on one network
affiliate in 1971-72; 57 leading female roles.

Alcoholism rarely occurred in the afternoon serial
dramas. When it did, there was rapid, unspecified
rehabilitation, or the character was written out of
the story.

415. Real, Michael R. "Marcus Welby and the Medical
Genre." In Michael Real, Mass Mediated Culture. Englewood
Cliffs, N.J.: Prentice Hall, 1977, pp. 118-139.

sample: 9 episodes of Marcus Welby broadcast between
January and May in 1975.

A qualitative analysis that revealed that seven of
the nine patients featured in these episodes were
wealthy and six out of the nine were missing a close
relative. The episodes usually had a patient who was
initially resistent to treatment, efforts by Welby to
help the patient face the disease, and a flawlessly
correct use of therapy and medication. Minorities
and women were cast in traditional roles: doctors
were white males, nurses were white females, and
orderlies were minorities (there were also two black
interns). The illnesses, contrary to reality,
usually appeared suddenly. Each episode ended with
the patient and family much happier because of the
intervention of Dr. Welby, even if a cure was
impossible. The focus on the wealthy reflected the
existing class bias of American health care.
Overall, the program favored established power and
stereotypes. Robert Young, star of the series,
averaged 5,000 letters each week seeking medical and
emotional advice. Also included was a discussion of
other medical programs, medically-related
documentaries, and health-oriented commercials (often
inaccurate and/or misleading).

416. Report on Alcohol, "Family Hour Reduces Drinking
Scenes but Coffee and Milk Still Less Popular than Alcohol
on TV." Report on Alcohol, 1975, 23(4), pp. 24-28.

sample: programs in the 1975 season monitored by
1,000 viewers in 32 states.

Although alcohol remained the most popular beverage
on television, the inception of the family hour (8
p.m. to 9 p.m. EST) lead to some reduction in
drinking scenes. From 8 p.m. to 9 p.m. there was an

average of 1.37 drinking scenes per hour, compared to
an average of 3.96 drinking scenes per hour from 9
p.m. to 11 p.m. The way alcohol was presented
(problem-solver, humorous context, and indication of
sophistication) was of considerable concern.
Overall, the portrayal of the consumption of alcohol
on television was unrealistic.

417. Report on Alcohol. "Having a Drink on Television has
a Serious Meaning." Report on Alcohol, 1975, 23(3),
pp. 22-32.

sample: 250 hours of television programming; 249
programs.

Reported findings of a survey of television
programming conducted by The Christian Science
Monitor. Liquor was the most popular drink on
television. There were a total of 507 drinking
scenes which took place in 80 percent of the
programs. Hard liquor (whiskey, vodka, rum) was
consumed in 62 percent of the programs. Liquor was
consumed 10 times more frequently than soft drinks
(in reality, soft drinks are consumed 16 times more
frequently than liquor). Also, liquor was used on
television 1.5 times more often than coffee (coffee,
in real life, outsells liquor 16 to 1). Four
concerns were voiced about the portrayal of
drinking: frequent use (often as a prop), humorous
drunkenness, use as a problem-solver, and use as an
indication of sophistication.

418. Schorr, Thelma. "Nursing's TV Image." American
Journal of Nursing, 1963, 63, pp. 119-121.

A discussion of The Nurses, focusing upon viewer
criticisms and the reasons behind program policy.
The producer, Herbert Brodkin, did not feel the
program presented nursing in a negative way but also
stressed that his first concern was to provide good
entertainment. The role played by two
nurse-consultants in script development and program
production was discussed.

419. Smart, Reginald G. and Mark Krakowski. "The Nature
and Frequency of Drug Content in Magazines and on
Television." Journal of Alcohol and Drug Education, 1973,
18(3), pp. 16-23.

sample: one composite week of late afternoon and
evening programs broadcast on each of six Canadian
television stations, including three American
affiliates, in 1971; 336 hours.

This study compared the extent of drug advertising on
television (pro and con) to print advertisements; it
also examined the extent of drug education available
through these media. In regard to drug education,
there were three items on news programs (advocating
drug treatment programs, the banning of amphetamines,
and drug education); three talk shows which included
segments on the dangers of drug use and heavy
drinking; and one 30-minute public affairs program
about heroin addiction and the need for treatment
facilities in the U.S. Drama programs rarely
presented criticism of heavy drinking.

420. Smith, Frank A., Geoffrey Trivax, David A. Zuehlke,
Paul Lowinger, and Thieu L. Nghiem. "Health Information
During a Week of Television." The New England Journal of
Medicine, 1972, 286(10), pp. 516-520.

sample: one week (December 13-19, 1970) of all
programming broadcast (6 a.m. to 1:05 a.m.) on
WWT-TV (NBC) in Detroit, MI; 130 hours.

All items (entertainment, news, commercials, etc.)
dealing with mental or physical illness, doctors,
dentists, medical treatment, smoking, or health were
logged and evaluated; cosmetics, physical
appearance, and food were not included.
Health-related content appeared in 7.2 percent of the
programming. Only 30 percent of this health time
offered useful information, and 70 percent of the
health material was inaccurate or misleading or both.
Television programming did not use the educational
capacity of the health professions to any notable
extent. There were 10 times as many messages that
urged the use of pills or other remedies as there
were against drug use or abuse. Although some useful
health information was offered, major health problems
such as heart disease, cancer, stroke, accidents,
hepatitis, maternal death, hunger, venereal disease,
mental health, sex education, child care, lead
poisoning, and family planning were practically
ignored.

421. Smythe, Dallas, W. "Reality as Presented by Television." Public Opinion Quarterly, 1954, 18, pp. 143-156.

*** see women ***

   sample: one week of dramatic programs broadcast on several New York City stations in 1953; 86 programs, 476 characters.

   Two percent of the characters in the evening programs and six percent of those in the daily serials were categorized as insane.

422. Wahl, Otto, F. and Rachel Roth. "Television Images of Mental Illness: Results of a Metropolitan Washington Media Watch." Journal of Broadcasting, 1982, 26(2), pp. 599-609.

   sample: one month of prime-time programs broadcast by five stations in 1981; 385 programs.

   The sample included 110 programs (29 percent) with some relevance to mental illness; 75 programs (19 percent) had minor references; and 35 programs (9 percent) contained mentally ill characters. Mentally ill characters usually were single males with no specific occupation; they were of various ages with an average age of 40. These characters occasionally had positive traits such as friendliness and loyalty, but they were most frequently active, confused, aggressive, dangerous, and unpredictable. Close to three-quarters of the mentally ill characters had no family connections and about half had no discernable occupation. Overall, television presented the mentally ill as a distinct and disenfranchised group of people.

423. Winick, Charles and Mariann P. Winick. "Drug Education and the Content of Mass Media Dealing with 'Dangerous Drugs' and Alcohol." In Ronald E. Ostman (ed.), Communication Research and Drug Education. 1976, Beverly Hills, Ca.: Sage Publications, pp. 15-37.

   sample: prime-time evening entertainment programs (with substantial drug use content) broadcast during the 1970-71 and 1971-72 television seasons; 56 programs.

On the average, one program about drug use was
broadcast every nine days. Of 50 characters who used
drugs, 24 percent were heavy users, 48 percent were
dysfunctional abusers, 22 percent were recreational
or social users, and six percent were experimenters.
Forty out of 56 programs depicted drug use as a
solitary activity, with heroin the most frequently
used drug. The consequences of drug use were
generally negative, both personally and socially.
Drug themes in programs usually were associated with
the police. Approximately 20 percent included a
theme of drug treatment. Two programs dealt with
alcoholism; alcoholism and drinking also were treated
humorously by several variety show entertainers.
Authors noted a decline in the portrayal of social
drinking and pointed out that this might be a result
of sensitivity to the problem of alcoholism. Eight
percent of all public service messages on television
were anti-drug abuse; PSAs also included informative
announcements about the incidence and health hazards
of alcoholism.

Author Index

Includes authors and joint authors.

Entries refer to individual entry numbers.

Subject Index

Entries refer to individual entry numbers.

About the Author

NANCY SIGNORIELLI is Communication Research Administrator at the Annenberg School of Communications at the University of Pennsylvania. She has contributed to such journals as the *Journal of Communication*, *Journal of Broadcasting*, and *Journalism Quarterly*.